Gender and Media
in the Broadcast Age

Gender and Media in the Broadcast Age

Women's Radio Programming at the BBC, CBC, and ABC

Justine Lloyd

BLOOMSBURY ACADEMIC
NEW YORK • LONDON • OXFORD • NEW DELHI • SYDNEY

BLOOMSBURY ACADEMIC
Bloomsbury Publishing Inc
1385 Broadway, New York, NY 10018, USA
50 Bedford Square, London, WC1B 3DP, UK
29 Earlsfort Terrace, Dublin 2, Ireland

BLOOMSBURY, BLOOMSBURY ACADEMIC and the Diana logo are
trademarks of Bloomsbury Publishing Plc

First published in the United States of America 2020
This paperback edition published in 2021

Cover design: Eleanor Rose
Cover image © Kreisler radio display, 1938, at Mick Simmons Ltd, Haymarket store /
State Library, New South Wales, Australia.

A catalog record for this book is available from the Library of Congress.

A catalogue record for this book is available from the British Library.

ISBN: HB: 978-1-5013-1876-4
        PB: 978-1-5013-1877-1
        ePDF: 978-1-5013-1879-5
        eBook: 978-1-5013-1878-8

Typeset by Integra Software Services Pvt. Ltd.

To find out more about our authors and books visit www.bloomsbury.com
and sign up for our newsletters.

Contents

Acknowledgments

I would like to thank the following people for their practical support and encouragement during the writing of this book:

- Colleagues in the Department of Sociology at Macquarie University, especially Harry Blatterer, Pauline Johnson, Gabrielle Meagher, and Alison Leitch.
- Other members of the Centre for Media History at Macquarie University, especially Bridget Griffen-Foley, Jeannine Baker, and Virginia Madsen.
- Researchers at the Centre for Transforming Cultures at the University of Technology Sydney, especially Devleena Ghosh and Katrina Schlunke, as well as Jan Idle, Jemima Mowbray, and Ilaria Vanni.
- Multifarious collaborators on "The Listening Project," especially Tanja Dreher, Cate Thill, and Nicole Matthews.

I would also like to thank:

- Lesley Johnson for her work that sparked this idea, as well as Helen Macallan for inspiring teaching and discussions over many years.
- Liz Jacka, Paul Ashton, and Paula Hamilton for their feedback on the project in its early stages.
- Katie Gallof, Susan Krogulski, and Erin Duffy at Bloomsbury for their professionalism and patience, and Shanmathi Priya at Integra for overseeing production.
- Barbara Szubinska, editor of *Storytelling: A Critical Journal of Popular Narrative*, for permission to reproduce sections of my article "Intimate Empire: Radio Programming for Women in Postwar Australia and Canada" from their Winter 2007 issue.
- The staff of the CBC Radio Archives; the University of Waterloo Archives; the BBC Written Archives Centre; the British Library; the National Archives of Australia, especially Edmund Rutledge and Craig Venson; the ABC Archives, Sydney, especially Sal Russo and Sabrina Lipovic; and library staff

of UTS, Macquarie and Murdoch universities, as well as the State Library of NSW, for assistance in tracking down materials.

- The staff of the Faculty Research Offices at UTS and Macquarie universities, especially Helen Thomson, Jaine Stockler, Gill Ellis, Christine Boman, and Glenda Hewett.
- My coeditors of *Space & Culture: The International Journal of Social Spaces*, especially Rob Shields for long-distance intellectual inspiration. I would also like to acknowledge the Department of Sociology, University of Alberta, for hosting me during a crucial moment of editing.
- Anonymous peer reviewers for this manuscript and also *Feminist Media Histories* journal.

The initial research for this book was supported by an Australian Research Council postdoctoral fellowship, "The ABC Women's Session, 1935–1973" (DP0450349) 2004–2007, as well as the Faculty of Arts and Social Sciences, UTS.

Research and writing time were also supported by a Faculty of Arts Mid-Career Fellowship from Macquarie University and a Visiting Research Fellowship at the Museum of Applied Arts and Science (MAAS/Powerhouse), Sydney, in 2016. I particularly wish to thank Kylie Budge, formerly of MAAS, for her kind support during a very enjoyable visit, as well as the staff of the museum, including Paul Wilson, Campbell Bickerstaff, Karen Biddle, and Matthew Connell for research help and chats.

Finally, but also beginningly, my family: my parents, Peter and Libby Lloyd, my brothers and sisters-in-law, Jamie Lloyd and Aoise Stratford, Daniel Lloyd and Katrina Retallick, and my nieces and nephews, Sam, Rowena, Maya, Gwen, Reuben, Hugo, and Miller for their encouragement and delightful company. And thank you to my partner, Juke Wyat, for both being there and never asking when the book would be finished.

Abbreviations

ABC   Australian Broadcasting Commission (Company 1929–1932, Corporation from 1983)

BBC   British Broadcasting Corporation (Company 1922–1927)

CBC   Canadian Broadcasting Corporation (from 1936)

CRBC   Canadian Radio Broadcasting Corporation (1932–1936)

Introduction: New Connections

The research for this book started by tracing the rise and fall of a set of programs aimed specifically at women audiences in the early years of public service broadcasting in Australia, Canada, and the UK. In doing so, I uncovered compelling narratives of working lives of the women who produced and spoke on the programs. The individual personalities and collective imagination of these women emerged in the details of their daily interactions with radio as well as their negotiations with management—the latter a force sometimes sympathetic, sometimes hostile to their ideas and innovations.

While I acknowledge and draw on the recent "biographical" turn in media history (Hendy 2012; Murphy 2016), this work investigates broadcasting history from the perspective of a "cultural circuit" that goes beyond individual life stories to look for connections between media production, consumption, distribution, circulation, and identification (Johnson 1986: 47). Going beyond a traditional audience or policy analysis, I place the individual career trajectories of these women within a different, more complex, story: how these programs, for both the audience and those who spoke on them, provided the ground for the emergence of a cultural form unique to a particular stage in the constitution of a middle-class female subject. This book asks the question of how this new subject position for women was constructed in the challenge that public service radio broadcasting made to divisions between public and private spheres: a new form of agency that was ultimately transformative of the opposition between these spheres. While this new agency began in personal experience and domestic space, it was not limited to there.

The trajectories of individual programs and media workers reveal that each broadcaster had very different attitudes to the content, format, and presentation of radio programming for women. Sharp contrasts emerge between each broadcaster's approach to women's programming. Each public service broadcast institution had very different interactions with civil society organizations and economic actors, which in turn also shaped the agenda of individual programs and therefore understandings of radio's transformative potential of the public sphere. While many of the women working in the programs forged their own paths and therefore shaped new forms of agency through their own individual efforts, the possibility of questioning the separation between public and private spheres was not always legitimated by internal management or program policy decisions. These programs carried the imprimatur of the state's broadcast institutions and patriarchal desires to ensure gender conformity, thus using the agenda-setting power of internal editorial policy to circumscribe topics that could be spoken about on air, especially whether news and current affairs were proper topics for women's programming. These editorial decisions, shaped in turn by cultural expectations around women's roles, framed and determined career opportunities available to women in media industries, as well the kinds of relationships that broadcasters were able to develop with the audience.

Certainly, resources were garnered for or taken away from these programs depending on the popularity of their hosts and guests; however, more subtle ideas of whether women's culture was worthy of airtime or even salient to a modern public sphere were also at play. Both the British Broadcasting Corporation (BBC) and Canadian Broadcasting Corporation (CBC), for example, devoted far more staff and programming resources to women's programming than the Australian Broadcasting Commission (ABC) was prepared to consider, as is evidenced by the success of BBC's *Woman's Hour* (broadcast from 1946 to present, discussed in Chapter 5) and the multitude of women's talks and diversity of topics allowed to be discussed by a bevy of women's issues commentators employed by the CBC in the late 1940s and 1950s (discussed in Chapter 4). By contrast, frustrated ex-hosts, women's organizations, and individual listeners alike voiced their concerns over the paucity of care and attention given by the ABC to its to the *Women's Sessions* for the three decades the programs were on the air (discussed in Chapter 3).

Analyses of the production contexts of the programs demonstrate that women as both audiences and producers actively negotiated the meaning of the programs and through their engagement with the medium of radio sought involvement in civic life during this period. Early and mid-twentieth-century women's culture has often been ignored in media studies written from a feminist perspective both because the evidence for its existence is harder to trace in comparison to the media-saturated gendered worlds of the 1960s and 1970s and because the era does not fit dominant narratives of gender and media, which are centered on the second wave and at times characterize the first half of the twentieth century as a time of passive feminine domesticity. For instance, the Australian Women's Broadcasting Collective (AWBC)—a pressure group of activist women within the ABC, which was formed following International Women's Day 1975—completely ignored the precedent of the ABC *Women's Sessions* in their own history. A twentieth anniversary book collection that provides an account of *The Coming Out Show*, a major project of the AWBC, is written as if women had never worked in the ABC except as typists before the mid-1970s (Fell and Wenzel 1995). Initially, I was curious as to why the history of women's programming was invisible to second-wave media groups such as the AWBC? To what extent did feminist broadcasting's sense of agency come from—even if purely as a resistance against—similar programming that imagined a specifically female audience? Did these previous programs have anything in common with a feminist media project and under what conditions were they discontinued? Initial answers to these questions raised further ones, particularly around why women's programming has persisted to this day at the BBC (which is addressed in Chapters 5 and 6) and on how and why women broadcasters thrived in *Women's Interests* at the CBC (whose stories are documented in Chapter 4).

While feminist programming itself has been dropped from many broadcasters in ongoing pushes toward "mainstreaming," the new range of voices and issues canvassed by these post-1960s programs challenged the politics of separate spheres at the same time that they emerged from it. While the story of *The Coming Out Show* and other similar feminist broadcasting projects are worthy of a study in themselves, and some of this work is already being done (Carter 1996, 2004; Friedman et al. 2009; Henderson 2006; Hilmes 2013; Veerkamp 2014), in order to understand any continuities between pre- and post-second-wave women's programming, I suggest that we have to understand on their own terms what the original programs were trying to do and what successes and failures they had in organizing listeners around the time and space of gendered radio. This aspect of media history has often been underestimated in contemporary debates about the reemergence of feminism in the second half of the twentieth century. The programs that are documented in the archives of the three broadcasters I focus on here represent the emergence of a new female subject who was addressed across class and geographic divides. I propose that such programs, as a keystone of public service radio broadcasting, helped form a female audience that was constructed through feminist challenges to divisions between public and private spheres, but feminists themselves were not able to fully realize this promise until the late 1960s, when the cultural form itself began to disappear. These programs represented a new kind of women's culture, which began in domestic and personal experience but eventually escaped its anchoring to the private sphere.

As mentioned above, while women's programming came under pressure for their coverage of news and current affairs, part of the issue with such content was often that it was too "international," hence exceeding the programs' highly gendered supposed domestic and strictly national agenda. Further complicating a focus on individual programs and workers is the question of how this deep transformation of gendered space relates to the fact that radio is in itself a transnational medium. Media histories purely at the biographical scale are limited in being able to explain how particular media forms reorganize everyday space-time and domesticate new social relationships (Badenoch 2005; Birdsall 2012; Cassidy 1998; Ehrick 2016). Critically, feminism has strategically used transnationalist appeals to build coalitions beyond national frameworks (McLaughlin 2004) as well as to highlight the spatio-temporal aspects of imperialism and capitalism (Keohane 2018: 176–177). While the choice of these three broadcasters was bound by considerations I discuss below, the tripartite, comparative structure of this book strikes a certain angle on the "transnational" that focuses on the historical legacies of one corner of the former British Empire but excludes others—an inter-Asian study of Australia, Malaysia, and India would find other fascinating links, for example. Yet the repeated gestures of reaching out beyond national boundaries by women producers and presenters within all three broadcasters discussed here underscore radio as a medium that cannot be stopped and checked at national borders. Radio as an always-already translocal and transnational medium obviously created new connections between places and actors that were taken up by producers and audiences. Several of the women who worked on these programs were also members of international professional organizations and networks, such as the International Council of Women and the Women's International League for Peace and Freedom. What was at stake in gendering international space through radio in this way? Looking beyond individual career trajectories allows us to see that all mediated spaces are politically inflected public spaces. The women whose radiophonic imagination I map here articulated their relationship with their audience and their own experiences in ways that contest the privatization thesis (Cassidy 2005; McCarthy 1995), which sees media as simply domesticating public space by bringing it into the home. Radio was, and still is, obviously a site of wide-reaching transformation of both domestic and public space, moving them closer and further apart in surprising ways.

The broadcasters examined here are linked by all three being part of an Anglophone public sphere that was predicated on imperial histories but that had to negotiate critical junctures between gender, markets, and state in each setting. All three were part of the public service broadcasting project, which at its broadest level can be interpreted as a configuration of economic, political, and social systems that target mass media as a key force in the democratization of everyday life (Scannell 1989: 136), and, as I understand it more specifically here, as the outcome of claims for universal access to media within arm's-length management and provision of centralized broadcasting infrastructure by the state (Scannell 1990). My original aim was to discern how the ABC as a public service broadcaster understood, formulated and defined a gendered constituency, and how this assemblage of gender and media changed over the period between the establishment of the ABC in the early 1930s and the decline of women's programming in the 1960s. Very quickly I realized that the very definition of this constituency was a site of struggle within public service broadcasting, as countless reports and suppositions of "what women want to listen to" attempted, rhetorically, to pin down the very purpose of the programs and what kind of ideal listener would be interpellated by them.

As I uncovered other instances of these kinds of programs in Canada and the UK, I found alternatives and possibilities that had been foreclosed in the Australian case. This diverse situation demanded reflection on particular political-economic contexts as well as theoretical explanation (Dahl 1994: 560; Gomery 1991). The three case studies allowed for differentiation on a key political-economic axes: one public service monopoly broadcaster that received no advertising revenue (BBC, a monopoly broadcaster from 1922 in radio until the introduction of Independent Local Radio in the early 1970s and in television from the 1930s until the introduction of the Independent Television Authority in 1955), one that existed in a mixed system alongside commercial players, but received no advertising revenue (ABC, from 1932 onwards), and one that existed in a mixed system alongside commercial players and also received its own advertising revenue (Brown 2009). Thus, the choice of broadcasters allowed for setting out a lineage of approaches to women's programming, as well as a litmus test on how such financial decisions play out within public service broadcasting as a sector that deals differently with commercial imperatives in specific national contexts. More importantly, the conditions of communication that have structured the threshold between the private and the public in each national context could then be teased out (Dawes 2017: 168). Each case provides an opportunity for careful empirical investigation into the mediated relation between a form of supposedly universal and therefore unmarked yet gendered, citizenship embedded within the public service broadcasting project and a key category of difference: women as having a particular stake in the ongoing democratization of everyday life (see Chapter 2). Finally, because the figure of the woman listener, imagined to be steeped in the space-time of everyday life, was recruited as a modern citizen in very different ways by each national broadcaster, critical differences emerge in how this figure was manifest in each of the programs. These contestations speak to contemporary struggles and hopefully will animate further reflection on taken-for-granted periodizations of feminist activity.

Thus, the case of women's radio culture between the two world wars and in the immediate post–Second World War period helps us understand that the exclusions of gender from the public sphere have been subject to ongoing negotiation from both inside and out, tested all the way along by audiences, producers, and institutions. This remarkable history has not always been matched by theorizing about media because of disciplinary boundaries between media studies, history, and sociology (Briggs 1980; Vipond 1997). Feminist media studies, at times, has not been able to account for the specific claims on the public sphere that women made during the postwar period, partly because studies have focused on historical breaks and generational shifts: the emergence of the figure of "the new woman" in early twentieth-century media (Leman 1980, 1983; Tinkler and Krasnick Warsh 2008), the second-wave feminist struggles during the 1970s (the latter of which gave rise to programs such as those produced by the AWBC), or the tensions of postfeminist media culture (Arthurs 2003; Brunsdon 2013; Moseley and Wheatley 2008; Spigel 2013). Such history has often told fine-grained stories of individuals and drawn out the influence of organizations and institutions, but done so without the benefit of theoretical frameworks developed by sociology, which aim to look for wider patterns and articulations of private experiences with historical change, and vice versa. The stories told in this book thus aim to draw these potentialities closer together: the political project of feminist media studies towards the "inside" story of historical experience and the "outside consciousness" of the sociological imagination.

Looking from this multisited perspective, the case of these programs tells us much about struggles for both coherent accounts of the public service broadcasting project and certainty around normative ideas of gender. Managements were always anxious about what held audiences together: a simple focus on gender never seemed to be enough to tie audience, format, and content into a neat package. This anxiety was there right from the beginning, for example, as early as 1938, when the ABC's middle management was uncertain that daytime radio sessions for women "served any purpose" (Inglis 1983: 58). The remit of such programming had to be constantly reiterated and rearticulated with the public service broadcasting project. While the demise of gender-defined programming in the 1960s can be seen to mark the end of the figure of the woman at home, steeped in everyday life as a time and place apart from public life, listening attentively to "educational" programming, this moment was not the end of the question of "what the woman listener wants." Talks for women as a locus of uneasy negotiations around such issues demonstrate that the trajectory of media historical research should end neither in policy nor audience research, but in the dialogue between media institutions and their reception in everyday life. While the constructions of women's work these programs put across may have been hegemonic (Boris 2004: 66), this is a dialogue that is always many-sided, a fact we should not forget, despite the technological form of radio as a broadcast medium.

In the process of documenting these dialogues, a variety of materials have been brought into play with each other: recordings of the programs have been used where they were available, as well as scripts where they were not. Newspaper and magazine coverage of the programs has been used to trace the efforts of the broadcasters' publicity departments to control the public perception of the program and garner listeners in a sometimes hostile medium. Print media has been investigated as a space for the audience to record their own responses to and desires for the programs, as well as for nascent radio celebrities, sometimes as fodder for the women's pages, to manage their own profiles and engage in a more formal dialogue with their listeners. Within the radio listings pages of daily newspapers, critics debated the value and direction of the programs and tracked the rise and fall of particular kinds of presentation styles. Institutional, as well as personal, archives divulged some of the "behind-the-scenes" work that went into the programs, as well as echoing many tussles over dominant perceptions of what women wanted to hear.

A range of repositories across three continents were used for building up this picture. Sound archives consulted include the archives of the ABC in Sydney, the BBC Sound Library at the British Library in London, and the CBC Archives in Toronto. Documentary research was conducted via the National Archives of Australia reading rooms in Sydney, Canberra, and Melbourne, the BBC's Written Archives Centre at Caversham Park, Library and Archives Canada's collection of CBC records in Toronto and Ottawa, and University of Waterloo's collection of personal papers of CBC women. Online archives searched for mentions of the programs and names of producers and presenters include "BBC Genome," which contains the BBC listings information from the *Radio Times* 1923 to 2009; the British Library's "British Newspaper Archive"; the National Library of Australia's "Trove" digitized newspaper database; and "Lantern," the University of Wisconsin-Madison Media History Digital Library (Pierce and Hoyt 2011). While this research has been as comprehensive as possible, there are still gaps in the records, new sets of documents to be unearthed and new angles to be thought through. Media histories are still being made and played.

Radio: Public, Private, Intimate

Introduction

On Armistice Day, 1939, Queen Elizabeth, consort to HM King George VI, broadcast a "Message to the women of the Empire" (Queen Elizabeth 1939). The speech, essentially a call to women in former and current British colonies to join the war effort, was transmitted via the BBC's shortwave "Empire Service" at Daventry in Northampton to local stations with BBC affiliation around the world. In Perth, Australia, for example, the broadcast appeared on the city's second ABC station 6WN on Sunday evening, after a performance by the New Note Octet of a tune entitled "Carnival" and just before the 7 p.m. evening news broadcast ("Your Radio" 1939). Reportedly written "by the Queen herself" (Alpen 1939) and relayed across stations affiliated with the BBC, this kind of broadcast built on earlier media rituals and "invented traditions" associated with the British Royal Family (Scannell and Cardiff 1991: 280–283).

Up until the 1930s, however, the international circulation of these speeches had only been possible via print, particularly newspapers. Such broadcasts rematerialized and retemporalized the colonial ties of the British Empire and reinscribed them within modern communication networks (Vipond 2006: 277). This kind of broadcast saw the BBC deliberately craft material for rebroadcasting by local stations, thereby appearing closer and more easily accessed by ordinary listeners than through its Empire Service (Potter 2012: 120). Simon Potter has described the BBC's use of broadcast media at this time as "an attempt to reinforce the unity of the British world in a pervasive atmosphere of imperial weakness," thereby reviving "an imperial order inherited from the Victorians" (2012: 2). Thus, the Queen's radio performance centered a racialized imaginary on Buckingham Palace in London as its natural "home" via a network of public service radio stations that materialized imperial connections by extending the reach of the (English) spoken word into homes of families with radio receivers across the former British Empire (Robertson 2013).

Like the King's Christmas messages, the Queen's message to women deliberately invoked homely and familial metaphors. Acknowledging that "war has at all times called for the fortitude of women," Queen Elizabeth's address continued the recent convention of the reigning British Queen making a speech on Armistice Day, established by her mother-in-law Queen Mary after the First World War. Speaking in November 1939, on the eve of the Second World War and only three years since her husband, second in line to the British throne, unexpectedly became King, the recently crowned Elizabeth used the new international medium of radio to signal profound changes in the situation of contemporary women. When she contrasted the role of women in the new war footing with "[the last war which] was an affair of the fighting forces only, [so] wives and mothers at home suffered constant anxiety for their dear ones, and too often the misery of bereavement," the Queen emphasized a new proximity of global events to the domestic sphere. The Queen remarked that women's "lot [in previous wars had been made] harder" because they felt that "there was little they could do beyond heartening, through their own courage and devotion, the men at the front." However, the Queen—speaking as an "ordinary" woman also caught up in the war—explained:

> This has all changed, and we no less than men, we have vital work to do, we have been given the proud privilege of serving our country in her hour of need. The call has come, and in my heart I thank you, the women of our great Empire, for the way that you have answered it, and tasks you have undertaken whether at home or in distant lands, cover every field of national service, and I would like to pay my tribute to all of you who are giving your splendid and unselfish help.

The *Australian Women's Weekly* (*AWW*) "Listening Post" columnist, in a report entitled "No Man's Land," described the speech as "intensely moving … Quiet, simple, charged with deep feeling, it came through like a breath of sweet sanity and clean courage" (1939). As with other media reports of the speech published at the time, the *AWW* underscored the personal impact of the war on the royal family through the figure of the Queen as a mother herself: "The King and I know what it means to be parted from our children." "Listening Post" noted the moment after this sentence appeared in the Queen's performance of the speech, when a "break [appeared] in the Queen's voice as she broadcast her Armistice message to the women of the Empire" and described her voice as "that of a woman conscious of a great task and a boundless debt to those she addressed." These reports confirm that the original intention of the broadcasts was reaffirmed by local print media. This intention of the BBC to use radio as a means to provide former colonies with news from "home" was achieved not just through the content of the broadcasts but also through a new sense of immediacy and simultaneity with this imagined home through radiophonic experiences of space and time that placed the listener alongside the Queen in the flow of world events.

The changes to women's role in wartime invoked by this speech indicated not just that women were called to participate in shoring up this order in new and dramatic ways through war and service work but also that their everyday lives had fundamentally changed. "At the same time," the Queen went on, highlighting the new closeness of the war effort:

> I do not forget the humbler part which so many of you have to play in these trying times ... I know that it is not so difficult to do the big things, the novelty and the excitement of new and interesting duties, have an exhilaration of their own but these tasks are not for every woman, it is the thousand and one worries and irritations in carrying on wartime life in ordinary homes, which are often so hard to bear.

Ending her speech by assuring "those who are feeling the strain ... that in carrying on your home duties, and meeting all these worries cheerfully, you are giving real service to the country," the Queen gave an injunction to the women of the empire to

> see to it, that despite all, that our homes do not lose those very qualities that make them the background as well as the joy of our lives. [In doing so] you are taking your part in keeping the home front, which will have dangers of its own, stable and strong ... it is after all for our homes that we are fighting. And we must see to it, that despite all that our homes do not lose those very qualities that make them the background as well as the joy of our lives.

By using the phrase "on the home front," popularized during the First World War (Andrews and Lomas 2017: 523; Grayzel 1999: 156), the Queen's speech both described and actively invited a newfound intimacy of distant events during wartime with the home.

Media and communication technologies have become increasingly intertwined with our everyday lives. This book considers how our contemporary situation has a longer history. The propagandistic gesture of the Queen's speech shows us that this history is in turn implicated with changing gender roles, as well as imaginaries of whiteness and territorial expansion, and of centripetal forces such as nationhood and empire. Given the complexity of its pleas to the emotional space of the home and family, and its circulation in places that the Queen would never herself visit in person, the Armistice Day broadcast, and the transformation of the spaces of everyday life it claimed, demands critical reflection on how such an event was produced and why it appeared at this particular time and place.

The five-minute speech from Queen Elizabeth was the latest missive from a long-standing series of negotiations between social forces that have sought to keep the private and the public in a proper relation. The transmission was the product of collaborations between broadcast engineers, colonial administrators, radio manufacturers, speech coaches, scriptwriters, studio producers, newspaper columnists, controllers of broadcasting, and, of course, the Queen herself, all of whom needed to come together to produce the event of the moment of broadcast. This chapter examines how these new social actors and political forces emerged at the same time as deep changes in the relationship between the domestic and the public. The chapter is especially interested in how these changes relate to tensions between gender and the public sphere, which we urgently need to address, in order to truly understand the potential that exists in our current moment to forge new ways of living and acting within a mediated society.

Spatial histories

Feminist scholarship has long troubled itself over the ideology of "separate spheres," which has at its heart a powerful dichotomy between male and female, public and private, rational and emotional. While the notion of "waves" of feminism is questionable—as feminism has been continuous with arguments for rights that trace back well before the "first-wave" feminism of the late nineteenth and early twentieth centuries—feminist activism has sought to constitute new social spaces within distinct traditions, which in turn have contested this binary ideology in different spatial modes.

First-wave feminism's claims were on the public sphere, the worlds of work and government, and its tactics were to radically rupture boundaries that excluded women from public institutions. Suffragettes—so named for their claims of universal suffrage or the right to vote for women—produced new and radical social spaces for women through the physical occupation of parliament and their interventions in other key sites of power, such as a transnational public sphere of communications between women's groups in separate nations (DiCenzo, Delap and Ryan 2011; Skoog 2011). Second-wave feminism's concerns, by contrast, centered on moving issues affecting women out of the private realm (unpaid work, gendered violence, the way that inequality is linked to care, embodiment, and so on) into the public, where they become visible, in order to demand change to taken-for-granted relations between public and private (Elshtain 1981; Pateman 1983). Most recently, third-wave feminists have pluralized and questioned these two strands, thus interrogating and linking the most distant, corporate, and military power with the most proximate, bodily autonomy (Pain 2015; Pain and Staeheli 2014; Pratt and Rosner 2006).

Within these waves, socialist-feminist analyses of societies organized along capitalist lines of male domination could also be read as moves to highlight how the "public" is implicated in class formations and how these formations vary across space and time. Contemporary feminism increasingly investigates how domains of the personal and the political intersect in everyday lives of women around the world, rather than understanding them as separate and noncontiguous. Likewise, black and postcolonial feminist critiques of the intersection of racialized and gendered exclusions call public power into question by asking how certain kinds of racial privilege erase other rights and relegate certain bodies to the private sphere (for example, Razack 2018). In settler-colonial societies, feminist critiques of the persistent authority of neocolonial institutions to intervene in the lifeworlds of indigenous communities call into sharp relief racialized divisions between private and public (Povinelli 2006). In these diverse ways, such feminisms share a project of spatial politics.

Despite this long history of feminist activism around the public-private divide, recently feminist scholars have highlighted that such distinctions are "unfinished business" (Higgins 1999–2000: 848). Many scholars, particularly those who have looked at the impact of current reallocations of private power and the rise of non-state actors in contemporary society, have excoriated second-wave feminist calls to erase the difference between public and private. As a result, this emerging feminist take on neoliberal gender politics has keenly highlighted how the canonical feminist strategies described above have at times paralleled classical liberal strategies to "privatise the public" (Cohen and O'Byrne 2013: 40). While not explicitly feminist, the programs that are studied here, and the people who worked on them, negotiated these complex relationships between the production, consumption, and distribution of media representations of gender. As DiCenzo has argued, by acknowledging the gendered nature of media and taking a historical approach to feminism itself, a more nuanced account of both media history and feminist historiography can emerge (DiCenzo 2004: 44). DiCenzo, writing in response to Curran, troubles the latter's description of a theme in media history that he terms the "Feminist Interpretation," which maps the "advance of women" (Curran 2002: 138):

> This [liberal-democratic] account contains an important element of truth. However, one of its defects is that it omits to mention that the "public" initially represented by the press largely excluded women. This is rectified by a different interpretation which narrates media history as HERstory. This simple shift of perspective produces a very different version of media history. (Curran 2002: 138–139)

Furthermore, Curran depicts the

> period from 1918 to 1968 [as] a time when the advance of women was to a significant extent contained … mainly because the success of the women's movement on the political front was not matched by a corresponding success on the cultural front. Most women continued to be socialized into acceptance of subordinate roles through family, education and peer group pressure. Women's culture, in the form of romantic novels, women's and girls' magazines, remained strongly influenced by traditional gender values. (Curran 2002: 139)

Curran's overarching narrative, while appealing, ignores the cultural construction of "traditional gender values" in radio and other broadcast media. Rather than simply seeing that "feminist history focuses on women, and largely excludes one half of the population (as does most media history, the other way round)" (Curran 2002: 149), it could be more productive to see gender as relational and the writing of feminist history as a project of diversifying and pluralizing gender itself rather than setting such clear boundaries and cohering around objects of study. As DiCenzo rejoins: "While feminist media scholars may privilege 'gender' as a category of analysis, this is not the same thing as looking exclusively at women" (2004: 46). The debate between Curran and DiCenzo is encapsulated here as an argument for complexity and nuance in the writing of media history. The material analyzed in this book resolutely shows that a great deal of ambivalence toward and questioning of "two-sphere" ideology did exist within the fifty-year span marked out by Curran as being complacent and conformist. The contradictions of the gendered media audience analyzed by US scholars, for example, have questioned the separation of women's interests from the "public" in the partitioning of daytime and evening programming during the 1930s (see Hilmes 1999; Wang 2002: 349; Wang 2018), when according to a CBS audience report, more women than men actually listened to CBS's evening programs (and 40 percent of men listened to morning and afternoon programs) ("Radio in 1936" cited in Craig 2000: 244, figure 13). Other scholars have highlighted how the silences and omissions of a gendered narrative distort other differences and through a focus on intersectionality have shown how this period was also marked by contestations of racial as much as gender ideologies, for example in Rooks's work on African American women's magazines (Rooks 2004).

What this book proposes is that these struggles over who or what should be private, of who or what belongs to the public sphere and therefore within it, are actually fundamental struggles over the particularities of power. Power delineates our understandings of place and space. Power constructs commonsense maps of the world, gives us our sense of who and what should be close, and who and what should be far away. Power gives shape to our sense of belonging to place and with whom we belong. This book argues that these struggles have been paralleled (but were not simply started) by the intertwining of media with our everyday lives. No longer able to "screen out" or "tune out" the voices of others entirely, media architectures are implicated in a profusion of complex and unresolvable claims on our attention, which throw us, whether we like it or not, into the entanglements of the public-private distinction.

The book draws on archives that register how these entanglements have developed over time (Bijsterveld 2016). The archives examined here show how powerful social forces have sought to properly discipline not only the relationship between the public and private by defining women's role in the home but also the ways that these definitions have been resisted by generations of feminists well before second-wave feminism. The material gathered together in this book explores programming for women from the mid-1930s until the 1960s on three public service broadcasters: the British Broadcasting Corporation (BBC, first as a Company 1922–1927 and then as a Corporation, 1927–present), the Canadian Broadcasting Corporation (first as the Canadian Radio Broadcasting Corporation (CRBC), 1932–1936, and then as CBC, 1936–present), and the Australian Broadcasting Commission (ABC, 1932–1983, first as a Company 1929–1932, subsequently as a Corporation 1983–present). This period was selected for examination because it was a time of tremendous change in social definitions of gender roles, audience expectations, and media forms, yet the ways this transition actually played out within media texts and institutions have not often been traced at a fine-grained level. The choice of these three broadcast institutions was made for both practical and methodological reasons. Firstly, the practical considerations of access to archives and my location in Australia drew me to investigate the ABC. I initially focused on talk programs as the ABC's archives were patchy to say the least for off-air or pre-produced recorded material until the 1970s, and only written scripts of full programs were available in the National Archives documents that had been transferred from the ABC. Talks were also the overwhelming genre through which the ABC made up its women's programming, partly because of funding constraints, but also because many of the early appointments at the ABC were linked to popular educational institutions such as the Workers Education Association (WEA). As I read around the topic and began looking through the ABC's collections, I realized not only that the AWBC's push toward feminist broadcasting during the mid-1970s was unique in the English speaking-world but also that the ABC's corporate attitude during radio's heyday had not been disposed toward progressive coverage of women's issues (as discussed in Chapters 3 and 6). Through digging into the document and tape archives of the ABC, I came across references to Canadian and British content that signaled a concerted, if not sustained nor mutually reinforced, effort to share program content between women's programs. I discovered that the BBC's still-running women's (although not explicitly feminist) program, *Woman's Hour*, had in many ways paralleled the ABC *Women's Sessions* but had taken the format in new directions. On a research trip to Canada, I came across the incredible stories of the CBC women discussed in Chapter 4. While all three institutions made attempts to define a gendered audience, these audiences were often not satisfied with the content and approach that were put across to them and in turn shaped the programs. What were the dynamics that pushed and pulled these programs internally across these different directions? What insights could be gained by a multicentered perspective, one that did not hold central one national context or another but followed the threads and tracks of the couriered tapes and scripts, as well as the ideas of gendered media as they went back and forth across these three countries?

I discuss both the birth and the discontinuation of these programs on these three broadcasters because the debates about what should replace them, as much as the ones that started them, demonstrate there was much at stake in the existence of these programs. At both ends of these program's lives, there was an intense consideration of the aims of the broadcasters and their responsibility to accurately represent women's experience, whether expressed as audience feedback on content or approach, or explicit feminist activism around media issues. The stories of these programs and the women that made them provide rich and valuable evidence of the dynamic relationship between media texts, producers, and audiences. Each chapter focuses on key moments in the establishment, consolidation, and decline of this programming. The discussion of program content and behind-the-scenes negotiations draws out what was at stake in tensions between the management of the broadcasters and their staff (most often female, but not exclusively) who attempted, and at times succeeded, in pushing the boundaries of what was considered "women's programming."

The answer to exactly why certain material and topics within the programs were challenging, or were seen to fall outside the prevailing narrow definitions of the audience for these programs, thus becoming so troubling to the management of these institutions, is complex. The key to answering this question lies in the specific contexts of each case and the individual women who challenged broadcasters' preconceptions—for example, Irene Greenwood's "Women in the International News" talks on the local ABC station 6WF in Perth, Western Australia, during the 1930s (discussed in Chapter 3). Uncovering the specifics of each moment is instructive, especially for the way in which changing political alliances, specifically the persistence of imperial networks alongside the foreshadowing of cold war politics, played out in each location. In debates over the "correct" format and content for programming aimed at the modern woman within the modern home, what seems at times to be merely aesthetic or personality-driven choices were in fact grounded in a paradox within the remit of these institutions: to use a public medium to define women as responsible for the space of the everyday life while bracketing out their involvement in public life. While public service broadcasting's take on the home as a feminized space was often understood to be self-evident and incontestible, and its activities natural progression that would inevitably direct home life in more productive directions while containing women within its demands for unpaid labor (Bailey 2009; Betts and Crowley 2005), this contradiction was central to the undoing of the programs as a "space apart" from the flow of public time and space.

Ultimately, this remit of gendered programming was fundamentally unsettled by radically different imaginaries of the connections between home and world that increasingly appeared in such programs. The nascent feminist arguments that the female producers and hosts attempted to make against these rigid ideas of home's role in modernity emerged within larger debates and were fed by connections between national and international women's organizations of the 1930s and 1940s. The "separation of spheres" was challenged through an alternative imaginary that sought to liberate women from their maternalist role, increasingly through a progressive alignment between gender issues and other political struggles.

So although this book is about radio programs for a particular listenership on a specific set of stations, it is only partially a history of radio programming for women on these three public service broadcasters as particular medium with an imagined audience. This book is also a history of a mediated relation. The relation in question is the one imagined by the state to exist between the public and the private. A key cultural form through which this relation can be understood was the "woman's program" on daytime radio as a uniquely intimate, self-sufficient, repetitive, and mundane space and time apart from the more dynamic and open-ended space-time of non-gendered programming. While generalized programming of current affairs, drama, and music of evenings and weekends was directed to an unmarked male listener, the relation between such programming and the "woman's program" makes sense only in relation to the broadcast schedule as a whole. Public service broadcasters clearly imagined and addressed their audience as solidly middle class—or if not already middle class, then in need of cultural uplift to become so—yet the relation between different social classes remains tacit in the way that public service broadcasting has formulated its project.

While the very meaning and viability of the domestic sphere as a classed, racialized, and gendered space was changing during this time, the model of what it should and should not include was also defined through "visual images and a social map where sex and class divisions are confined to specified physical areas … *mean[ing] that it takes a special effort to see the model from the outside*" (Davidoff, L'Esperance and Newby 1995: 67, emphasis mine). While the idealized image of the domestic sphere was defined through such heroic metaphors as "the home front," the model was not necessarily taken as given by the women who worked on the programs I explore here. The themes and topics that they included in their programs were defined by programming policies that were beyond their control, but they often, in the day-to-day work that they undertook for the programs, stretched and pushed at the boundaries of the model, reflecting wider tensions and ruptures in the model itself. The book is an exploration of how such tensions and ruptures were felt and lived through the voices recorded in the scripts and memos, fragile scraps of paper left pinned to the files, that have been drawn from the archives here. While much wider than broadcasting itself, these struggles are writ large within the medium of public service radio, a technological form produced by the modern state, and consumed in the modern domestic, as a progenitor of a modern, mediated society. Radio programming aimed at, and presented by, women during the twentieth century was a unique moment of critical importance understanding the role of media in contemporary life. The decline of the programs also tells us much about how media forms mesh or jar with collective understandings of gender. Through an analysis of the debates over the form and content of this programming, I demonstrate how these programs reflected crucial changes in the cultural spaces available to women during the mid-twentieth century.

Histories of intimacy

Throughout this book, I use the notion of the "intimate" to describe a constitutive dynamic of closeness and distance. In this aspect, the book builds on a long history of feminist work to transform the separation between the public and the private by bringing into clearer focus the ethical aspects of everyday life (Elshtain 1981: 335). Inquiry into this relation is important and valuable because what kind of nexus there is between the personal and the political, the individual and the collective, is a question that remains at the heart of contemporary social relations. While this question has been explored in important work inspired by new social movements that seeks to unpack the heteronormative assumptions of intimacy (Gabb 2008: 77–78), more work needs to be done to pick up the threads of the role of media in the "intimate turn."

To this end, this book explores a moment when broadcast media became part of the social architecture of the home. The historical moment when the electronic medium of radio was enfolded into the everyday time and spaces of the modern home tells us a great deal about contemporary mediations of everyday life because radio broadcasts constructed an immediacy and semblance of presence that had never before been experienced in the domestic sphere. Radio's coincidence with maintenance and transgression of social boundaries has long been highlighted by media historians (Hayes 2012; MacLennan 2013; Moores 1988; Razlogova 2003, 2006, 2011; Scales 2010, 2016; Smulyan 1993; Valliant 2013). While modern print mass media (books, newspaper, magazines) had already been "at home" for some time, radio's reception has been associated with an "intimization" of public address, as institutions such as national governments (Lacey 1994, 1996; Nicholas 1996) as well as commercial interests (Johnson 1983; MacLennan 2013) and civic associations (Goodman 2007) sought to access new constituencies in novel ways. Most notably, public figures such as politicians struggled to find ways to adapt to and control their message in the new medium (Loviglio 2005). As many of these scholars have pointed out, this "intimization" has a longer history, which is not unique to broadcast media such as radio (see, for example, Illouz 2007). These accounts work against the technological determinism of much scholarship and provide a clearer sense of the agency of individual listeners and their specific social contexts, as well as how these new formations of media and the home paralleled changes in broader economic and political structures. This section provides an account of these changes through the lens of "the intimate sphere," which underpins the politics of everyday life that is the topic of the book.

Indeed, media had already been enfolded into the private life of the European bourgeois family from the seventeenth century onwards, a time characterized by what Jurgen Habermas (1989) terms the "structural transformation of the public sphere." In Habermas's account, a long transformation took place in the everyday life of the middle classes of Europe during the seventeenth and eighteenth centuries. This transformation was felt as a new kind of interface between the world of politics and the family, out of the courtly society of the early seventeenth century to the coffee shops and public houses of the early eighteenth century, then into the home, all the time facilitated by the mass distribution of print material, particularly the dissemination of popular novels that dealt with domestic subjects in an epistolary style (Habermas 1989: 49–50). Habermas describes media's imbrication with domestic life in passing via the rare explanations he gives of the concept of the intimate sphere within his wider analysis. Paying attention to these explanations opens out a productive space for a new kind of analysis of the relationship between media and everyday life.

A closer reading of Habermas provides the ground for a fundamental re-interpretation of the relationship between home and world in the formation of modern sociality. In the first section of his second chapter on "Social Structures of the Public Sphere" entitled "The Basic Blueprint," Habermas identifies historical development of the public sphere with the decline of the privatized power of the monarchy, as authority was "depersonified" and became more widely shared and checked by emerging class formations. The bourgeois public sphere, according to Habermas, is revealed sociologically

> in the recognition of the fact that it was private people who related to each other in it as a public. The public's understanding of the public use of reason was guided specifically by such private experiences as grew out of the audience-oriented

(*publikumsbezogen*) subjectivity of the conjugal family's intimate domain (*Intimsphäre*). (Habermas 1989: 28)

This developmental framework is challenged in a later section "The Bourgeois Family and the Institutionalisation of a Privateness Oriented to an Audience," in which Habermas provides an account of the transformation of the bourgeois home into a more solitary, individualized environment. Habermas thus complicates the way in which this temporal progression plays out by highlighting the spatial simultaneity of public and private in the same site. While Habermas sets up the private domain of the bourgeois family as a precondition for the emergence of public, rational debate, these two forces are not so easily separated: "The line between public and private sphere extended right through the home" (Habermas 1989: 45). The early institutions of the public sphere were "held together through the medium of the press and its professional criticism" (1989: 51). Important strands of media sociology, particularly those that stem from anthropological views of how modern technologies are intermingled with enduring rituals of the maintenance of community and the reproduction of the social order, have emphasized the role of media in bringing together individual actors into wider entities. A limitation of these traditions is their unquestioned functionalism—their tendency to posit the maintenance of monolithic, unquestionable social structures over the analysis of issues of difference and inequality that these very structures create.

Habermas's work cuts against this functionalist tendency as he demonstrates the emergence of class formations at the same time as media forms. Habermas explains:

> The sphere of the market we call "private"; the sphere of the family, as the core of the private sphere, we call the "intimate sphere." The latter was believed to be independent of the former, whereas in truth it was profoundly caught up in the requirements of the market. (1989: 55)

Later in the book, he further describes the modern intimate sphere as different from preexisting forms as it intersected with an "audience" and is "public-oriented": "The consciousness of [universal humanity] grew up in the patriarchal conjugal family's intimate sphere that was oriented to a public" (1989: 85). Eventually, he laments, in a dystopic vision of a post–Second World War suburbia based on consumer culture, "The intimate sphere dissolved before the gaze of the 'group'" (1989: 157). Against the claim that the intimate sphere has "dissolved" without trace, the trajectory of "intimacy studies" is crucially foreshadowed in Habermas's oblique references to the mutual constitution of the intimate and the public.

As feminist scholars have sought to elaborate, Habermas's notion of "intimate sphere" (*Intimsphare*) is crucial to his understanding of the public sphere, yet it is an elusive concept. It is important here to acknowledge that the "private sphere" has internal distinctions that match the complexity of notions of "the public." As Fraser has suggested, castigating feminists for their use of an undifferentiated notion of "the public sphere," the "private" also requires analytical distinctions between "private property in a market economy" and private life, as in "intimate domestic or personal life, including sexual life" (Fraser 1990: 57).[1] The tension between these two components of "private life" gives rise to the Habermasian argument that modernity is experienced as a radical upheaval in speaking and listening in public through sentimental and individualized forms.

While the transformation of the public sphere was "structural" in the sense of a structural conflict between different social classes, as Habermas argues, it was also lived and felt through cultural production. Appearing in the watershed year of 1750, the cultural form through which a new interface between public and private manifests is the "mediocre" domestic novel *Pamela* (43). The new configuration of the domestic and the political embodied in such texts, and understood by their readers, is diagnosed by Habermas as potentially permeable to a range of voices with less regard to status than had previously been possible. While the radical ideal of the bourgeois public sphere was its "openness to … popular participation" (Calhoun 1992: 4), feminist scholars have long since complicated this story and questioned whether Habermas's analytical category of the public sphere actually rests on idealized claims to universal participation that were never realized and, further, reproduces the gendered assumptions of the public-private binary (Fraser 1989, 1990; Landes 1995; McLaughlin 1993, 2004). While Habermas does not go so far as to designate, as Nancy Fraser (1990: 62) does, the notion of the public sphere as *bourgeois masculinist*, rather than simply *bourgeois*, he does clearly imply that the emergence of this public sphere was within a gendered space. He sees the experiences that sought expression in a public sphere of private individuals as flowing from "the wellspring of a specific subjectivity [which] had its home, literally, in the sphere of the patriarchal conjugal family" (Habermas 1989: 55). He diagnoses this family "turned in on itself" as based on a newly "permanent intimacy" (44), which both challenged the ruling elites and demanded new kinds of political subjectivities.

It is important to remember that, as historians of everyday life have traced, the concept of the domestic as a private space is only a recent phenomenon and emerges at the moment when specific spaces in the modern European household were linked to specific activities (Ariès 1962: 392–393):

> In the eighteenth century, the family began to hold society at a distance, to push it back beyond a steadily extending zone of private life. The organization of the house altered in conformity with this new desire to keep the world at bay .... It has been said that comfort dates from this period; it was born at the same time as domesticity, privacy and isolation, and it was one of the manifestations of these phenomena. (Ariès 1962: 398–399)

Michel Foucault described Ariès's work on this history of the spatial patterning of the modern family as key to his understanding of space, power, and knowledge. In an interview with novelist Jean-Pierre Barou and feminist labor historian Michelle Perrot, Foucault cited this passage from Ariès's book as inspiration for a "whole history [which] remains to be written of *spaces*—which would at the same time be the history of *powers* (both these terms in the plural)," arguing that "anchorage [of subjects] in a space is an economico-political form which needs to be studied in detail" (Foucault 1980: 149, emphasis in the original).

Following these debates, it is the premise of this book that the binary of public and private has always been socially constructed, and that in these attempts to define and give proper place to the intimate, important historical contestations and negotiations—which have been ongoing well before second-wave feminist critiques—have been elided. This book gives an account of how relations between public and private were imagined and fought over during times that have traditionally been understood as proto- or even antifeminist. By looking in close detail at the content and context of broadcasting for and by women in the mid-twentieth century, I argue that what has been considered as the preeminent struggle by feminists in the late twentieth century—the public-private distinction—was not new and has actually been erased in many accounts of feminist historiography (Rakow 2008). Here, it is important to acknowledge that while such erasures have been blind spots within feminism, many contemporary feminists are working with exactly this dynamic—to revisit past periods and to retell stories differently—and are capturing previously untapped energies of past incarnations of feminism and rethinking current ways of understanding relationships between gendered spaces and social domains (for example, Carmi 2015; Johnson 2010; Rooks 2004).

The arrival of radio in the domestic sphere in Western societies in the period just after the First World War had an asymmetrical impact on gender relations across the world, as women's very selves were being increasingly defined through the home in particular ways (Hilmes 1999). Many nonelectronic and oral cultural forms (storytelling, jokes, singing) have been intrinsic to family and domestic life, and still remain so, but in the early twentieth century, the arrival of radio figured a new constellation of social forces in the daily lives of men and women. When radio found a place in the home within the flow of domestic events, it spoke directly—even if such radio was prerecorded, even if many other people were listening to the same program, and even if there was a model, "stand-in" audience for the program in the studio—to the listener-at-home. While other mass-reproduced visual media (books, photography, newspapers) had already represented places and times outside the home, radio offered a much more immediate access to these external places and times, and to the people who inhabited, felt joy, and suffered within them. In what follows I suggest that we are only able to understand our contemporary situation by grasping the significance of this process. These changes become evident only through close attention to the changes in the relationship between public and private that were forged at this time. By taking a historical perspective and taking into account the complex negotiations of the public and private that new media forms throw up, we are able to revisit the public-private distinction with fresh eyes. This revisiting is a key means of advancing the spatial politics of the feminist project. In order to do so, I propose a framework that abandons the absolute and binary nature of the public-private distinction while still allowing us to understand that this distinction has immense power and material force via the relationality that such difference implies.

"Intimacy," I argue, has the potential to operate as a third term that unsettles clear divisions and taken-for-granted hierarchies between public and private. Studies of intimate life help us understand how power constructs families, sexualities, social labor (Jamieson 1998), as well as life plans, emotional commitments, and a politics of love (Plummer 2001, 2003). The radical potential of the intimate sphere is key to understanding a broad set of power shifts in contemporary culture, shifts that continue today, as new cultural forms invoke new relationships between intimate and public discourse. In the following chapters, I connect these tensions with a series of case studies of the circumscription of women's participation in the public sphere to show broadcasting intensified a gendered politics of the domestic that had been bubbling up since the privatization of domestic space described by Habermas and highlighted as historically contingent by Aries and Foucault.

Inciting intimate geographies

For these reasons, I suggest that we can better understand the role of radio in the twentieth century through the lens of "intimate geographies." This notion helps move beyond a simplistic public-private distinction—and indeed one that is based on abstraction—to be able to understand the historical development of intimate form of broadcasting as a concrete and specific networking of public and private spaces that helps foregrounds the collective subjectivities at play. More than ever, we need to see more clearly how the public and private are interrelated and mutually constitutive (Stewart 2003). Intimate geographies are thus spaces constantly being rewritten and open to new relations, full of human agency and the potential for civic action. Intimate geographies branch out from privatized lifeworlds in unexpected and inspiring ways.

Some examples of these potentials can be found in recent work by feminist cultural geographers Rachel Pain and Lynn Staeheli (2014), who propose a radical coupling of "intimacy-geopolitics" that connects everyday experiences of violence with a multiplicity of spaces, thus refusing "scalar or spatial hierarchy" (Pain 2015: 72), and instead speak out loud that Foucauldian injunction to *write a history of spaces and powers simultaneously*. As Anna Parkinson has recently argued in a study of the structures of feeling exhibited by Theodor Adorno's post–Second World War broadcasts on West German radio, the socio-spatiality of media provides concrete means to reshape our notions of where and with whom we belong (Parkinson 2017). Parkinson's definition of "intimate geographies" builds on Pain and Staeheli's work to think through

> the space that one inhabits and through which one receives the social coordinates anchoring the individual to certain communities. [Intimate geographies] are particular intersubjective spaces and communicative modalities through which discussion, conflict, and behavior are negotiated, and act to reproduce or, at times, to alter a society's habitus or social norms and ways of existing in the world. (Parkinson 2017: 2)

This lens of the intimacy of media space is useful to look at not only radio geographies but other media geographies as well, such as film (Lloyd 2014) and digital and social media (see Chapter 6). In this book, I focus on gender and radio in order to offer a medium-specific history, one that gives a rich and complex view of the social processes surrounding the changing materiality and practices of the modern home. In order to explore this new intimacy of public space through media, and the transformation of gender politics that coincides with it, the next section outlines the arguments of key thinkers who have traced intimacy as a site of power and production of selves in contemporary society.

Lauren Berlant's extensive writing on the intimate public sphere (1998, 2000) has reworked the public-private distinction in provocative and fundamental ways that inform the notion of intimate geographies. Berlant together with her coauthor Michael Warner (Berlant and Warner 1998), and her interlocutors included in the 2000 edited collection *Intimacy*, tell stories of "how hard it is to adjudicate the norms of a public world when it is also an intimate one" (2008: 2). Berlant diagnoses the intimate public sphere as a recent phenomenon and implicates contemporary mass media, starting out from Habermas, in preparing persons "for their critical social function in … the intimate spheres of domesticity, where they would learn (say, from novels and newspapers) to experience their internal lives theatrically, as though oriented toward an audience" (2008: 3). Yet as Berlant and others have teased out, the public sphere is not a singular entity, and it is built on multiple exclusions, not the least of which is founded on gender.

By introducing a queered and gendered perspective on Habermas's important work, as Berlant does, the potential for a new critique of media's spatiality and the formation of modern subjectivities that are simultaneously public and private, and unequally intimated, emerge. The problem posed by normative models of the public sphere is that the publicness of the public sphere is taken for granted, and its nomination as a "sphere" posits its existence as a homogenous and autonomous thing (compressing the complex processes drawn out from Habermas's work outlined above). These models have a reifying force that masks public concentrations of power's relationships to the private. Berlant argues that intimacy is not given to any one place or site and as such is not equivalent to the private sphere. Instead, intimacy is "mobile," "portable, unattached to a concrete space: a drive that creates spaces around it through practices" (2008: 4). Thus, intimacy arises through practiced geographies. It is this fundamental relationality of intimacy as a "third term" that bridges and questions the public and private divide that provides a key for a different take on media history, one that integrates the spatial and the social.

Yet the key tension highlighted by feminist critics of universalist notions of the public sphere remains. As feminist thinkers such as Landes have pointed out, the notion of "the public sphere and the conditions for publicity presupposed a distinction between public and private matters [thus] it was ill equipped to consider in public fashion the political dimensions of relations in the intimate sphere" (1995: 97). Such feminist critiques highlight how notions of the private perpetuate the original meaning of privacy, a state "de-*prived*" of public relevance. This history is recorded within the etymology of the term "privacy," which indicates "private" phenomena as those places or states "lacking" public significance (Bok 1982: 290). These recent critically informed and historically based reconfigurations of intimacy, which go beyond a model of privacy as "lacking" public relevance to look at intimacy as a relational space (Blatterer 2010), in parallel with the model proposed by Landes, show how the exclusion of women, among others, from the mediated public sphere was a constitutive move, one that paradoxically enabled claims to universalism. Framed by other patriarchal social institutions such as the family, radio programming for women struggled to overcome these exclusions. As the following chapters show, women producers made valiant efforts to democratize radio but repeatedly encountered assumptions that, on the one hand, everyday life lacked political relevance and, on the other, that gendered programming was not able to speak about wider issues of public relevance. Such efforts to democratize radio for women foundered, however, on the strategies employed in doing so, which were based in "maternalist" or "feminine" viewpoints, which clashed with deeply held ideals of both the new cultural form of radio as a universal public and the possibility of women's programming speaking to a collective subject who had more than a narrow set of interests in domestic and familial topics. This contradiction, I argue, partitioned off women's programming as a "semi-private" space (Rooney 2002, 2004) that, while it held multiple and conflicting investments for different collective subjects, remained unassimilable into the dominant mode of radio as embodying public time and space.

In this *feminine* public sphere, broadcasts to women were developed to subjugate the private to the public: oriented to bring the knowledge of experts to bear on household management and to make for maximum efficiency in use of commodities and the optimum productivity of domestic labor, topics that were discussed as the "modernization" of the home. Important work by scholars in the 1980s and 1990s has mapped how an intimized media address has manifest in moments of active depoliticization such as in Nazi Germany

(Lacey 1994, 1996) as well as in liberal-democratic societies such as the United States (Steiner 1995) and Canada (Crean 1987; Taylor 1985). Women's media in this mode has also been argued to contain cultural forms that deliberately invite intimate connections between audiences and commodities, for example in women's magazines of the late nineteenth century as an "intimate imagined space" (Duffy 2013: 31–32). Australian feminist historian Marilyn Lake argues that pairing of women and home was loosened during the Second World War, in tandem with the rise of consumerist cultural forms aimed at women. Such forms directly evoked and addressed female desire, rather than duty, especially within cinema and commodity advertising. She challenges historians of gender to take account of the "changing structure of femininity itself, the interplay of cultural forms and self-definition, and the way that changes in discourse [are] secured by the specificity of ... [historical] conditions" such as wartime (Lake 1990: 267).

Looking at women's programming on radio through this lens, a new set of questions emerge outside a purely biographical or media historical perspective: What kinds of changes in the structure and discourses of femininity were contained with radio as a cultural form? The intimate address of public service radio programming for women sought to be an inspirational companion, or knowledgeable friend, supporting the listener through daily life, providing expert knowledge on homecraft, personal relationships, and child-rearing. While at times this friendly voice encouraged women to take up their role in the public sphere, as members of civil society in women's organizations or local government, very rarely did this vision of friendship extend to workplace solidarity in the sphere of paid employment. Within this emergent *feminist* public sphere, women producers and hosts worked both overtly and covertly to discuss material about current world events and political organizing with their audience. These women worked from the inside-out of the public-private distinction: through media production as a form of social action, they aimed to move private, individualized experience into the open, thus complicating the public-private divide and questioning the taken-for-granted legitimacy of women's exclusion from the flow of public time and occupation of public space, as has been argued by a body of work conducted since the 2000s by generation of historians who have revisited these programs with a view to uncovering previously hidden gendered histories (Lesley Johnson's 1988 *The Unseen Voice* and Kate Lacey's 1994 *Feminine Frequencies* are both groundbreaking in this regard). This crucial work has been continued most recently in the UK, through extensive archival work, particularly around the programming policies and career biographies of women involved in the BBC's programming for women. Recent publications by Kate Murphy (2016), Kristin Skoog (2009, 2010, 2011, 2013, 2014, 2017), and others (Andrews 2012a, b; Bailey 2009; Rewinkel 2013) have worked with the BBC's extensive Written Archives to tell previously untold histories. In Canada, recent and thoughtful work on women's contributions to the CBC by Kate Zankowicz (2015) and Barbara Freeman (2011) has uncovered key figures and unearthed important connections between women working in public broadcasting and civil society groups, both nationally in the case of work by Zankowicz (2015) on the CBC's Kate Aitken and internationally by Freeman (2001, 2011) in her account of Elizabeth Long and others' involvement in transnational media associations. In the Australian context, Jeannine Baker's recent study (2017) of figures such as Irene Greenwood's work on commercial radio has contributed to this project. Outside the scope of this book, such work in non-European countries has been focused on the United States (Ganzert 2003; Hayes 2012; Smulyan 1993), while other important critical historical work continues to be done in Latin America by Christine Ehrick (2016) in particular. This book comes out of this distributed and ongoing work. In what follows I seek to add to these national histories and forge new encounters between them.

Media's Domestication as Intimate Geography

Introduction: Not a technical article

In 1922, the US magazine *Radio Broadcast* published an article entitled "O Woe! Radio." The article was introduced by the magazine's editors as "a cry of despair, a burst of laughter, a tragic comedy and a sly, sound estimate of human character, all rolled into one" (Bourke 1922: 107). They promised that because the article presented "as accurate and entertaining a picture of the effects of radio in the home as we have seen" it would find its echo in "thousands of homes." The article's author, Alice Bourke, described the arrival of a birthday gift from her husband of a "radiophone" when

> during the forenoon the radio man and his assistants came. They had a heavy forty-foot mast with them, and immediately commenced adapting the landscape scheme of the far corner of my garden to their pedal extremities and the pole. They assured me that a good antenna was of the utmost importance.

At this point Bourke asked her readers not to "throw the magazine away until you get your money's worth" certifying upon her "honor that this is not a technical article." She then proceeded to outline all the visits from neighbors that the installation provoked, with the result that by 8.30 that evening "a passerby would have thought the Bourkes were holding a mass meeting":

> When my husband came home to dinner I was waiting in my pink organdie and new white pumps. With my very own hands I coaxed from the rubber-bunioned, carbolic-scented mahogany box the facts that Liberty bonds were going strong, and that it would be cooler tomorrow with variable winds.
>
> We did not Fletcherize [i.e. chew slowly and carefully] dinner that evening. We impatiently awaited the eight o'clock concert. It was not to be. The thoughtful little people who had paid [us a] noontime visit had a rather neat little broadcasting system of their own.

> At five minutes to eight, the Jones and Smith families presented themselves in complete editions on our front porch. It was quite a coincidence that both Mrs. Smith and Mrs. Jones had believed I might like a little fresh lettuce!
>
> Their remembrances made me very happy, but piqued my curiosity, inasmuch as we have such a large lettuce bed ourselves. Ah! How young I was then!

Despite Bourke being proficient at tuning the set, one of the male neighbors continually questioned her abilities:

> I've tried a million odd times to justify my manipulation of the set during atmospheric disturbances, and have spoken to him so learnedly about "static" that a college professor would hang his head in shame, but does this doubting Thomas believe? His eyes say what his lips yearn to: "You can't fool me. You gotta bum set, and don't know how to work it!" (109)

Bourke ended the article with a sign of things to come:

> Do not, I pray you, labor under the delusion that only my evenings are devoted to Public Service. Far from it. In the morning, just about the time I am beginning to wonder how in the name of Heaven John can poke such big holes in his socks, the door-bell rings, and one of my fellow Household Slaves enters. The *Jacksonville Bazoo* has inaugurated a woman's hour from nine to ten. Would I please etc? I accommodate, but the ether does not. She goes home possessed of two eggs, a cup of my butter, and the belief that I wouldn't let her hear Jacksonville because I did not want to be bothered with her. (109)

This beautifully written story of the interplay of social practices and technology, of the intersections of home and public, provides an insight into the moment of radio's domestication during the early 1920s. The process of incorporating radio as a technology and a set of new practices of the circulation of information within the home as a social space was bound up with shifts in gender roles in profound and unpredictable ways. While the "radio-phone" that Bourke receives as her birthday gift is assumed to be a "masculine" technology, her adeptness at "switch[ing] the kazazzies around [to] produce entertainment" (108), as one of her husband's friends from the "Elks club" describes it, produces a different, more open-ended construction of the medium.

Bourke would go on to have a career as a night-rounds police reporter on the *Chicago Tribune* during the 1920s and early 1930s. In 1930 she became known by her call sign W9DXX and thus described in ham radio speak as a "YL [i.e. female, from the morse-code friendly initials for 'Young Lady'] 2-meter operator in the Illinois area" (Woodruff 1951: 4). After she resigned from the *Tribune* around 1933 to take care of her husband during an extended illness ("How a YL Police Reporter Works" 1934), she became more active in ham radio and during the Second World War was trained in cryptography, becoming the only female radio operator in the US Army Reserve (Bien 1941; "Built by Amateur Radio Operator" 1940). While these new roles were yet to come, in 1922, when Bourke wrote about the interest that radio sparked with her neighbors, she was already implicated in the new intimate geographies of everyday life that domestic radio reception afforded. In the early 1920s, firm boundaries between collectively consumed publicly circulating information and the privacy of the modern home were changing, as Bourke so comically describes of her new radio-inflected household's routines.

The domestication of radio in this period challenged existing understandings of the home as self-enclosed space, and by extension, women's role as self-evidently situated within it. Bourke herself was markedly enthusiastic about the new medium, against its disruptive effects on her family's domestic routines and the interruptions that her neighbors make on her and her husband's time for listening. Contra the discourses that heralded a pre-given, non-technical role for women within the home's incorporation of radio, Bourke, like many other women of the time, was actually an active agent in radio's domestication. Describing the pre-radio era of her life, she harks back to traditional gender values during that "happy period when we had a Home, and when the only tobacco ashes I was obliged to sweep from the roof of the piano belonged to the Boss." But in the next breath subverts these values in a parenthetical aside:

> (I put that last line in because he may see this article some time. Of course I am the boss, but it shows a nice disposition on my part, and incidentally it is handy in many ways to let him think he is the Great Voice around this radio-devastated remainder of What Was.)

Writing at the cusp of the transformation of radio into a fixture within the modern home, Bourke was far from a passive recipient of radio as a technology and medium of public information. She was proud of her ability to use her hands and ears to "coax" signals from the "mahogany box."

The article ends with the visit of a "fellow Household Slave" in the shape of her neighbor, which heralds the arrival of more than an unwanted daytime visitor. This liminal stage of the first encounters with radio—when the nature of radio's connection to everyday life was still being negotiated and women were not yet clearly marked out as an audience—was coming to an end.

Gendered programming was about to actualize a new mediated space-time of individualized domestic reception. This form of reception was achieved by recuperating traditional gender roles from print media: parodied by Bourke in her neighbor's interest in the *Jacksonville Bazoo*'s initiation of a "woman's hour."

Making time for women

The "woman's hour" appeared in programming schedules as soon as radio became a broadcast medium and part of an industrial system. The use of radio for civilian purposes had been limited by national governments during the First World War (Baudino and Kittross 2015: 48), and up until the 1920s radio had mainly been a point-to-point form of communication between individual low-powered amateur radio operators (Johnson 1988: 12). The early 1920s is a key point in radio history, when regular programs began to be broadcast from a central point and could be heard on "receivers" (unlike ham radio, designed to be one way and unable to transmit) produced on a mass scale.[1]

In the United States, the University of Wisconsin station WHA, whose license held had been converted from "experimental" to "educational" by the US Commerce Department in early 1922, may have been responsible for the first women's program. WHA's schedule included midday and evening educational broadcasts for "homemakers," including an evening lecture by Miss A.L. Marlatt on "The Profession of Homemaking" in early June 1922 (Davidson 2006: 251, 373). The earliest mention of a women's program in the pages of the US *Radio Digest* was in November 1923 when KGW, a commercial station based in Portland, Oregon, broadcast a woman's program. Owned by the publisher of *The Oregonian* newspaper, its slogan using its call-sign initials to spell out "Keep Growing Wiser," KGW carried a woman's program every day from 3.30 to 4 p.m. except for Sunday. The program was KGW's only daytime programming, apart from "weather" at 11.30 a.m., and was followed by a break in transmission until "markets, weather" at 7 p.m. ("Radio Broadcasting Stations" 1923). WHA's sister station, KSAC, broadcasting under the Kansas State Agricultural College's noncommercial "educational" license, started its *Housewives' Half Hour* in February 1925 (Slotten 2009: 45). The same month, KOA, a commercial station owned by General Electric and based in Denver, Colorado, began broadcasting a "matinee for housewives" every weekday. In October, *Radio Digest*'s listings showed after more than three hours of "Rialto theater musicale," the half-hour "matinee for housewives" was broadcast at 3.30 p.m., followed by "fashion" at 4 p.m. and "Herbert White and his Silver State Orchestra" at 6.30 p.m. ("Advance Programs for the Week" 1925).

Many early women's programs in the United States were linked to the growing interest in radio from the advertising profession as a means to reach women as consumers (Wang 2006: 78–79). As Susan Smuylan has documented, Anna J. Peterson, "our radio mother," broadcast menus and recipes for the People's Gas Light and Coke Company on Chicago's KYW in 1925 (Smuylan 1993: 305). From 1926, WHA broadcast the *Homemakers Hour* six mornings a week, through its title and timing effectively "denying the fact that many female farmers worked alongside men in physically demanding settings outside the farmhouse" (Valliant 2002: 80). By 1928, the program was WHA's most popular broadcast and held its own against similar commercial programs such as NBC's *Women's Magazine of the Air* and CBS's *Radio Homemaker's Club*, the former initiated in the spring and the latter in the autumn of that year (Hilmes 1997: 149; Valliant 2002: 81).

The first programming for women on a nationally funded public service broadcaster began in the UK on May 2, 1923, the day after the opening of the BBC's Savoy Hill studio that had included "Lord Birkenhead … inaugurating the 10 pm *Men's Hour*, which had only a short life" ("Women's and Household Talks" n.d. 1936–1938: 1). At 5 p.m. on May 2, HRH Princess Alice, Duchess of Athlon, delivered the BBC's first afternoon talk for women, speaking on the "Adoption of Babies" and Lady Duff Gordon followed on "Fashions" ("Women's and Household Talks" n.d. 1936–1938; see also Murphy 2014: 31). Later that year the first edition of "the official organ of the BBC," the *Radio Times*, advertised that *Women's Hour* from 2LO London on 1 October would comprise of "Ariel's Society Gossip" and "Mrs C.S. Peel's Kitchen Conversation," also at 5 p.m. ("Women's Hour" 1923).

In Australia, the 1929 "wireless programmes" listing in Melbourne's *Weekly Times* advertised the *Hattie Knight Talk* on the commercial Australian Broadcasting Company station 3LO from 2.24 to 2.40 p.m. ("This Week's Wireless Programmes" 1929), and Knight had a regular weekly afternoon talk one day a week during the late 1920s and early 1930s. Together with women's sports enthusiast and physical education teacher Gwen Varley, Knight was also instrumental in organizing the Australian Broadcasting Company's "Women's Association" that first appeared on the Company's stations in May 1929 ("Broadcasting Today" 1929) and continued on the Commission station for another six months until late 1932 ("Broadcasting Programmes for the Week" 1932). Originally founded by Varley in 1928 as the 2BL Women's Amateur Sports Association, the ABC Women's Association programs mixed domestic instruction with reports on much more popular sports and social activities such as golf and tennis competitions and "motor picnics," all coordinated via radio (Consandine 2006).[2] After July 1932, when the Federal Government took over the Company stations and the Australian Broadcasting Company became the Australian Broadcasting Commission (ABC), the Women's Association broadcasts continued on Melbourne's 3LO until November ("Broadcasting Stations: 'A' Class Stations" 1932), when they were replaced by various personality-based programs such as "A Chat with Jane" in April 1933 ("Broadcasting Programmes" 1933). Varley also moved to the local Sydney ABC station, 2FC, where from May 1933 until the mid-1930s she hosted sports and health broadcasts aimed at women ("Radio Session Had 14,000 Members" 1953). During 1934 *Women's Sessions* reappeared on 3LO, and Hattie Knight continued to broadcast within them, with a regular talk entitled "Sidelights," presumably a theater segment ("Listening In" 1934).[3] By 1939 the *Women's Session* on 2BL was fixed in the ABC's national morning timetable, promoted for the new season in August of that year as around "a 40-minutes morning-tea 'spread' entirely for lady listeners" from 10.20 to 11 a.m.: "On Monday and Wednesday it is conducted by 'Jane' who is Mrs. Reg. Wykeham; on Tuesday it is in the hands of Noelle Brennan; and on Thursday of W. Burston," W. Burston being music educator and concert pianist Winifred Burston, who by 1940 was given the whole of the Thursday edition for a "musical session" ("Highlights of the ABC: Morning Women's Session" 1940).

The first women's program in Canada appeared in 1935 with a Montreal-based production for women. Promoted by the national public broadcaster, the Canadian Radio Broadcasting Corporation's (CRBC) Department of Public Relations described "For You, Madame" as a half-hour feature ("'For You, Madame' ... " 1935). During October 1935 CBRC's program department was "busily putting the final touches" to the program and it was broadcast at 9 a.m. October 17 on the CRBC national network. Records of the program do not say whether the broadcast was in English or French, despite its use of "Madame" in the title. It started with "a sketch prepared by Miss Barre, in the nature of a Cavalcade of Womanhood, a tribute to their courage and achievement since the beginning of recorded time," thereby addressing Canadian women within a unified national category across linguistic and geographic divides. A "brief message to the women of Canada" from Canada's only woman Senator Mrs Cairine Wilson as part of the programme was also "eagerly anticipated." These kinds of programs came and went during the 1920s and early 1930s and were usually designed as one-off "talks" and "features." When Elizabeth Long, whose work on the CBC is discussed in Chapter 4, joined the broadcaster's newly created Talks and Public Affairs Department as assistant supervisor of *Women's Interests* in 1938, the CBC "had only two programs directed to women listeners—'The History of Dress' and 'Touring English Cathedrals'" (Taylor 1985: 64).

By the mid-1930s, formulated as daily programs, talks for women represented a new settling of the possibilities of radio into a structured set of expectations and programming policies. The BBC took up this approach early on when Mrs Ella Fitzgerald was appointed on April 5, 1923, as "Central Organiser, to undertake the provision of material for the *Children's Hour* and to organise the *Women's Hour* when it began." The Women's National Advisory Committee that she had set up in January 1924, however, advised at its second meeting that the "term *Women's Hour* be abolished, although the talks given should deal mainly with topics which would particularly interest women" ("Women's and Household Talks" n.d. 1936–1938: 1; see also Forster 2015: 180–181). So from March 1924, therefore, the "Women's Hour" title was dropped, and the two 5 p.m. talks were incorporated into the afternoon concert, from 4 to 4.30 p.m. These talks were the template for later, more regular and enduring, incarnations of women's programming on the BBC, and, as later chapters will show, the CBC and ABC also followed this model of factual spoken word programs for women.

Why this format was so favored raises other questions about the domestication of social power in the form of expert knowledge about the proper conduct of everyday life in modernity. Women's programming as a series of talks by knowledgeable people on disparate topics linked together only by their general interest to women as the bearers of the responsibility for the modern home seems to have been such a "taken-for-granted" situation that very little comment is made on the suitability of this format in the production and listener research documents housed in written archives. Certainly a decisive factor would have been the relatively low cost and efficiency of production (see Chapter 5 for discussion of the "magazine" format at the postwar BBC), another was the paternalistic assumptions of public service programming in general, which aimed for cultural and moral instruction, especially in the Reithian dictum as it was taken up at the BBC and ABC. Yet another impetus was a form of market differentiation, in that commercial stations in Australia and Canada carried more radio plays and serials than radio talks (as discussed in the next chapter in the Australian case). Appearing at the intersection of these factors, service talk format was a cornerstone of women's programming in public service broadcasting from the 1930s onwards, and many thousands of hours of such talks were produced within and across all three broadcasters.

Apart from these instructive and didactic modes of address, women's programming was differentiated from entertainment and news along another key dimension of radio's interweaving with everyday life: time. The scheduling and formats of programs from the 1930s onwards coalesced to code the "public" flow of time in the evenings as masculine. The women's programs examined in this book were all broadcast during weekday mornings or afternoons or at the latest, in the CBC's case, the early evening. Hilmes has identified a shift to ideas of broadcasting time as gendered in the early 1930s, observing of US commercial programming that "only after 1933 does a firm distinction between day and nighttime programming take hold; for example, until the middle 1930s, several women's serial drama shows aired in the evenings" (Hilmes 1999: 26). The period of the 1920s then was one of flux in categories of gendered radio time and space, as mediated everyday life took shape. Exploring these new formations of gender, time, and space and how they were settled into the cultural form of women's programming is the task of this book. A brief survey of recent radio historiography in the following section will help explain the gendered nature of this historical convergence of intimacy and publicity.

Writing radio histories

A set of important works have revisited the debates around the introduction of radio into the home and the particular stakes that women had in negotiating its arrival. Johnson's groundbreaking work on women and Australian radio has shown how commercial stations in Australia recognized "the housewife as a specific object of interest" (Johnson 1981: 169) for advertisers who wished to place radio programming in the background of domestic work and, further, how the informality of radio presentation style was the "result of a long period of development partially characterised by a struggle between the Australian Broadcasting Commission and its commercial rivals to capture the interest of the steadily growing radio audiences" from 1923 onwards (Johnson 1983: 43). In 1988 Johnson published her important book *The Unseen Voice: A Cultural Study of Early Australian Radio*, which described the rise of the intimate, informal radio voice and the way that broadcasters developed techniques to produce this voice at the same time as listeners learnt "how to be listeners" (Johnson 1988: 70). Gill's PhD thesis *Ideology and Popular Radio: A Discourse Analytic Examination of Disc Jockeys' Talk* built on Johnson's work to look at how the feminization of the radio audience and the integration of radio into the pattern of women's domestic lives were central to the capture of time and space in the home (Gill 1991: 133). By the mid-1990s, the contours of a new body of sociological work on women's relationship to radio were emerging, with Leman's book chapter on class and gender in BBC wartime programming for women (1996), based on her 1983 MPhil thesis at the University of Kent, and in the same year, Lacey's magisterial *Feminine Frequencies* (1996). In the following decade, other work such as MacLennan's analyses of Canadian radio has shown how broadcast schedules of the 1930s attempted to interface with and shape listener habits (2001, 2008, 2013). Recent work incorporating sound studies approaches with radio histories of political cultures, such as Birdsall's *Nazi Soundscapes* (2012) and Razlogova's *The Listener's Voice*, has been groundbreaking for the ways in which it has shown that listeners actively negotiated "forms of sound perception and social order" (Razlogova 2011: 5). Wijfjes (2015), Valliant (2013), and Scales (2016) have investigated national and transnational histories of broadcasting that tell us much about the politics of radio in the twentieth century and the problematic of maintaining public-private divides in such technological complexity. Hayes (2012) and Robertson (2013) have shown how racial and gender categories have intersected, and been kept apart, in US radio serials and the BBC's "Empire Service," respectively. While radio offered new connections between the temporality of the home and expanded the scope of the public sphere, this work reminds us that new media are not always opened equally to new subjects and new ways of speaking, and power relations frame all technological change.

The (gendered) democratization of everyday life

As Kate Lacey has written, the promise of radio in Weimar Germany was coincidental with an opening up of the public sphere to new groups, including women, and creating a new sense of time and space for the home within broadcast networks (Lacey 1996: 17–55). Whether radio was seen as site for a new set of women's agencies within modern life or as threat to the stability of the home depended on ideological battles over to what extent the new medium would and could either overturn or reinforce "the public-private divide in female experience" (Lacey 1996: 38–39). As Moores has argued, a set of "wider social transformations put the mother at the centre of the privatized family" while the discourse of radio sought to "re-position ... [her] at the centre of the broadcasting audience" (1988: 34). Radio became both a conservative touchstone and a sign of a radical moment in the 1930s, as the medium was brought from the gendered space of the amateur experimenter's "radio shack" and into the family living room (Haring 2003, 2008).

Paddy Scannell's phenomenological work on broadcasting's transformation of speech and hearing explains that by their openness to a diverse set of social actors, radio and television have brought about new public textures of listening and speaking (1979, 1995, 1996). Scannell (1979), together with Cardiff (1980), has identified very clearly how radio in the 1930s changed notions of issues of public relevance. Which topics could be talked about and how they were to be discussed were recast when radio configured new subjects for discussion across classed and gendered boundaries in the first few decades of radio (1979). Scannell also focuses on new formations of public and private in what he terms "the democratization of everyday" life (1989: 136). Interestingly, to illustrate this process he draws on an example of a woman talking in 1934, while her husband was out of work during the Depression, on the BBC National program's *Time to Spare* about her attitude toward pregnancy and the lack of availability of birth control (Scannell 1980: 19–21). Scannell gives a lengthy quote from a talk in this series by Mrs Pallis, the wife of an unemployed ship's riveter. Mrs Pallis's fifteen-minute unscripted and unedited talk as part of this series was reprinted on the front page of the BBC magazine *The Listener*.

Scannell highlights to what extent inviting working-class people to speak about their life experiences extended "radio's social range" (1980: 24):

> Nothing is more interesting, and nothing more elusive, than the domain of the "merely talkable about" and its historical development in broadcasting. When it started up in the 1920s, there was so much that could not be talked about in public, or at least not in front of women, children and servants. In a class-divided society like Britain one of the things that had, in the novel context of mass democracy, to be claimed and asserted, *was the entitlement of all to have opinions, to have them heard and to hear those of others.* Here is a woman from Sunderland, whose husband is out of work, talking on radio in 1934 of her feelings when she finds she is pregnant again: "I know I've cried when I knew I had to have another baby, not for myself, but for what they have to be brought

into—no work, no means, no jobs for them. But it means expense to avoid them. I know all about the avoidance part, but I haven't the means to carry it out. It costs money … I think we ought to have information from somewhere given to us. It's ignorance on some people's part; or, for people like myself who know, we haven't got the money." (*The Listener*, May 16, 1934: 812 quoted in Scannell 1989: 144, emphasis mine)

In the magazine, Pallis's talk, transcribed from her radio broadcast, is followed, as it was on the air, by a brief postscript given by "A Doctor," whom Scannell describes as a "suitably official person [employed] to point out the moral of [the speaker's] tale" (Scannell 1980: 20). Eventually, and despite the clear public relevance of this testimony, this first-person narrative of a woman speaking about reproductive rights, as well as other testimonials in this series, resulted in debates in parliament on the availability of birth control advice and the family's access to other forms of support, as well as listener complaints, and finally extensive political pressure on the BBC to halt the broadcasts (Scannell 1980: 22). Some thirty years before the cultural form of second-wave feminist programming existed, the representation of personal experience in a public medium was a contentious issue.

David Cardiff's early and important work on the cultural form of the BBC radio talk, developed together with Scannell, invites us to consider the role of the women who worked in radio in understanding these new possibilities of the medium. Cardiff argues that "in encouraging listeners to become 'citizens of the world,'" BBC's first director of talks Hilda Matheson (see also Murphy 2014: 35) "fostered the art of the spoken word as a means of domesticating the public utterance, as an attempt to soften and naturalise the intrusion of national figures into the fireside world of the family" (Cardiff 1980: 31). This potential is highlighted in Matheson's own words, reflecting on the oral bias of the medium of radio, that "broadcasting is clearly rediscovering the spoken language, the impermanent but living tongue, as distinct from the permanent but silent print" (Matheson quoted in Cardiff 1980: 31). Elizabeth Long, CBC's supervisor of *Women's Interests* from 1938 until the 1950s and appointed to the role because of her experience as a newspaper women's editor, attributes the discovery of the central importance of voice and address in forming the sound and style of women's programming to an incident in late 1938, when, after formal testing of their microphone manner, two future CBC women's talks presenters, Mattie Rotenberg and Margaret MacKenzie, believing that the audition was over, interviewed each other about their families:

We were all fascinated. The women had suddenly come to life. Their voices, their language had changed. Somehow any two women meeting on any remote jungle path, or on a frozen Arctic shore might pause to exchange the same information in that same warm voice … I never knew whether Donald Buchanan [CBC's Supervisor of Public Affairs Programming] scheduled the two speakers in his political forum, but that day I learned that woman-to-woman language was wanted for women's radio programs. (Long quoted in Graham 2014: 150)

It was this rediscovery of the power of the ordinary and of orality that was to energize women's programming and its relationship with its audience, as later chapters will show.

Yet the assumption of what women were interested in and how the programs should convey content often placed the institution and individual programmers at odds, particularly at the more conservative ABC. Catherine King, the popular host of the ABC Perth's *Women's Session* from 1944 until 1976, as part of an fiftieth anniversary program for the station in 1982 told a story on air of how she evaded the more stringent edicts about what could be discussed on her program. ABC Headquarters in Sydney was more able to control content on stations in other capital cities such as Melbourne and Brisbane, which fell within the same time zone, but ABC Perth, two hours behind the Eastern states and several days away by rail, was less easily brought into the fold. Unlike the east coast version of the program, which King characterized as "supposed to be on lovely topics like 'how to breastfeed' and suitable topics for women like 'dresses' and 'cooking,'" her program followed in the tradition established by figures such as Irene Greenwood in the late 1930s and early 1940s (discussed in detail in Chapter 3) to ensure the public relevance of the Session. King strongly resisted such domestic fare and made clear to the station as a whole and her audience that she had a very different vision for the program (Lewis 1979). King explains to the interviewer how she negotiated attempts to limit her program to a narrowly defined set of "women's interests," with the cooperation of her station manager, Conrad Charlton:[4]

I remember a disc that came from Sydney, "How to Make the Better Biscuit." Well, I didn't care about making my biscuits better, and also how to make a little suit out of your husband's shirt-tails. In fact they sent those over from Sydney and I was supposed to use them. And I took them into Mr Charlton and said "If Sydney wants me to do this, I don't want to be associated with it, but you can put them on two days and I'll do the other three days, because I won't have a bar of this in the *Women's Session*."

So he said ... "Give me the memo," and the memo said three days [of the daily session per week] is ample for Mrs King to arrange.

I said "What will you do with it?" and he said "Put it in the urgent basket."

Then ... I said "What will you do with the discs?" and he said "I'll break them."

And that was the end of any suggestion ... that was just so utterly against the conceptions I had. (King 1982)

This account of a collaboration between a woman producer and host and her station manager to resist centralized control of her program signals the extent of the reach of the ABC's gender ideology, but not total acquiescence. King's program philosophy in the mid-1940s reconfigured taken-for-granted divisions between public and private, as well as what could be considered a women's issue. When asked in the same interview about problems she encountered, King reflected that "they finally defeated me over international news" (King 1982), referring to a battle she had with the ABC station manager who followed Charlton over the inclusion of international news within her program. The next chapter will explore why international content was so problematic for the ABC and the controversy surrounding one particular broadcaster, Irene Greenwood, who preceded King on the ABC's Perth station.

Conclusion

Media studies and media histories in particular have described the changing modes of presentation on radio and their gendered histories and effectively questioned the valence of public-private divide (Badenoch 2005: 590–591; Loviglio 2005: xv; Smulyan 1993: 300). The gendering of the new medium of radio within existing notions of the home as the domain of national family was also given new meaning and import through the rhetorical expansion of family of empire (as seen in the Queen's speech at the beginning of the last chapter). Thus, radio was able to engender a peculiar kind of intimacy. The medium, through its domestic reception and daytime address to women, neither "publicized" private space nor created new forms of publics, but shifted the relations between public, private, and intimate. The intimate and confessional mode of radio was on a continuum with the bourgeois public sphere that was connected by Habermas to the personalized, literate cultures of the eighteenth and nineteenth centuries. Yet, as the examples discussed in this chapter illustrate, radio for women within public service broadcasting became the site of a new, excessive imaginary of gender, one in which women were not addressed as the privatized, excluded other of the terms "bourgeois" and "hommes" but were now indeterminately positioned as connected to other places in a simultaneously intimate and public space: the broadcast relation of listener, institution, and host. The broadcast (and now networked) public sphere is increasingly accessible and personalized and thus takes on the "traits of a secondary realm of intimacy" (Calhoun 1992: 24; Habermas 1989: 172), yet as long and continued feminist work has shown, the "personal" is not necessarily equivalent to the private, and this disjuncture is a powerful political space from which coalitions and solidarities can emerge and also intervene.

Anything but the News: Defining Women's Programming in Australia, 1935–1950s

When you switch on your radio set, the valves slowly warm up and the full flow of power sweeps in to give you the programme you want—so the power of the mind flows in to help us in our tasks, responding to the thoughts we hold. But it is our job to turn on the switch.

"Beauty in Life," talk by Mary Grant Bruce on September 20, 1940, 3LO Melbourne, quoted on the "Women's Page" of the *ABC Weekly* (Bruce 1940)

Introduction

As argued in the last chapter, the arrival of radio as a technology and cultural form heralded a new, potentially democratic configuration of the home and the institutions of modern public life. During the 1920s live music, news, parliamentary broadcasts, child and adult education, political talks, and celebrity culture all became accessible in the home, if that home could afford a radio set. Women's programming on radio was a troubling innovation, however, from the perspective of cultural authorities such as politicians, educators, and newly minted radio critics. What kind of relationship should women at home have to these newly accessible public worlds? Should radio programming for women simply support existing assumptions of women as responsible for domestic labor or could it be taken up to modernize these ideas? And if women's domestic role was to continue, could radio be used to instruct women in the most efficient and up-to-date ways to run their homes? Or rather, should radio open up women's worlds and speak to their curiosity about and involvement in the public sphere on a national, and even world-wide, scale? As foreshadowed in the last chapter, these were the questions that created constant struggle within the public service broadcasters canvassed here, which, like the societies that gave rise to them, encompassed all of these different and conflicting ideas of women's futures. These debates waxed and waned at the Australian government-funded broadcaster, the Australian Broadcasting Commission (ABC), for the entire four decades of its *Women's Sessions*.

In this book, to provide important context on the individual careers of women broadcasters, I survey internal attitudes toward women's programming on three public broadcasters in Australia, Canada, and the UK. The case of the ABC *Women's Sessions* and their troublesome history demonstrate that women's programming raised issues of gender and genre within broadcast media that were hotly debated from the early 1930s onwards. As the evidence discussed here shows, this contestation did not stop in the 1950s, despite its received understanding as a highly apolitical period. This chapter first looks in detail at the brief career of feminist activist Irene Greenwood within ABC Perth's *Women's Sessions*. This chapter focuses on how she crafted a globally intimate voice within women's programming, as well as how she came up against limits on discussions of international politics on the public broadcaster as a result. Then I outline some of the contemporary commentary from both within the ABC and without surrounding the its persistence with women's programming well into the 1950s. Sources such as national and local newspaper coverage of radio listings, as well as internal documents and correspondence, are used to map the trajectory of the sessions, which placed the ABC out of kilter with the wider Australian radio industry in the postwar period, when such programming declined. These materials are used to tease out the radically different understandings of gender, home, and world that emerged in discussions between the women who worked on the programs and the ABC's management. The programs' implicit assumptions that daytime radio programming should be used to encourage women at home, suitably assisted by experts, to learn more about domestic science and family psychology were contested by many of the women that worked on the programs and thereby picked up on debates prevalent in the wider public sphere at the time. This chapter therefore explores issues at play for this study as a whole: What was at stake for women within mid-twentieth-century media in transgressing gendered divisions between public and private spheres?

She will be missed ...

Pasted inside a scrapbook covered in blue and green floral-patterned paper, in an archive in a University Library in Perth, Western Australia, is a cutting from the *West Australian* newspaper published on October 2, 1940 (Halsted 1940). Headlined "Well-known broadcaster,"—with a phrase from the article "She will be missed ... " repeated in handwritten pencil below—the cutting appears in a scrapbook documenting the radio career of Irene Greenwood, nee Driver, who appeared on Australian radio for more than twenty years as a presenter from the early 1930s to the 1950s. In her radio broadcasts on both public and commercial radio, Greenwood, who later described herself as a "second-generation feminist" (Greenwood 1976), drew on her involvement with a range of women's peace and Indigenous rights organizations, including the post-suffrage Women's Service Guilds of Western Australia, the Women's International League for Peace and Freedom, and the Australian Federation of Women Voters (Baker 2017; Fisher 2017). During her 60s and 70s, she was involved with establishing what would become the Family Planning Association in Western Australia, as well as the Abortion Law Repeal Association, the Women's Electoral Lobby, and the United Nations Association (Baldock 1993). During the late 1980s, Greenwood donated this scrapbook to the Murdoch University Library as a record of her work in broadcasting and involvement in the Australian women's and peace movements from the 1930s (Greenwood "Women in the International News").

Until they were abruptly discontinued in late 1940, Irene Greenwood's talks from 1936 to 1940—"every Friday at 11 am" (Greenwood 1976)—within 6WF Perth's *Women's Session* stand out against the backdrop of women's programming on this and other ABC local stations. In contrast to the programming that was "geared towards the domestic and supportive role of women with an emphasis on home hints, child care, and self-improvement of a superficial kind" (Lewis 1979: 29), Greenwood regularly emphasized women's role in international politics and the possibilities of broadcasting to explore questions of social justice and promote world peace. Greenwood's talks started in July 1936 after she had approached ABC Perth's station manager Conrad Charlton, when Greenwood's husband's mining speculation was at its least lucrative in the height of the Depression and she needed to supplement the family's income (Greenwood 1976; Murray 2005).

While the details of talks recorded before mid-1937 are not documented in her archives, Greenwood promoted the possibilities of radio to organize women internationally throughout her career with the ABC's Perth station.

Participating in a broadcast to celebrate "International Women's Night" in 1937 hosted by the Federation of Business and Professional Women, she reported that her commentary had been broadcast throughout the United States "in nation-wide hookups that reached England and France" (Murray 2002: 147). She told her listeners on her local program that "on this evening women threw a girdle of thought around the world; they linked themselves together in a chain of friendship and cooperation. The theme for the celebration was this year 'Women in Governments the world around'" (Greenwood 03/05 1937, quoted in Murray 2005: 75). She highlighted the potential of radio to develop solidarities between women and to coordinate feminist activity across national boundaries:

> Even although these national and international link-ups in broadcasting are becoming quite frequent, they can never lose the romance—with the sense of distance overcome, the belief in difference is over-ruled by a realization of fundamental likeness which is stronger than superficially different characteristics. (Greenwood 03/05 1937, quoted in Murray 2005: 76)

The subjects of Greenwood's talks throughout the late 1930s focused on inspirational and path-breaking women in the news, for example "China-Mme Sun-Yat-Sen, Mme Chiang-Kai-Shek" on August 27, 1937. In late 1937, her talks focused on notable international women such as Belgian feminist Baronne Marthe Boël, "new President of the [International] Council of Women" (September 24), Natalie Kalmus, American color film pioneer, Rosita Forbes, English explorer and travel writer (both October 1), and the "New York World's Fair and Monica Walsh (Director, Women's Participation)" (October 15). In 1938, Greenwood profiled British Labour figure and Fabian socialist Beatrice Webb (March 18), followed by Czech feminist Františka Plamínková in a talk on "The Czech Women: Their Country, Their Customs and Their Outstanding Woman-Senator Plaminkova" (May 27). Other progressive women activists and politicians appeared in a talk entitled "Dr Edith Summerskill, Mrs Elsie Parker, Miss Caroline Woodruff and Mrs Stein" (June 10). Summerskill was a British Labour politician; Parker was Secretary of the New York branch of the National Municipal League, an urban reform organization that later became the National Civic League; and Woodruff was a Vermont-based public educator and campaigner for pensions for teachers in female-dominated profession.

Talks following the outbreak of war in 1939 maintained their international focus, but turned to more patriotic topics such as "A Surface Survey of Women's National Defence Work" (November 3), "Leaders of Women's Voluntary Services,

Great Britain" (November 10), and enlistment of women (November 17). In 1940, subjects of talks included "Miss Ellen Wilkinson, Miss Caroline Haslett— Key Women in the National War Effort" (June 21), "Princess Alice of Athlone, Hut-Clubs for Englishwomen, Sabiba Goksen on Turkey's Women" (July 5), with her final talk on the ABC on July 26 "On Books, Libraries, and Women Librarians" (Greenwood 1937–1940).

Despite this huge range of topics and the reported popularity of the programmes among WA listeners, Greenwood is not mentioned in Ken Inglis's official ABC history *This Is the ABC*, which covers the first fifty years of the broadcaster and was published to coincide with its fiftieth anniversary in 1983. Inglis only briefly mentions 6WF Perth's women's programming of this period as "talks directed at women about health, hygiene, beauty, fashion, sewing, cooking and household management [which] were put on mid-morning and mid-afternoon, when they were assumed to be taking tea" (1983: 14), leaving out from this list the events of worldwide "feminist interest" (Halsted 1940) that so exercised Greenwood. Inglis does mention 6WF's Dorothy Graham ("6WF" 1936) as an exception to the usual round of speakers in this session being "from such a body as the Housewives' Association or the Country Women's Association," because Graham was "on the staff … as Women's Session announcer and soprano" (1983: 14), yet does not mention the topics she broadcast on.

This absence of Greenwood in this official history is especially striking given the local and national impact of the organizations she was associated with. Her colorful talks on women's achievements, steeped in the progressive politics of the 1930s, go against the uniformly domestic characterization of women's programming on the national broadcaster as established by Inglis. These talks were topical and addressed a heartfelt need from activists, Greenwood included, for making international connections between women's organizations, as well as questioning the idea of individual, ordinary women's concerns as separate from the flow of international events. Greenwood was involved with these issues outside her radio work and was a keen organizer of political education through local women's organizations during the 1930s. Indeed, as an item in Perth's *Daily News* noted in 1938: "One of the results of the international strife this year is the keen interest taken by women in foreign affairs … Young women in trams and buses read the foreign news in the papers, and take part authoritatively in discussion" ("International Affairs and Women" 1938). As a result "a new Women's Group" was being "formed for women interested in international and cultural studies" and had started meeting monthly at the YWCA. Greenwood participated as the first speaker and went on to "suggest to the group avenues of study and books for reading and discussion along economical, social, political and international lines." The article finished with details of the next meeting, which would discuss *Are Women Taking Men's Jobs?*, a recent book by Australian trade unionist and founder of the Council of Action for Equal Pay, Muriel Heagney ("International Affairs and Women" 1938).

Greenwood's involvement in politics had begun in her teens, influenced by her mother's involvement in the League of Women Voters (later the Women's Service Guilds). At the age of 21, in her first job as shorthand typist in the Department of Agriculture in the West Australian public service, she was involved in the high-profile West Australian civil servants and teachers' strike of 1920 (Baldock 1993: 1). During the early 1930s, Greenwood became involved in international peace campaigns when she travelled to Sydney with her husband and was involved in radio broadcasting with leading Sydney feminists, including international socialist feminists Jessie Street and Linda Littlejohn (Baker 2017). Her role as both broadcaster and activist would single her out for attention, especially after June 1940, when against the backdrop of Italy's entry into the Second World War and Soviet Russia's annexation of the Baltic states, the Menzies Federal Government banned the Communist Party, as well as Italian Fascist and other organizations. Although she never publicly declared her membership, from the early 1940s Greenwood reportedly was a member of the Communist Party (Kotai-Ewers 2013: 117; Oliver and Latter 1996: 179). Interviewed in 1976, Greenwood said that because of her political activities leading up to the Second World War she had

> suffered calumny, criticism … it was a hard road to hoe. I have known what it meant to be suspect in the period in Australia when any who stood for peace were dubbed Communists. I have known, with others, what it meant to have my house raided, papers seized, books taken. (Greenwood 1976)

These strands of feminist and socialist internationalism that Greenwood drew together in her talks set her not only against conservative, economically liberal governments such as that led by Menzies but also against the tide of pre- and postwar Australian feminism. Drawing on the work of Marilyn Lake, Australian historian Ann Firth has argued that after gaining the vote in the 1920s, Australian feminists concentrated on recognition of women's maternal citizenship within the nation-state and made political claims through the figure of "the wife" in parallel to male citizenship framed in the role of "breadwinner" (Firth 2004: 203). During the 1930s Australian feminists collectively reframed rights for women "as workers," and although this political subjectivity was not taken up in postwar public policy,[1] and although Greenwood herself was part of the movements for equal pay from the 1940s onwards (Murray 2002: 197–202), these struggles were also within a national frame.

It is against this background of struggles to reshape women's citizenship toward both the home and the nation that the discontinuation of Greenwood's talks in the early 1940s is set. The internationalism of a certain strand of feminism of the 1930s, which would determine the individual career of Greenwood, was at odds with the cultural form of women's programming in the Australian context, which emphasized women's domestic role as a contribution to the nation.

Woman's place is in the world

Greenwood was aware of the isolation of Australia, and Perth in particular, from world events during the 1930s, and Perth women's organizations made many efforts to bring international politics home through circulation of a diverse range of voices. Geographically isolated before frequent air travel and unable to join in live ABC networked programming from the Eastern States because of a two-hour time difference, ABC Perth used its international connections to leapfrog the centralizing effects of program control from ABC HQ in Sydney by emphasizing its own programming and personalities. Enthusiastic correspondence from a range of listeners attests to the way in which Greenwood's call for women to be involved in public life resonated with her audience. Her appeals to think beyond the national interest while valuing home life as a source of democratic possibility appears to have encouraged a personal connection with middle-class women in particular. On February 21, 1938, for example, 6WF *Women's Session* listener Effie Long wrote to Greenwood commending her for her recent "most delightful" talk on "Madam Cheang Kai-Shek" and asking about a book entitled *China at the Crossroads* that Greenwood had mentioned in this broadcast, saying, "I have endeavored to procure this book, but my efforts have been futile." Long asked if there was "any possible means of my purchasing your talk, as I am desirous of passing this information to the girls of my [secondary school] class." Demonstrating the new configurations of international, domestic, and gendered space that such broadcasts afforded, as well as attesting to Greenwood's resourcefulness against the difficulty of finding ways to access publications in prewar Perth, Long finished by inviting Greenwood to take "afternoon tea one afternoon at 4 o'clock this week, then you could tell me the ways and means of gaining this information."

Highlighting the confluence of feminism and international politics, a report in Perth's daily broadsheet, *The West Australian*, in November 1938 flagged a meeting that had brought together local women around their interest in world events. Greenwood had asked members of the Perth Women's Service Guilds to bring to a meeting at its Nestle House headquarters "any letters received from overseas during the past few weeks which contain interesting impressions of current events and which might help to provoke general discussion":

> Some letters received have treated the subject lightly and have endeavored to see the brighter side of things, discovering humorous incidents. Others have reflected the war-fever which cannot fail to attack any community in the midst of trench-digging and other air raid precautions activities, while others, again, have philosophized on the shortcomings of a civilization that can allow such situations to arise. Some letters, more particularly those originating in Central European countries, have been heart-rending in their poignancy, and one recalls reading only this week a pathetic little missive from an elderly Hungarian Jew (a relative of a Perth family) describing the plight of himself and his eight children—all out of employment because of their religion and faced with destitution and poverty. Between the lines could be read a story of despair and abandoned hope and of a fear of such dimensions as to be difficult for us in Australia to imagine. (Halsted 1938)

Greenwood explicitly crafted this form of globally intimate voice at the end of the 1930s and wrote about her ideas for linking "Women, World Events and Radio" in *The Broadcaster* in February 1939:

> "The world is only as wide as your own imagination," says an old Arab proverb. If this is so, then we today, however limited our imagination may be, can live in a limitless world, and for us in Australia, our much talked of isolation becomes a thing of the past. ... *I could go on and on, telling you of women who gave contributions of service to their respective countries last year, and whose activities were brought before the people through radio ....*
>
> One fact emerges; women all round the world are building for the betterment of conditions—socially and culturally. They have been *aided in their work of construction by radio, and through it their good deeds have been made to shine, not merely like a little candle, but as a great beacon illuminating the world.* (Greenwood 1939: 30–31, emphasis mine)

This international vision was echoed by a range of women's groups who gathered to celebrate International Women's Day (IWD) in Perth in March 1939 in a coalition that would not be repeated during or after the war years, when divisions between conservative, socialist, and feminist groups would later emerge over issues of women's paid labor and reproductive rights (Reekie 1985). IWD in Perth in 1939 involved an all-day conference followed by an evening public meeting. While left-wing and union-affiliated women's groups were present, including the Women's Organising Committee of the Communist Party, the Labor-affiliated Modern Women's Club, Chinese Women's Refugee Helpers' Band, Council Against Unemployment, the Spanish Relief Committee, the Women's Auxiliary of the Mining Division of the Australian Workers' Union, many other nonaligned, non-feminist, and Perth establishment groups also participated such as the Women's Christian Temperance Union, Women's Guild of University graduates, Theosophical Order of Service, Young Women's Christian Association, the Council of Jewish Women, and the Women's Justices' Association. The WA Communist Party's *Workers' Star* reported that "no less than 21 women's organisations participated," and Greenwood, representing the Women's Service Guilds (WSG), gave a talk on "economic trends in world politics" ("Woman's Place Is the World!" 1939). The role of radio, in Greenwood's vision, was to rematerialize the activists' networks developed by transnational women's organizations in the post-suffrage era in order to advance world peace (Fisher 2018; Hensley 2006). She believed that radio would have a positive role in a modern women's movement, encouraging the international exchange of information and political education. In this facet of her work on radio, she drew on the already existing networks of the WSG, which in turn built on aspects of the League of Women Voters and the Women's Christian Temperance Union before them (Coltheart 2005). The template for the kind of feminist internationalism that Greenwood pursued in her long career as an activist emerged in the late 1930s in reference to these nineteenth-century feminist networks, built upon "Western imperialism and Christian evangelism" (Coltheart 2005: 182; see also Keating 2018), but she also used the medium of radio and the format of the talk to speak in new and inspiring ways to individual women listeners, who were in turn encouraged to see their own everyday lives as intimately connected to world events.

The plight of the home

Greenwood, apparently a canny self-publicist, and, perhaps with good reason, assuming that she needed to prove her indispensability to the station, passed

Long's letter on to Conrad Charlton, ABC's manager for Western Australia. Charlton replied on March 11, 1938, saying he was "very pleased to know that your talks prove so interesting, especially to one who is a teacher of secondary school girls" while saying that it "would be impossible to do anything in the nature you suggest at the moment, but I will not lose sight of the opportunity to go further into the matter with you when the second transmitter is operating."

Exactly what Greenwood's suggestion to Charlton was is not recorded in their correspondence, but it is likely that Greenwood was wanting to expand her airtime, and possibly her salary, as around this time—in what were to be recurrent episodes of financial stress—Greenwood appeared to have money problems while her husband Albert pursued risky mining ventures. Greenwood kept a meticulous record of freelance payments for her talks, and most talks on the local station received a payment of 2 pounds, 2 shillings, with talks on the national ABC network 3 pounds, 3 shillings. At a rate of one talk per week throughout the year, these payments would have amounted to about two-thirds of the average wage for women in a white-collar occupation at the time (i.e., 146 pounds, 13 shillings, 6 pence, still less than half of the average male wage of 1940 (*Victorian Year Book 1941–42* 1944: 495)). In early February 1939, Charlton, writing back to a letter sent by Greenwood on January 30 about her money worries, responded that there was no chance of employing her daughter at the ABC and that it would be "unwise to stop her progress through the University, especially if you can obtain financial assistance." Greenwood had apparently asked Charlton about employment for her daughter with the Commission and had mentioned to him that her daughter might have to discontinue her university studies due to the family's financial pressures.

While the opening of hostilities between Great Britain and Germany in August 1939 opened up new frontiers for Greenwood's focus on women and international politics, it also ultimately closed down her talks on the local station. On August 16, 1940, Colin Badger, Broadcasting Division of Department of Information, Melbourne, wrote to Greenwood offering her extra work above and beyond her local talks by requesting her involvement in a series for the ABC's overseas shortwave broadcast service in which Australia was "trying to answer [Goebells and Co's propaganda] for the Pacific region in several ways … immediately by a series of talks directed to showing what [its] effect … has already been on Germany and on Europe":

> We mean to do this in a fairly conventional way by showing the effect of Nazism on particular classes of the community like scientists, teachers, lawyers, business people and so on.

We want to include in this series a talk dealing with the position of women under the Nazi regime, and I know you have plenty of material at your hand on this subject. We do not want to make the talks too bitter in tone, but rather reasonable and persuasive. We don't want to excuse or palliate what has happened; on the other hand we want to avoid a too violently propagandist tone. The argument might be to make with a brief statement on the contrasted positions of women in the democracies and in the Fascist countries; then perhaps developing the fact and instances [*sic*] the Nazi view of the proper position of women, and perhaps finishing on the note that any tolerable position for women can only be achieved if the Hitler movement is broken now.

Greenwood sent her finished script back to Badger on September 1, explaining that she wanted to, more complexly, contrast pre-Hitler Germany with the rise of Nazism rather than "simplifying the subject to merely contrast women under Nazism and in, say, Australia today—a simple comparison of life under Nazism and Democracy ... Weimar had to come in to show the depth of the fall. I hope you agree with this point." The script "Women under Nazism" ends with the "plight of the home" in a Fascist society, where she still contrasts barbaric Nazism and civilized Australian democracy, but does this by making the "the German woman" a tragic figure who has given up her freedom in order to survive, thereby humanizing German women:

Most tragic of all is the plight of the home. It soon became unsafe to voice any criticism of the system for fear of the Gestapo without or a member of the family within. Home, as a haven and a refuge, as we know it, has ceased to exist in Germany. Supplies of food, clothes, household equipment, are in such short supply that housewives must stand for hours in queues for merest necessities ... What is a home with an empty hearth, a bare table, its members seldom in it, its door always unlocked, and Fear its most constant visitor? To contrast a happy Australian home with that of the German woman, to realise that here is the means and the measure of her degradation—for it was for a home that she sold her birthright of freedom. ("[Women in] Hitler's World and Ours", 1940: 4, in Greenwood 1938–1946)

The script concludes that German women "are cogs in the great Nazi war machine!":

[They] have lost both their worlds [i.e. both public and private]. We still have ours. The lesson, surely, is plain. We must guard jealously our democracy, which alone guarantees our freedom and standards of life, and we must help break the regime which holds women in bondage. For only then can they win back their former position among the civilised women of the world. ("[Women in] Hitler's World and Ours", 1940: 5, in Greenwood 1938–1946)

Badger, however was not satisfied, on September 4 wrote to Greenwood to ask her to further rewrite this "script to focus more on Nazi treatment of women." Badger's request would draw the focus away from the historical context that Greenwood originally wanted to include, as well as to mute her not-so-subtle call to her intended audience to realize their own freedoms and the need to uphold them within an increasingly polarized society. While Greenwood was eventually able to satisfy the Department of Information requirements, this moment of possibility for radio to reshape gendered domestic imaginaries was interrupted by shifts in international and national politics that came to a crux around Greenwood's ABC broadcasts.

Censorship and the women's cold war

When Greenwood's talks in the 6WF *Women's Session* were cancelled by the ABC in October 1940, the *West Australian's* "Women's Realm" columnist noted that "it would be with regret that listeners to Mrs. Irene Greenwood's weekly broadcasts in the Women's Session from national stations each Friday will learn that this feature is to be discontinued" (Halsted 1940). Greenwood was to be heard for the last time at the end of the week, when she was to "review the achievements of women during the four years that she has been broadcasting." The article's author sounded very close to Greenwood when she reported:

> Few events of particular feminist interest have taken place in the world during these four years without calling for her comment, and her extensive reading of current literature dealing with international affairs has kept her abreast of developments at home and abroad. Since she gave her first broadcast on this session in July 1936, she has been on the air without fail every Friday morning, with the exception of Good Fridays, and has thereby perhaps established a record. Her broadcasts will be missed by those country women who, in their busy lives, have little time and few opportunities of keeping themselves up to date with developments in the women's movement both in Australia and overseas.

Conrad Charlton, ABC's manager for Western Australia, had written to Greenwood on September 10, 1940, communicating a decision, without explanation, from ABC "Head Office … [that there were to be] no further engagements of speakers to broadcast talks in the Women's Session ... for the present" effective from early October. Greenwood's leftist politics must have been a factor in the discontinuation of the talks, as discussed below, but her approach also deeply challenged the notion of separate spheres. Isabel Johnston, state president of the Women's Service Guilds, writing to the editor of the *West Australian*, reported that members of her organization were "much perturbed" at this news that there would be "no further engagement of speakers to broadcast talks in the Women's Session":

> We feel quite sure that there will be a unanimous protest from the women in our rural centres that, evidently on the grounds of economy (for it can be for no other reason) they are going to be deprived of many of the weekly talks of speakers which they have enjoyed for many months, and in one case for a number of years. If the new policy of the ABC is given effect to, it means there will be a decided deterioration in our Women's Session. Matter will be put over secondhand, such as book readings, and no matter how good these readings may be, they will lack the appeal, and individuality of the women speakers. *Household recipes and household hints have a part to play in a Women's Session no doubt, but the quarter-of-an-hour's cultural talk included in the session* is what women look for and need at this time. There has been a reduction in the licence fee of 1/. The fee is now £1, instead of £1/1/, as formerly. But the women of the State, we feel sure, would rather not have this reduction in fee, if programmes are to be adversely affected, as [this] policy indicates. (Johnston 1940, emphasis mine)

Keeping the pressure on the ABC via the local press, a carbon copy of a letter titled "No question of merit" from the "Secretary WCRU, 14 Aberdeen Street, Perth" to the Editor, *The Daily News*, Perth, dated October 14, kept by Greenwood in her files highlighted rumors about the decision to "get rid" of women speakers "because of their voices, views, or some such other considerations."[2] However, the letter-writer reported:

> On making enquiries, I was told that the question of merit does not arise. All women speakers have been put off all National *Women's Sessions* in Australia. This hits Western Australian women hardest because of their isolation, and petrol rationing will make it even harder for them to get to their centres and will throw them back on their radios for the programmes which it is the business of the ABC to provide.

In the meantime, Greenwood continued to submit talks on "Women in the International News" for VLQ, the ABC's newly established shortwave station broadcasting to overseas and remote areas, broadcast via its "All Australia Women's Session" ("Today's Radio" 1941). She also continued to submit talks to the ABC National Programme during 1941, with talks broadcast on July 15 and August 12 "on Miss Gertrude Bell and Mrs Emily Pelloe respectively," according to a letter from B.H. Molesworth, federal controller of talks, on July 2. Correspondence with Molesworth in preparing these talks in May and June allowed Greenwood to re-open the discussion of the reinstatement of her talks, and on May 25, Greenwood repeated her appeal to Molesworth, saying she "recently had letters from Secretaries of CWA groups who tell me of the dreadful cultural isolation of women in our outback districts today … and where ever I visit groups of women to speak, that they do miss the old women speakers."

This letter prompted the following response from Molesworth, who faced down Greenwood's continued pressure about "re-introducing talks into the Morning Women's Session in WA":

> Actually, there is a talk now being broadcast in WA and which is relayed from the Eastern States at 11.15am WA time. It is not directed only to women listeners but is the talk which is included in the *Town and Country Hour*. This should help some of the women listeners in the country to whom you refer because this whole session *Town and Country Hour* is arranged with the object of trying to provide something of interest for country listeners as well as town listeners.

Attached to Greenwood's letter was a typescript of talking points that outline her arguments for bringing back the local *Women's Session* (and that perhaps were used in her appearance before a Commission hearing about this issue in Perth in May 1944)[3]:

> This policy seems first of all to regard women listeners as the least important section of the listening public.
>
> It also overlooks completely the special needs and conditions of women in the State of Western Australia … [where due to dispersed population and petrol rationing women] will find it harder to get newspapers, periodicals or books—country towns are poor in library facilities. They will get into their centres for their meetings, discussions etc. less often. *Radio therefore becomes an intellectual and cultural necessity* … [emphasis in the original]
>
> It must be remembered that the time of the Women's Session in WA is particularly suitable, and is part of a valuable block listening period from 20 to 11 (*The Watchman*) through 11.00-11.30am (*Women's Session*) to the schools broadcasts from 11.30 to 12. Women listen right through this period as it suits the country-woman who is preparing her big meal of the day and has her

wireless close at hand. Letters and reports from CWA groups all stress this. The removal of speakers, interviews with visiting celebrities, travellers and so on will cause a blank at this time, which is greatly to be deplored.

The connections that Greenwood saw between her talks and those of "The Watchman" are not mentioned in any other correspondence but are telling. These talks by Edward Alexander Mann, the ABC's chief commentator and a hugely popular broadcaster, were based on his previous experience as a center-right, anti-Labor Nationalist politician from Perth in the Federal parliament in the 1920s. His daily sessions "At Home and Abroad" and a weekly program "The News Behind the News" were commentaries on world affairs that were agenda-setting for the national scene and described by Inglis as being legitimated "from the vantage point of a robust liberal imperialism and Christianity acquired in the time of Queen Victoria" (Inglis 1983: 63). The ABC programmed his talks anonymously, until his identity was revealed in Parliament in 1939, because they were seen to be contentious given his political background. Greenwood portrayed her talks in the *Women's Sessions* as a continuation of Mann's remit to talk about international politics from an Australian perspective and thus aligned them also as equally patriotic.

This reading of "censorship" of Greenwood, despite Charlton's ostensible explanation that all talks were to be cut at this time, is supported by later research by other scholars, especially that of Richardson who found that Greenwood, as well as other left-leaning writers for the ABC, had scripts changed or cut, especially when writing about Soviet Russia in the period after the Menzies Government banned the Communist Party in Australia in June 1940 and before the German invasion of Paris in June 1941 (Richardson 1988, 1989). During May 1940, Communist Party organizations and media outlets, including Perth's *Workers' Star* (briefly renamed *The Clarion* in anticipation of the ban) as well as the homes of key members, were raided by plainclothes policemen ("Police Raid Communists" 1940). Fisher notes that Greenwood, later recorded by the Australian Security Intelligence Organisation (ASIO) as a member of the Communist Party of Australia from 1942 and party official from 1943, "was periodically under surveillance by the security services ... [and a]lthough she was sometimes asked to censor material in her ABC radio talks owing to their pro-Soviet messages, she became adept at navigating editorial policy while still promoting her agenda" (Fisher 2017). Lesley Johnson records a parallel instance of censorship of international talks in the national *Women's Sessions* in the late 1930s, when Constance Duncan, peace activist and YWCA leader, was told in

July 1938 that her weekly talks on international affairs in the session were to be terminated (Johnson 1988: 181–182). ABC management told Duncan that *The Watchman* and other current affairs talks from the BBC were deemed sufficient coverage, but a confidential internal report mentioned her "political sympathies" and her belief in "some form of 'Christian Communism'" (Johnson 1988: 182).

Greenwood's supporters also believed the discontinuation of her talks to be a form of censorship. On May 26, 1941, Gertrude à Beckett, the wife of Melbourne establishment lawyer William Gilbert à Beckett, wrote to Greenwood describing the discontinuation of her talks as "censoring of your talks [which] must be terribly annoying to you in your work, but carry on, you must be putting something across the air which is worthwhile, or I, for one, would not have noticed what I did in your talk as being as I said 'above the average.'" À Beckett also mentioned that she had corresponded with ABC Brisbane broadcaster Elizabeth Webb "speaking from 4QG and found she too was an ardent supporter of Douglas." This reference to Douglas, as well as to recent books by Colin Barclay-Smith later in the letter, was to the international Douglas Social Credit Movement, a scheme for redistribution of wealth through debt-free credit and centralized control of pricing.

Not to be deterred, Greenwood attempted to put further pressure on the ABC by correspondence with the Labor opposition leader John Curtin in early November 1940, which resulted in him making representations to the Postmaster General, as the public servant responsible at the highest level for broadcaster. She also proposed to Curtin to set up a rival program on Labor's planned Perth-based radio station (Greenwood "Short-Wave Talks over Station VLQ"). Appealing to regional independence and the mythical figure of the isolated rural woman listener, she described the effects of the ending of the talks to Curtin as in a letter on November 1, 1940:

1. The new arrangement keeps a skeleton session run by one woman (here it is Mrs Dorothy Graham). No special speakers to be employed in future. However the ABC is advising women to listen in to a relayed talk which goes over all States—here at 1.30—once daily.

2. This disregards the special needs of West Australian women listeners, who are more dependent on their radios than those of the Eastern States. 1.30 does not suit them. One farm woman writes that husbands are in for dinner at that time and they will not listen to a woman but turn to music, market reports etc. The women thus lose doubly by the new arrangement.

3. The whole point is that it is another example of domination from the East by persons who do not know WA conditions, and that if economy is the excuse there are other avenues where it could be practised.

Greenwood emphasized that she wanted "this matter [to] be made one of principle rather than a personal one" and was confident that "my talk, 'Women in the International News' established itself, and had such a wide following, that if women speakers are re-instated, I am sure to come back." On the same day, the *West Australian* reported that the Australian Labor Party, on behalf of the Subiaco branch, had recently asked the ABC if "reports stating that, in the interests of economy, women speakers were being discontinued," and at its October 31 meeting the branch had discussed a letter from the ABC "stating that the Commission had decided that, from October 7, women speakers would no longer broadcast talks in the Women's Sessions" ("Women Broadcasters" 1940).

Appealing to Curtin as a former journalist in labor movement media outlets and editor of the union-owned *Westralian Worker* during the 1920s, Greenwood ended her letter by raising the "possibility of organising the Women's Session on the new Labor Station to be erected" in Perth. Greenwood cited "the work of Mrs Isobel Grey in Sydney on 2KY" that she believed "to be the best B Class [commercial] women's session in Australia." She also emphasized her qualifications for the role based on "many ideas from extensive reading of up-to-date methods of broadcasting and feel that it is a great opportunity of giving the women of WA something that is sadly lacking present radio programmes." While Curtin was not able to meet with her while in Perth, he wrote from the Federal Member's Rooms at the Commonwealth Bank Building on November 6, 1940, acknowledging her letter and saying that he had "noted [her] remarks, however, and will bear them in mind." He suggested Greenwood follow up about the new Labor Party-affiliated commercial radio station in Perth with the station's management, the People's Printing and Publishing Co, publisher of *Westralian Worker* and owned by the Australian Workers' Union. The new radio station was eventually opened by Curtin's former employer in October 1941 as 6KY, to match the 2KY call sign of the union-owned Sydney station, which had operated since the mid-1920s. While Greenwood wrote to the People's Printing and Publishing Company in February 1941 applying "for position of organiser and announcer of the Women's Session of your station" and again to the station manager on July 30, also applying for an announcing role (see also Richardson 1989: 14, fn 13), and stating that she was "known as a speaker to groups all over the State, and can meet the needs of informal discussion as well as from prepared scripts," she was not successful. The station's opening line-up in October did not include Greenwood, and Perth's *Mirror* ahead of the opening listed "Mavis Ruck [as in] charge of the women's session" ("6KY Soon on the Air" 1941; "Announcers at 6KY" 1941). While Ruck had no apparent connection to any local women's organizations, she did have previous experience as a broadcaster on Perth commercial stations and was an elocution teacher and, perhaps more importantly, daughter of a Labor party councillor for North Fremantle, Stan Ruck.

While Greenwood did not give up on returning to the air, she switched tack, and in January 1941 applied to the Fellowship of Australian Writers (FAW) as an associate member of the WA branch. Clearly anticipating that as a radio broadcaster she might not be considered a "writer" by the FAW, she made a case for her eligibility based on the craft of writing for the ear that she had mastered in her radio work, as well as the scope of work that she had done:

> As you are perhaps aware, it is necessary to understand the technique of phrasing the spoken word and placing it within the framework of written phrases. This, I claim, is an art in itself, and until there is such group as the Fellowship for radio speakers, I must seek association of those who live as I do by writing and speaking on the fellowship of Writers.
>
> My work has recently been extended to talks over some 10 or 12 transmissions of the Australian Short-Wave Station VLQ. The most recent of these talks is a series programmed for January on varying aspects of life as lived by women in Western Australia. Perhaps your group would consider this and some 200 filed talks would entitle me to become an associate member. If so I should be grateful.

Whether she was immediately accepted or not is not recorded in Greenwood's correspondence, but she was highly active in the Fellowship from the late 1940s until the late 1960s and made a life member of the Fellowship's WA Branch in 1975 (Fisher 2017; Kotai-Ewers 2013: 303–307).

Resuming transmission

On August 4, 1944, Greenwood wrote to Molesworth about some issues with the sound of her voice on a recent recording of a talk on "People in the International News" and described, yet again, her hopes that "Women's Session may be resumed here, and I can return to the microphone," and highlighted the discussions she had provoked during the Commission's visit to Perth in May of that year:

Mr Moses [ABC General Manager] said that WA is the only State without a Women's Session, and something should be done about it on his return [to Sydney]. Since he was here, the Advisory Board has put in a recommendation, and Mrs Ivy Kent (who is a member) told me personally that she had my talks in mind when she said that women listeners should be hearing what is being done by women elsewhere. (Greenwood "Short-Wave Talks over Station VLQ")

A few weeks before the Commission's visit, in April 1944 a letter from a "Housewife" was published in Perth's *Sunday Times*' "Women's Opinions" column. The letter's writer echoed Greenwood, saying that when she heard "the dulcet tones of the [ABC] announcer informing me that 'this is your national station … '" she responded by thinking "Is it?" and suggested she "would be snubbed if I wrote to them saying that as it is 'my' station, according to their own announcement, I demand that they put on a more entertaining and helpful women's session during the mornings!" (Housewife 1944)

Despite Moses's personal support of Greenwood (Lewis 1979: 31), she was not chosen as host of the reinstated sessions, and Catherine King was appointed instead. King had been the instigator of successful children's programming on the local ABC after kindergartens were closed down in Western Australia under threat of Japanese air raids during early 1942 (Inglis 1983: 103). On August 30, the *West Australian* announced the reintroduction of 6WF's *Women's Session* with "Mrs Alec King" as host, and described her as "setting out to give her listeners something to think about rather than something merely to entertain them" ("New ABC Session: Many Interests Covered" 1944). Dated the same day, an unsigned letter in Greenwood's archives to the manager of *The Broadcaster*, a weekly radio journal published by the *West Australian*, on behalf of the Women's Service Guilds (most probably written by Greenwood herself from the identical paper and typeface as other signed letters in the same file), started by endorsing King as the host of the new program and then finished with a pitch for Greenwood to return:

At the time, we … wrote deploring the cessation of the talks by Mrs Irene Greenwood, on Fridays' "Women in the International News"; and we hope now at a live women's session is envisaged we may soon have Mrs Greenwood back on the air again, and benefit from the wide store of knowledge she possesses of women in International affairs.

A similar letter, again not personally signed, was addressed to King on the same day, and while congratulating her on her new appointment also mentions the

Guilds' role in the reestablishment of the session and at the same time took the opportunity to make a final pitch for the return of Greenwood to the sessions.

On September 7, 1944, Charlton wrote to Greenwood, highlighting her approval of "our choice of Mrs Catherine King to take control of the Women's Sessions in this State" and requesting "four talks at fortnightly intervals, on the subject of 'Women in the International News' on ABC Women's Session … to start on September 20th." Greenwood wrote back agreeing to do alternate Wednesday talks on "Women in the International News." The positive relationship continued through the mid-1940s with Greenwood on August 27, 1946, conducting interviews with Indian women delegates at the feminist organization-led Australian Women's Charter Conference in Sydney for broadcast in the program, and in September 1946 preparing a script for a talk giving further news of international political participation in the conference, reporting on the visit of "Mlle Jeanne Chaton, [French] Resistance Leader visiting Australia for the New Education Fellowship Conference" as well as Dr Maria Zebrowska, "first official representative of the new Polish Government to come to Australia, Professor of Psychology at Warsaw University and eminent children's psychologist" (Greenwood "Short-Wave Talks over Station VLQ").

The problems of international content in the programs, however, continued under King. Without naming Greenwood, or any other broadcaster, when later asked about skirmishes with in a 1982 talkback session as part of the ABC Perth's fiftieth anniversary programming highlighted struggles she had with management over such talks, recalling:

> They finally defeated me over [talks on] international affairs … They felt it was not the place … in Women's programs. They thought [the women] could listen to *Notes in the News* at six minutes past one. But my feeling was that one wanted to look at every aspect … And I was on the point of resigning over that if they were going to do this to me, but my father [English professor Walter Murdoch], who was always a mediator with me … said that there were ways around it, instead of having straight talks called "International Affairs," I could just do interviews with people who were authorities in international affairs, which of course, was quite wise. (King 1982; see Andrews 2016: 34)

King's own interest in radio as a forum for discussing international issues and politics paralleled her involvement with the International Association of Radio Women (IARW), which she helped pioneer in 1950, according to an item published on the *Sydney Morning Herald's* women's page in 1953 ("Women's Interests on the Air: Hebrides Flying Doctor" 1953). A visit to the IARW's second meeting in Amsterdam featured on her program in 1952, and a script that King attached in a letter to IARW cofounder Lilian van der Goot is discussed by media historians Kristin Skoog and Alec Badenoch in their work on the IARW as a transnational feminist network. Skoog and Badenoch describe how King's report on the 1952 conference "made it sound almost like a meeting to which [her listeners] all had been invited, and she ended by asking listeners to write in with what controversial topics they would like discussed in future" (2016: 205).

Despite these attempts by King to include this kind of content, by 1948, Greenwood had left the ABC and started her own program "Woman to Woman" on the Whitford's 6AM-PM commercial network, broadcasting five days a week on one metropolitan (Perth) and three regional stations (Geraldton, Kalgoorlie, and Northam) until 1954. The scope of the program, away from the far more bureaucratic—and nationalist—ABC, was both local and international, enabling "listeners to inhabit several spheres simultaneously" (Baker 2017: 304). The gaps in Greenwood's appearances on the ABC recounted here, and the ensuing absences of international content in women's programming, are inextricably linked with tensions within the ABC as a key institution of the public sphere during the 1930s and 1940s.

The potential during this period for radio as a medium to facilitate transnational connections and for the ABC in particular to open up a worldview that went beyond dominant understandings of gendered media content were constrained both by nascent cold war politics on an international scale and by a centrally bolstered insistence on women as passive recipients of instructional programming. The ABC's attitude was most baldly stated in November 1943 when Basil Kirke, the ABC's manager for NSW, forwarded a report on the national *Women's Session* (which was not taken in Perth due to time differences) to the federal director and controller of talks. He had asked Miss Margaret Fraser, one of the ABC's "Presentation Officers," to give him "some ideas about the manner in which the Women's Session should, in future, be conducted" (Kirke 11/15 1943). Fraser's report asked "what do women really want, and not what they should have." From "observations and talks" Fraser conducted "with women of varying stations and abilities," she ascertained that what they wanted during such a daytime session was:

1. Light gay music
2. A warm personality conducting the session, who, in time, becomes their microphone friend ...

3. Chatty hints for use around the home, without a suspicion of preaching or teaching
4. A funny story or incident that is found to be a relief ...

Fraser considered:

> Any form of solid education, news review, music primarily for the music lover, forum (meaning "After the war—Then What?" type of broadcast) or wholly cultural talks are wasted time in this session. The busy housewife has only half an ear on the radio, because she is thinking of a dozen things in her daily round. She wants to be mildly entertained without using her brain to any appreciable extent.

While the main *Women's Session* on ABC Perth during the 1940s may have paid only lip service to this policy, as reported in the previous chapter by Catherine King in her account of her encounter with the fragile discs intended to instruct West Australian women to make a "better biscuit," Greenwood's agenda went beyond stereotypical notions of gendered programming to explore new kinds of intimate geographies mediated by radio, in particular its potential to transgress national boundaries.

Wishy-washy sessions

As Andrews's (2016) account of the postwar ABC working environment for women shows, conventions around what kinds of work women were allowed and not allowed to do within broadcast institutions, and also what women's programming was allowed to contain, were well entrenched by the 1950s and 1960s. The case of Greenwood and her continual struggle to stay on air at the ABC show that such conventions were being contested at the time that they were being established. The further entrenchment of women's programming within public service broadcasting during the late 1940s and early 1950s as centered on women's unpaid work in the home is therefore important to understand the gaps in second-wave feminism's memory around the careers of women such as Greenwood and her vision for broadcasting. The struggles over *Women's Sessions* on the ABC actually ran parallel to a wider withdrawal from programming centered on women's interests in general within the radio industry in the postwar years. Programming for and by women in particular all but disappeared from daytime programming on most commercial stations during the late 1940s.

During the late 1940s and early 1950s, Elizabeth Webb, former ABC *Women's Sessions'* broadcaster ("Elizabeth Webb" 1940) turned journalist, media commentator, and art critic, drew consistent attention to women employees' battles for editorial control of the ABC's Sessions in her "Radiopinion" column in Brisbane's *Sunday Mail*. Webb had pioneered a form of intimate political address in her own program, *Speaking Personally*, which was broadcast nationally from Brisbane on daytime ABC radio in the late 1930s. Described as a "formidable journalist and a superb communicator" by Sharyn Pearce in one of the only studies of her broadcasting career, Webb's own program had been "a complete departure from the format of her commercial competitors" (Pearce 1995: 47). Australian commercial broadcasters during the 1930s conceptualized their "daytime 'women's market'" to match the needs of advertisers by "broadcasting light and breezy interviews with visiting overseas film stars, health, household and beauty tips, news commentary from a 'woman's perspective' together with the occasional contentious debate" (Pearce 1995: 47).

In mid-1946, the ABC tried to capitalize on its national reach by appointing Clare Mitchell as national organizer of *Women's Interests*. Mitchell was a former home economics educator and broadcaster, most prominently as the host of a "Banish Drudgery" segment promoting the use of electricity in the home sponsored by the Sydney County Council's electrical arm on commercial station 2GB during the late 1930s ("Stars of the Air: Claire Mitchell to Conduct New National Women's Session" 1946). This national approach met with local resistance, however, because it did not allow for regional diversity where capital city-based hosts could garner loyal audiences and make promotional visits to local communities statewide, as King had so effectively done in WA (see, for example, "Women's Realm: Country Needs" 1945; "Countrywomen's Interests: Women Must Contribute to Local Government" 1947). In February 1947, Webb found that the ABC's increasingly centralized women's programming demonstrated that the broadcaster no longer "bothered itself with the question of what women want to listen to in the mornings" (E.C.W. 02/02 1947). Rather "its idea—and it's been experimenting with a National Women's Session for a number of years—appears to be to keep any one personality from becoming really popular with the public, and, at all costs, to maintain its imperial dignity":

> So it gives out entertainment plus enlightenment as it believes the public ought to like it … [to] Mitchell … has fallen the unenviable task of trying to keep everyone happy. As I see (or hear) it, she's got a rough row to hoe—because listeners are still smarting under the shock of losing their individual State personalities and

heartily resent having everything thought up and dished out from Head Office. I hear a lot of complaints that all the friendly personal warmth has vanished under such meticulous, clear-cut, business-like manipulation. That's what this National women's feature lacks: warmth; that little personal touch fostered so charmingly by the late and much mourned Jane ... Clare Mitchell sounds just too good to be true; a little too perfect, and as if she knows ALL the answers. (E.C.W. 02/02 1947, emphasis in the original)

As Webb hinted at here, Mitchell's didactic presentation style was seen to symbolize ABC paternalism, and in her September 28 column Webb described Mitchell's national *Women's Session* as marked by "a rather chilly impersonal dominance of all States [which] is apparently not appreciated here [in Queensland]":

Evidently other States feel the same about their own personalities. One interstate complaint to this column says: "Our session has lost the personal touch. It's now like a row of tenement houses." Actually the context [*sic*] of the *Women's Session* is good, packed with psychology and enlightenment, but ABC can't (or won't) see that a number of women busy with household chores don't want instruction so much as a friend who drops in to tea. It shouldn't be difficult to adjust matters, to please all tastes. Why not split even and give each State full time and control at least twice a week? (E.C.W. 09/28 1947)

Mitchell would not last long as compere and organizer as she soon, like King in WA, clashed with ABC management over editorial policy. Also like King before her, Mitchell appears to have tried to include news and political content in the session with mixed results. For example, in October 1947, the ABC *Women's Sessions* had introduced a current affairs segment, hosted by Dorothy Duncan of the Bureau of Current Affairs, which had developed in the UK from an Army Education Unit that was set up to provide reading material and training of civilians in postwar home and public life (Duncan 10/02 1947). In a more openly feminist vein, in the last *Women's Session* for 1947, Mitchell saw an opportunity for the Session to start a debate about housewives' "working conditions," advocating for housewives to organize around a "Sixty-Hour Week" on the eve of the introduction of the five-day working week across Australia on New Year's Day 1948:

Next week the Forty-Hour Week comes into force for most workers in the Commonwealth, except of course for housewives, who might be in a majority numerically, but it's an unorganised majority. Estimates of the hours housewives work vary between one hundred and seventy five. Anabel Williams-Ellis, an expert in women's work, who visited us from England this year, said women should press for a sixty-hour week. *New Year resolution—why not form ourselves into a union? It could become the most powerful body in the land. But it would be frowned on, naturally, by our men.* (Mitchell 12/31 1947, emphasis mine)

Mitchell suggested that the burden of housework was preventing women from being able to take a more active interest in public affairs:

> If only we could free ourselves from the burden of chores, the inexorable tyranny of meals, of washing up, house-cleaning and laundry, we might have time to take a more active interest in public life. If only there wasn't always the children's sewing we could perhaps read more. (Mitchell 12/31 1947)

A few days later, Mitchell announced her resignation (Inglis 1983: 169). While the programs described above were not specifically mentioned as the reasons for her departure, an article published in the *Sunday Telegraph* (just underneath that week's page 5 "Beach Girl of the Week" photo-feature) on January 4, 1948, quoted Mitchell as saying that she did not approve of "wishy-washy sessions designed only for women," which focused only on "household hints" and thereby "pandered to women with girlish sessions" ("Woman Broadcaster Leaves A.B.C. after Clash" 1948). She explained that while she respected the "Commission's viewpoint" she could not "subscribe to views that I consider old-fashioned ... I believe that women's sessions should be of general interest [and] should not be designed only for women" ("Woman Broadcaster Leaves A.B.C. after Clash" 1948).[4]

Perhaps indicating the kind of internal discussions that gave rise to Mitchell's departure, in January 1948 a Parliamentary Standing Committee on Broadcasting meeting at Hobart heard of a widespread lack of public interest in broadcasts of parliamentary debates, especially from women ("Interest in Debates on Air Assessed" 1948). Mrs Lynda Heaven, ALP member (and during the early 1960s elected first Labor Female Member of Tasmanian State Parliament on a recount for a vacancy caused by the death of a sitting member), Federal Secretary of the Australian Housewives' Association, State President of the Women's Christian Temperance Union, and foundation member of the Women's International League for Peace and Freedom, representing the Housewives' Association at the hearings, took the opportunity to single out the ABC *Women's Sessions* that she thought "were excessively cultural and psychological, and lacked practical use": "Very few women are interested in parliamentary broadcasts, because they are not interested in politics, and this is a reflection on them"[5] ("Interest in Debates on Air Assessed" 1948).

Pursuing her ongoing critique of the "service talks" model of gendered programming promoted by Heaven, in February 1948 Webb highlighted a recent guest-edited version of the *Women's Session* by print journalist Sadie Parker, who was filling in after Mitchell's departure as "near perfect a woman's programme as radio could produce":

> She culled "Things women want to know from the world news," including resume of personal life of blind philosopher Helen Keller, insight into Vivien Leigh, women's attitude to prize fights and problem of youth delinquency, ending with interview with the [Anglican] Dean of Sydney [Stuart Babbage] on workability of his Marriage Guidance Bureau. Instructive, interesting and intelligent. (Webb 02/29 1948)

In March she bemoaned changes implemented after Mitchell's departure when despite the "ABC's momentous decision to call its women's session, *Women's Magazine*," recent changes had "fortunately done little to alter what is still (in spite of persistent male interference) the best women's session on our air." She implored "Now, for Pete's sake, leave it alone!" (E.C.W. 04/11 1948).

Profound changes were taking place outside the ABC, where women's programming was shifting to use supposedly more popular male announcers. By December 1949, Webb's column would declare "Male Announcers Move in on Kitchen Sessions." While she was thankful that the days when *Women's Sessions* were "recipe-ridden and the highlight was a hint on how to remove stains from sinks" were "mercifully past," she wanted to know the "average woman's reaction to Brisbane commercial radio's 4BC's Household Service Bureau, 11.30 a.m., in which male announcers give domestic hints and recipes to what is presumed to be an entirely feminine audience":

> Being allergic to airborne recipes myself, I was delighted recently with an excellent delivery of beetroot in gelatine from one of the most verile [*sic*] and robust male voices in radio to-day. Now, just before the 12.30 news on 4BK, we're being treated to a sponsored recipe—recommended by leading Brisbane chefs. Once again the recipe is man handled. And they're doing all right. Straight to business. No "mucking" about. And with a conviction which almost persuades us they actually know what they're talking about. But it takes some getting used to have a male plead with us to sprinkle shredded lemon peel or split blanched almonds on the cake before using. (E.C.W. 12/11 1949)

Sydney newspaper *Truth* also reported in March 1950 that 4KQ, the Australian Labor Party-owned station in Brisbane, had dropped women announcers from its regular morning *Women's Sessions*. KQ's manager, Les Andrews, told *Truth*: "I want to use all male announcers on the station from now onwards" ("Short Waves" 1950). The station's decision mirrored the decision in 1949 of other Brisbane commercial stations such as 4BK and 4BC to restrict the airtime of women announcers and where they did appear, to pair them with male announcers:

> Now we come to the question: Do women listeners doing their household chores like to hear women announcers—or do they prefer to hear about a sale of scanties, etc., from the lips of embarrassed males? It's a moot point—but Sydney stations have found that men have more appeal to the ladies on their sessions. It's up to the Brisbane gals to decide for themselves! ("Short Waves" 1950)

This removal of women announcers from daytime programming on commercial stations continued during the early 1950s with Webb noting a "growing trend in radio to 'wipe' women's sessions" while the ABC's "altering *Women's Magazine* to *Morning Magazine* rings no changes ... A heap of variety still with feminine influence" (E.C.W. 07/22 1951). Taking over the "Radiopinion" column from Webb, former ABC Brisbane film reviewer Joyce Stirling told her readers in July 1953 that the removal of female announcers was a backwards step, in a piece entitled " ... Male Announcers ... [need to] Give That Gooey Nonsense Away." Stirling contrasted the style of female commercial radio hosts such as Mavis Riding on 4BC and Irene Tucker on 4BH, as well as the ABC *Women's Sessions*— "one of the most enjoyable of the day from anybody's listening point of view"— with the approach of male announcers who

> treat their women listeners with that dreadfully patronising "microphone manner" ... Some of that gooey nonsense that goes on in certain housewives' sessions ("Come on, Mrs. Fitzwizzlebreeches, don't be shy. Try hard and win five shillings for Daddy") is very hard to take. We don't like it, boys. After all, most of us HAVE come of age. (Stirling 1953, emphasis in the original)

The increasing marginality of women's programming to Australian daytime radio also upset conservative critics, who lamented the loss of focus on women's domestic role. In February 1952, Lesley Morris, radio critic of the Melbourne Catholic newspaper *The Advocate*, described daytime radio as universally dull, entirely composed of "pops" interspersed with "serials," with the exception of the ABC, which was "the only one on the air worth a hearing, once again because the Commission uses experts, and because it is prepared to concede intelligence to its audience" (Morris 02/28 1952). Her diagnosis of commercial stations' dullness was "due to the fact that, in the mornings, at least, the housewife, the listener at whom the programmes are aimed ... is [considered by programmers to be] too busy to treat programmes as anything but a vague background to her work," yet she also saw the serials as detrimental to female listeners by being overly melodramatic and "heart-wringing":

> It is interesting to note that most of the old-time women's sessions have vanished—the cosy gossips spiced with fashion news, recipes and household hints no longer exist, except on the ABC, where they assume a more sophisticated form ... Purely feminine interests are catered for, but the session rises above the usual "all girls together, let's talk cooking" atmosphere. Of particular interest are its talks on interior decorating and on books.

A few months later in July, Morris returned to the topic, again baffled at "the disappearance in recent times of the woman announcer": "Three years ago, at the outside, every city commercial station had its feminine personality. At KZ she was a straight announcer, but the other stations built special sessions around their women announcers" (Morris 07/31 1952). She singled out the ABC *Women's Sessions* for praise in their persistence with the sessions, and by implication, with the home-maker ideal:

> Good listening for anyone, but ... naturally, stresses the feminine point of view. [Assuming] that its listeners are intelligent and interested in current events; it recognizes that, while women will always listen to talks dealing with domestic doings and child care, their horizons are not necessarily bounded by these interests.

Singling out the "standard of [audience] letters" read out in the program, especially when compared with those read out in commercial stations, she "hoped that the tendency to eliminate women's sessions stops before it reaches the ABC."

The national *Women's Session* changed names in mid-1948 to *Women's Magazine*, hosted by Sheila Hunt, a former ABC News typist, who had moved into announcing during the Second World War to replace male members of staff on defense leave (Hunt 04/06 1948; Inglis 1983: 105). By June 1951, the ABC program had changed name again to *Morning Magazine* (Hunt 06/08 1951), and a new host, Ida Elizabeth Jenkins, former ABC Children broadcaster, took over (Inglis 1983: 169; Quinn 1951). From 1953 a *Country Women's Session* was scheduled for fifteen minutes once a week to be hosted by Lorna Byrne, regular guest on ABC women's national programming ("Turn on the Wireless: Lorna Byrne to Country Women" 1939) and former head of the women's extension service of the NSW Department of Agriculture.

The beginning of ABC Television broadcasts in November 1956 saw the initiation of the afternoon TV program, and the ABC's women's TV program began in late November.[6] Hosted by Mary Rossi, high-profile Catholic and "mother of 10" (Musgrove 1968), later described by her daughter Claudia Rossi Hudson as "no women's libber" (Carroll 2011), the program's audience was "tiny" and it went through a series of name changes, ranging from *Mainly for Women* in 1962 and *Matinee* in 1963, until it was discontinued in 1969 (Inglis 1983: 213). In May 1958, the radio sessions were again changed, with Jenkins's departure as full-time host, and Ruth Stirling, sometime cooking contributor to the sessions ("Radio Items: Women's Session Diary" 1955), took over. Described as "plump, brown-eyed Mrs Stirling, mother of 13-year-old Susannah" by the *ABC Weekly*, she was portrayed by this ABC publicity as arguing for women to have careers, as long as they were still good home-managers ("Save Your Husband's Life—with a Salad" 1958; see Inglis 1983: 239, 475). "Housewives are wonderful," Stirling was quoted as saying, "and being a good wife and mother is most important":

> But if a woman is a person as well, she can be a better wife and mother …
> Perhaps she might write a short story-and then immediately tear it up.
> Or she might begin designing the children's clothes.
> … If mother is a good manager and makes her family feel that they are sharing her big new adventure. it can only be good …
> A slovenly woman will have an untidy home and badly brought up children whether she goes to work or not.

Stirling herself was shocked by the attitude of ABC managers to the program and recounted in an oral history interview that she was "furious" at the way that the program was starved for resources and threatened to walk out of a meeting because of the dismissive attitude that male executives had toward women as an audience (Stirling quoted in Andrews 2016: 35). It would take another decade for the ABC to finally—yet cautiously—eliminate its radio *Women's Sessions*, as will be discussed in the final chapter. Evidently, the generic name for such programming continued well into the 1960s, with job advertisements still referring to the position of supervisor of "*Women's Sessions*" on a "Federal basis" in 1961 ("ABC: Four Vacancies at Sydney Head-Quarters to Work in Radio and TV" 1961).

Conclusion

Ultimately, the official remit of gendered programming was fundamentally unsettled by wider changes to the media landscape, which were a result of collective efforts by social movements to reshape discussions about gender and work, and to decouple women's assumedly natural role from the space of the home. The nascent feminist arguments that women such as Greenwood attempted to make at the ABC against such rigid ideas were fed by connections between radio and women's organizations of the 1930s and 1940s. The groundbreaking work of women such as Greenwood indicates that the medium of radio provided way of networking homes through the figure of the personality broadcaster. At the same time as the idealized image of the domestic sphere was defined by the very remit of the programs to explore only domestic and individualized experience, dominant ideologies of home as separate from public life and women as unpaid workers in the home were not taken as given by women broadcasters such as Greenwood, Mitchell, and King. Critics such as Webb drew attention to the potential of radio to speak to women about new topics and in new and pioneering modes of interpersonal exchange.

The themes and topics these broadcasters included in their programs were often shaped by programming policies that were beyond their control, but in their day-to-day work they stretched and pushed at existing intimate geographies, reflecting wider tensions and ruptures in the location of everyday life itself. Radio itself operated as both a means and a metaphor for understanding the new transparency of domestic space in modern culture. The long-held "separation of spheres" could be challenged through alternative, mediated imaginaries that sought to liberate women from their maternalist role. For feminists such as Greenwood and King, this was increasingly achieved through a progressive alignment between gender issues and international solidarities. It was these early possibilities that would grow into further critiques of the connections between patriarchy, colonialism, and nationalism in the 1960s and 1970s (Grimshaw 2017). In this aspect, much was at stake in women's intersubjective dialogue and the tabling of female lived experience, as will be shown in more detail in the next two chapters.

For now, this story tells us much about factors determining the shape of women's programming at its peak, including widely held ideologies of separate spheres and contradictory notions of the value of domestic labor. This chapter has explored the relationship between the home and the world that was so much in contest and manifest in both gender and class politics. Some of the broadcasters discussed here understood their imagined audience of women at home as collectively waiting for a revolution that would liberate women from their domestic role. The daytime radio imaginaries constructed by these women intertwined the public and private in ways that signified a new kind of gendered space, yet the full promise of this space was yet to be realized.

Mental Health on a National Scale:
The Women of the CBC, 1940–1953

Here's to a lady that's sure got guts
If it weren't for her we'd all go nuts
Mental Health on a national scale
It's Marjorie's baby an' hear it wail
Ah, woe, woe is me
Shame and sorrow to de family
The formidable teamsters James and Long
Treat all de ladies to a morning song
Fine commentators de country wide
Are held in check and respectful guide

    chorus

As for de female afternoon
We feed it to 'em on a wooden spoon
Who dreamed up de monster I wouldn't say
But no matter how you slice it
It's still TC Matinee

"Staff Poem" [about *Trans-Canada Matinee* given to Marjorie McEnaney] n.d

Introduction

A new role for radio was secured during the early 1940s when the national broadcasters became the mouthpiece of the "war effort." Radio was recruited to bring home and public life closer together and was part of a unified approach to organizing the national economy. In Canada, CBC relied on the "talk" format very heavily for its in-house daytime programming during the war.[1] Two staples of morning programming during the late 1930s were *Woman's World* "conducted by Roxanna Bond" on CBO Ottawa, from 10.15 to 10.45 from January 1939 until June 1940 (Bond 1939–1940), and *Monica Mugan* on CBL Toronto, from 11.30 to 11.45 Monday to Fridays from September 1939 until the early 1940s.[2] During 1940, *Woman's World* was replaced by *Wartime Housekeeping*, hosted by Ethelwyn Hobbes from Montreal on the national network, and complemented by afternoon "service" programs scheduled to follow the afternoon news from 4.18 to 4.30 p.m., which included topics such as *Sewing is Fun* (September 25, 1944) and *The Post-War Woman* (September 28, 1944).

Some women's programs blended informational and serial formats. One very successful example of this, in its homely construction of public events in the Canadian context, was *Our Knitting Circle*, a wartime program written by advertising copywriter Jean Hinds, then freelancing for the CBC. Hinds was invited by Elizabeth Long, who had taken up the newly established role of director of Women's Programs in 1938, to "lighten up" the talks format. Monthly episodes portrayed "an imaginary group of typical Canadian women who discussed neighbourhood affairs over their war work" and was "based on odds and ends of amusing information garnered from personal experience [of Hinds] in groups where knitting-needles and women's tongues flew equally fast" ("Personality of the Week in Radio" 1947).

In her account recorded as part of a special documentary retrospective on daytime and women's programming prepared for CBC's twenty-fifth anniversary in the early 1960s, Hinds gives a sense of the possibilities that this new genre of informational programming, centered on a serial format, afforded:

> I can't remember what most of [the afternoon talks before I started working for the CBC] were about, because I never heard them, I was busy in the office, writing ads for such things as smooth-fitting rayon stockings. But the talks must have been fairly serious because Elizabeth wrote and said she wanted to get some humour into the series. Would I write a series of stories about a women's knitting circle, clicking their needles for the war effort, as well as muddling through a lot of other patriotic enterprises? ... So I wrote the first episode and it was broadcast in May 1940. (Morrison 1961)

The program was exceptionally popular, and Hinds continued to write one episode a month in the evenings after she had finished her work at the advertising office. The episodes linked the rhythms of domestic work with the flow of the events of war, cementing women's everyday activities with the world of conflict and geopolitics, brought home in radio news broadcasts and policy.

> I sought ideas for "Knitting Circle" stories from the news ... My September talk
> of 1941 had the women sitting round but dropping their stitches as they listened
> to the radio and counted the German planes the Spitfires and Hurricanes
> brought down. (Morrison 1961)

According to an article published in CBC's in-house magazine, Hinds's *Knitting Circle* series "was so successful that she was engaged [in 1944] for a daily commentary for Prairie women on current events and matters of topical interest" ("Women Workers" 09/25 1942). The *Knitting Circle* had finished broadcasting by 1942, but the CBC continued to use the domestic and familial as a site of nation-building through the genre of talks that spoke to and on behalf of women in the postwar era. Thus, the end of the war in 1945 did not see the end of public service broadcasts to women. The project continued because radio lent itself strongly to a social objective to "nationalize" domesticity in the postwar era. Canadian Anglophone broadcasting as constructed by the public service broadcasting project served to subsume and negotiate regional, linguistic, economic, and political differences under a centralizing figure of "the national woman." Daytime radio, as an intimate medium that spoke to the rhythms of everyday life, was seen as key to defining a proper place for women within the national project. However, this certainty about women's roles was not as clear as a universalist, nationalist drive to coherence may have aimed for.

This chapter documents the innovative radio work undertaken within CBC's phenomenally successful and incredibly prolific talks for women under the auspices of its Women's Interests Department. During 1950, for example, 2,700 talks were produced by the department annually, a figure that represents over fifty individual talks per week, or more than seven per day (Long 1950). The chapter covers the period from 1940, when the talks for women were initiated, until 1953, the year after CBC's first television broadcasts, when the Women's Interests Department took a different direction by initiating its first daytime magazine program on radio. The chapter focuses on not just the content but the actual formal qualities of this talks programming, which embodied in introductions and openings moves between different dimensions and scales within radiophonic space. The programs employed sound techniques and effects to move between "private" and "public" worlds in ways that are highly revealing of the narratives that structured a relationship between masculine and feminine radiophonic space. The unique access to technical and staff resources that these programs enjoyed, especially in comparison with the under-resourced Australian examples, contributed directly toward the kinds of experimentation and creative use of the medium that these programs developed. This support for women's programming existed because CBC's programming was partly privately funded through sponsorship and advertising within a government-owned network with a public service remit (see Boardman and Vining 1996).

This hybrid public and market-based model gave relatively high status to women's programming through the figure of the woman consuming responsibly in the national interest while attracting long-term program sponsorship from food, and to some extent, fashion, industries. This combination of address to women as both consumers and citizens allowed CBC's women's programming to go from strength to strength during the postwar years and eventually transcend its relegation to the domestic. The case of CBC women's programming shows that traditional understandings of the separation of spheres could not be clearly maintained in the case of radio. The very performance of domesticity within these radio programs, and the energy and invention of the women who produced them, opened up an ambiguous imaginary space for engagement with the listener that was multivalent and unpredictable, rather than clearly public or private.

Caught in the act: Monica Mugan

CBC's Toronto-based morning host Monica Mugan, as mentioned above, ran a self-titled daily morning program during the early 1940s. Her program opened with a waltz tune (Noel Coward's *I'll See You Again*), which faded under the voice of a smoothly spoken man who announced: "It's 10.45 and again we take you for a brief interlude at Monica Mugan's." In the only copy of her program kept in the CBC archives in Toronto, Monica Mugan is broadcasting from the Women's Institute Convention held in Toronto in January 1943. The introduction by the male announcer positions the listener as "being taken for an interlude" at a woman's house and creates the impression that the audience is "eavesdropping" on a private gathering. This was far from the case, as Mugan's spoken introduction to the program bears out:

> This is Monica Mugan saying good morning and speaking to you this morning from the convention floor of the Royal York Hotel, where I'm attending a session of the Women's Institute Convention. I haven't counted heads this morning, it's a very large room of women, but there are around four hundred women. (Mugan 1943)

The program then proceeds with Mugan interviewing representatives of the Women's Institute and reporting on the results of an election. The intimate address of the male announcer is used to create an atmosphere of privacy and domesticity, which is undercut by the sounds of a large meeting of people in a semipublic place: the Royal York Hotel. This reconfiguration of public and private—with a gendered twist—was recounted in an article in the CBC program guide, connecting listener and host in a literal manner.

The publicity article showed a photo of a young man in a suit, named Eric Hardy, pouring a cup of tea for Mugan, and the photo's caption explained that he was one of "several young college men [who] were emerging from a scarlet fever quarantine" during which they had become "Monica-conscious when they listened by accident first and then by choice" ("Monica Misses Her Cue" 1942). The students recreated the event of "dropping in" at a friend's house for morning tea in their college residence and invited Mugan along: "They purchased a smart recorded arrangement of her theme music, 'I'll See You Again'; set the hour, had their kettle boiling, and as their petite radio friend marched in slightly out of breath, they set the gramophone going." When they asked Mugan if she liked the recording, "Monica had to admit that the whole date was so much off the beaten track she had lost her celebrated aplomb, [and] hadn't recognised the Noel Coward tune with which her programme opens every day." The unstable spatial moment of a radio program that imitated the event of morning tea with the neighbors, as well as the intimate presence that Mugan as host provided, provided the possibility of remaking domestic space along more open, inclusive lines.

They Tell Me: Claire Wallace

In August 1942, former newspaper journalist Claire Wallace's Toronto-based program *They Tell Me* went national, expanding its aim to go "behind the scenes" of public life into new dimensions. The program was sponsored by the Canadian Federal Government's National War Finance Committee, which used the program to raise war bonds (Wallace 1942), and the program's connection with listeners was seen to be an asset to funding. Wallace herself was described as "versatile" with a "flair for digging up intimate personal news of interest to women" and the program's "keynote" as "informality." The program was designed around real people's stories and to create a sense of a dialogue between listener and host: "to remove the certain amount of stiffness that accompanies a straight monologue talk, Claire has the able assistance of personality man Todd Russell" ("They Tell Me" 1942).

Wallace's program experimented with radio style, encompassing location-based, verite-style reporting such as "going undercover" as a store detective or as a maid to learn about the conditions of domestic work (Crean 1985: 87). She was heralded by the CBC as "Canada's news snooper and story scooper" ("They Tell Claire" 1942), spending a night in a run-down historical Toronto house on one occasion to gather material for a story on ghosts and on another putting an advertisement in the paper for a gigolo that received 300 replies (Crean 1985: 87–88). The program was broadcast on private stations as well as the CBC, sometimes on multiple stations in one city, and was promoted by newspaper advertisements as well as personal appearances by Wallace (Chamberlain 1943). "Little booklets" on future trends were offered to *They Tell Me* listeners on various topics, predicting "world air travel," the "place of plastics in the world," and "the world of the electron" (Glover 1967). Her programs were incredibly popular. In the early 1940s, Wallace's program was reportedly the most listened-to Canadian afternoon program of the year, with an audience of nearly half a million listeners, according to analysis for the Canadian Association of Adult Education of a radio listener postal survey conducted by the Elliot-Haynes Company. This survey concluded that *They Tell Me* was heard daily by one-quarter of the available audience of 1.8 million radio set owners in Canada in late 1942 and early 1943 (Chamberlain 1943: 18).

The program's production was imaginative and deliberately blurred boundaries between public and private time and space. The program's opening created a move "inside" within the temporal flow of radio, which was coded as masculine, to a space defined as privileged, not publically accessible, female, and intimate, and claimed to be a meeting point for "the women of Canada." The program theme started with sound effects of the tick-tock of a clock, then a male voice saying, "Again it's time for Claire Wallace, shall we go in?" followed by the sound effect of a door opening, then a track of a general buzz of female voices talking in a large room, and eventually the sound of a bell being rung. The unidentified male announcer (either Russell or Elwood Glover) then introduces Wallace—apparently always in a smart chapeau (see "Bright and Breezy," 1943)— addressing listeners dispersed across Canadian national space: "From Milltown to Grand Prairie, from Sydney to Nanaimo, the women of Canada meet again to hear *They Tell Me*, a program of stories *behind the stories*, presented by Claire Wallace" (Wallace 1943).

Wallace, who worked outside the CBC as a travel agent (Glover 1967), then gave an overview of the highlights of the program and set out the places that the audience would be "taken" during her show. Listeners were encouraged to understand themselves partaking in the broadcast, as both active listener and potential participant, as part of the war effort. The formal quality of being "taken" to a gathering by permission or invitation of a male announcer was shared with the introduction to other CBC women's talks, such as Monica Mugan's program, but in the case of *They Tell Me* this speaking position was given a national reach and geographic mobility by Wallace's access to a cosmopolitan worldview. Indeed, a CBC publicity story heralded Wallace as "first Canadian to fly by Clipper to Europe and the first woman to fly across Canada" ("They Tell Claire" 1942). This article, while emphasizing the access to scales beyond the local that Wallace's travels encompassed, also portrayed the "intimate and local" approach of Wallace as potentially reaching out through the interconnected media of radio and telephone to make contact with the listener themselves:

> From Halifax to Nanaimo, Claire is digging up the human interest angle in today's news. Listeners may hear things they never knew about Canada, or even about the people living right next door … after seven years of broadcasting, she is on a coast-to-coast hook-up bringing to the women of Canada, stories with a twist. Claire went down 3,000 feet in the Hollinger Gold Mine … *one of these days your telephone may ring with Claire waiting to ask you questions about something that you do that the women of Canada should know about—all part of winning the war.* ("They Tell Claire" 1942, emphasis mine)

The program, perhaps because of its high profile, and certainly because of the success of its female host, attracted controversy. In June 1944 *They Tell Me* was discontinued after negative media coverage of a National Radio Committee proposal to raise Wallace's salary. Reportedly, after Wallace's assistant quit from exhaustion, and in the absence of any request from Wallace, the program's sponsor, the National War Finance Committee, was asked to increase her salary by $30 per week, from $170 to $200 (Lang 1999). The ensuing barrage of commentary on her proposed salary rise in Canadian newspapers invidiously contrasted her salary with a reported male journalists' total weekly income of $40 to $50 by highlighting that her eventual salary would be quadruple that of an upper-level male journalists' salary. Such reports depicted Wallace as unpatriotic in her demand of higher wages during wartime (although this ostensibly had not been her own request but that of her sponsor). This debate also drew highly gendered criticism of women's programming as frivolous and inconsequential by depicting Wallace as a "radio gossiper" and the program as "chitchatter" (Lang 1999: 130–131). This debate reveals that the journalism practiced by men—and therefore their work as a whole—was seen to be more worthy of payment and recognition as contributing to the war effort. When the series resumed after the end of the war in January 1946, it was sponsored by Robin Hood Flour Mills (Cooke 2003; "'They Tell Me': Claire Wallace Broadcasts from a Plane in Flight" 1946), presumably with an appropriate salary for Wallace ("Claire Wallace in New Series" 1947).

In September 1947, Wallace was made a "Princess of the Mohawk Nation" during a broadcast from Oshwegen, near Brantford, Ontario ("Princess Gaw-Go-Wan-Na-Rya-Nee" 1947). Wallace's Mohawk name "Gaw-go-wan-na-rya-nee," translated as "Princess Loud-Voice-Heard-All-Over-The-Land," underscored the role of radio, and the genre of informality and intimacy her program had developed within it, as a way of domesticating the Canadian nation. Described as "one of the few white women ever given this honor by the Six Nations Council," Wallace's radio persona as a mobile adventurer provided a site of both gendered and racialized identifications—drawing women into the imaginary of settler-colonial space. Wallace's travels opened up spaces and times that were not usually represented but also reimagined intimacy within a range of collectivities that were elsewhere absent for Indigenous people. While the act of appropriation of indigenous identity and exoticization of nonwhite others has a long and problematic history, and cannot be brushed aside, the program's aim to go "behind the scenes" also reached beyond established geographies of intimacy and connection. By articulating her role as a radio host who used the inside-outsideness of the radio medium to create a decentered, travelling subject, Wallace's program called into question taken-for-granted arrangements of self and other, private and public. As a host who performed "informality" and proximity with her listeners, she also was allowed to take them to unexpected, unfamiliar, and complex places.

Wallace, reflecting on the program in the late 1960s, cited this broadcast and being "given a Native American name" as one of the most memorable stories she did (Glover 1967). This reach of the public world of radio into the national home had unexpected consequences, creating new flows of identification beyond the nation, as will be explored in the next section that looks at the international dimensions of women's radio programming through another key CBC figure, Kate Aitken.

Leftovers and politics: Kate Aitken

For the new season of 1948–1949 the *CBC Times* announced the arrival of Kate Aitken's program under the headline "Your Women's Editor—Kate Aitken of the *Standard*," heralding her role on the *Montreal Standard* as Woman's Editor. The program was to feature a regular segment "launched by" her sponsor, Ogilvie Flour Mills: "Kate Aitken Home Service Department." A second feature involved "a weekly award of $100 for the 'Outstanding Community Project of the Week,'" which was to be presented "in recognition of the worthy community work being carried on in hundreds of Canadian centres which aim to provide better cultural, recreational and educational facilities for citizens," as well as Aitken's regular coverage of "fashions, current events and arts" ("Women's Programs to Feature Kate Aiken [*Sic*]" 1948).

A broadcast by Kate Aitken on the last day of 1948 that listed notable women of the year set the pattern for a consumerist address, which linked the unnamed woman-at-home with public sphere, primarily through consumption practices but also in a surreal political configuration of the nation-state and world politics. Sponsored by Ogilvie Flour Mills, Aitken's talks simultaneously combined radically different, and at times conflicting, scales—domestic, local, regional, national, and international—by situating the listener as being connected to a mediated world of celebrities and commodities in ways that both drew on existing frameworks from print media (Clampin 2017) and anticipated television's uptake in the home during the 1940s and 1950s (Wood 2015).

The broadcast begins with Aitken appearing to have a casual chat with her male cohost "Mr MacCurdy," who she calls "Mac" during the talk. After this awkward introduction, she gives a roll call of "the outstanding women of the year." This list of women in national and international news ranges from the "mother of the year, Princess Elizabeth," who had produced "the baby of the year," to the "woman athlete of the year" to Madam Chiang Kai-Shek, "the ... well ... sad woman of the year" (presumably in reference to the Chinese Civil War and the imminent exile of her husband's Nationalist government to Taiwan) and included Mrs RJ Marshall, president of the National Council of Women, but also "head and founder, and really ... the 'sparkplug' of the Consumer Association" (Aitken 1948). During this listing of names, she is asked by "Mac" to name the "world's best dressed woman." Aitken responds:

now look, for my money ...

Here she is Mac, her name is Smith or Jones, or Brown. She has a husband, a nice dad, she's crazy about him! She has three children, she gets, ohh, about $25 per week to spend on groceries, and milk and butter and food.

She wears a clean housedress in the morning, sometimes she's so busy she just puts on another clean housedress for supper, then covers it up with a frilly white apron ... white as snow. She doesn't wear a mink coat, she doesn't wear glamour clothes, but she's smart and neat, she keeps powder on her nose, she has her hair cut short and curled: she's Mrs Canada. And for my betting she's Canada's best dressed woman.

Mac responds straight from the program sponsor's advertising copy:

I'll bet a girl like that knows her way around. She knows it's smart to use Ogilvie's readymix cakes ... A woman like that could walk into any grocery store and point up at the shelf and say "I'll take that there, Ogilvie's Gold and Chocolate Cake."

In this script "Mrs Canada" is positioned as "Canada's best dressed woman" because she makes do with what she has ("25 dollars a week for groceries" and "a clean housedress" and "a frilly white apron"), rather than requiring "glamour clothes." The thrifty, proud, and decidedly Anglo-Saxon female citizen is depicted as requiring only cake mix to complete her self-contained world of family, but at the same time the framing of this sponsored punchline, however implausibly, ties the site of the domestic to the swirl of world events and public figures via the shop counter.

This excessive spatiality sets the structure for Aitken's programming, which initiated a genre of news and current affairs grounded in the routines of everyday life. In September 1949, "Your Women's Editor—Kate Aitken" was advertised by the CBC as returning to the air "with more news of interest to the woman who runs a home" in her thrice-weekly program:

Discussing her program plans for this season, Mrs Aitken said she would divide her broadcast time between news about world events which directly affect the housewife, human interest stories, personality sketches of people in the news, fashion trends, and information about housekeeping. ("Kate Aitken Begins New Radio Season" 1949)

A broadcast by Kate Aitken in 1953 exemplifies how this programming philosophy would manifest in evermore bizarre juxtapositions. Rather than generating a cosy fit between gender and domesticity, these 1950s broadcasts create a disjuncture between the flow of public time in the "course of world events" during the cold war and the home (see Mislán 2017 for a contrasting case in the writing of Trinidadian-born Claudia Jones in the postwar United States). More critically, the broadcasts encourage women to feel that they are agents in these events but without offering them a way to participate in the public sphere outside consumerism. The broadcast lists "the housewife" at the end of a list of public figures, mostly presidents and prime ministers of countries with relationships to Canada. While interpellated as "important" and "included" in "setting the course of world events," ultimately the chief role of women in this sequence seems to be to successfully create interesting dishes from the remains of their family's Christmas celebrations.

The talk starts with "a particularly happy good morning to the gentleman who we have in our midst" to which a male voice replies with a non-sequitur, perhaps as a result of Aitken going off-script: "yes, I certainly do" (Aitken 1953). Aitken continues:

> They're not often in on the morning broadcast when it hits the air, so how are ya, boys? ... We were all wondering about the progress of the year that's coming in ... now we know this, that the people that set the course of our world's events, well, we could possibly count them on the fingers of two hands.

Mac's voice breaks in and says, "Well, Mrs A, this morning let's name them:"

KA:	Well, ladies first, young Queen Elizabeth, definitely ...
Male host:	and ... Stalin!
KA:	and Malan [Prime Minister and the architect of the system of apartheid], of South Africa
Male host:	... Eisenhower, of the United States.
KA:	... and the research boys, scattered as they are over every large nation, it's to them we look both collectively and individually.
Male host:	... there's General Mao, of China.
KA:	and Nehru, of India.
Male host:	... and Canada's Lester B. Pearson.
KA:	... and Churchill, of course, and another smart Britisher, called Butler, he's the lad that's going to handle the money!
Male host:	... and Peron, in the South American continent.
KA:	... and for goodness sakes, let's include that person whom we vaguely describe as the housewife. Some of us call her mother, some of us call her mum, or even disrespectfully, from the head of the house, sometimes she gets this: "the old girl"
Male host:	... or "the missus"

KA: [laughs] the missus! or "meet the wife"! Yes! I expect one of her
             good resolutions today is "I'm going to make the food on the
             table more attractive" … Well, if it is, this broadcast is right in
             there with you pitching and punching!

Aitken then gives a recipe for using up leftover fruitcake, which involves combining steamed stale cake with red and green jell-o, "You know what it is— it's a 'stop and go' dessert, you stop just long enough and then you go until the last crumb is eaten, it's good luck!" Just as thrifty and resourceful as "Mrs Canada" of the 1948 broadcast, the anonymous "housewife" of this later broadcast stands in contrast to "the research boys" to whom Canadians were imagined to "look collectively and individually." The housewife here is spatially contained to the kitchen, while the other figures mentioned in the broadcast have access to the world stage.

Aitken's program ultimately connected women's interests internationally within an imperial framework. In 1954, Aitken returned to CBC Trans-Canada, with a daily program Monday through Friday titled *Your Good Neighbour*:

> She plans on travelling over 75,000 miles by airplane during the coming months and will visit British Columbia, Newfoundland, Jerusalem, the Soviet Union (where she will make a factual report on how 285 million people, live, eat, shop and educate their children), Western Europe and South America … report[ing] on her travels and talk about people, places, food, fashion, grooming and many other items of interest to Canadian women. ("Kate Aitken" 1954)

The scale of one of her trips during 1954 is recorded on Aitken's Canadian Overseas Telecommunication Corporation "Cable Transmission Card." Her itinerary is listed as "UK-India-Pakistan-Burma-Ceylon-Malaya-Australia." The countries were linked by historical ties as part of the empire, where, as the card noted, possession of a "Press 'Cable Transmission Card'" would allow "the bearer to send telegrams to CFRB 37 Bloor West Toronto without charge 'via Imperial Cables' or 'via Imperial Wireless' of all classes—including 'Urgent Press'" (Canadian Overseas Telecommunication Corporation 06/30 1954). Aitken used the interconnection of the national and international, here materialized in postwar Commonwealth exchange of information, people, and communications, to create a visibility and legitimacy for women's domestic labor. The radical potential of this configuration was limited by a gendering of domesticity that, while it "stretched" (Zankowicz 2015: 12) across supposedly separate spheres of public and private, did not work toward reconfiguring the relations between them. It would be up to other women broadcasters at the CBC to experiment with these possibilities by bringing visions for peace and international politics more directly into the scope of women's programming.

"Housekeeping Plus": Mattie Rotenberg

One of these women Mattie Rotenberg, described as "a graduate of the University of Toronto [who] received her degree there while working on special research in Physics on a fellowship given by the National Research Council of Canada," began broadcasting on the CBC in January 1940 ("New CBC Talk Series Listed for Women" 1940). This introduction to Rotenberg's talks in the pages of the *CBC Times* noted that "since her marriage, [Rotenberg] has had a special interest in educational problems and is a director of the Hillcrest Progressive School [a Jewish day school], Toronto." The program called out to women to recognize their work in military terms during wartime: "While sons and fathers are at the fighting front, mothers and housewives are enlisted for service at home. The executive duties and responsibilities of the home front fighters will be discussed." The first talk in this series, "The Family Cook House," discussed "the special problems of feeding the family during war emergency." Subsequent talks were titled "The Home Troops' Kit," "The Family Billet," "The Junior Corps," "The Safety Patrol," and lastly "The Fun Parade." In April Rotenberg was to speak on "What's Home to You?" Now described as "an outstanding authority on domestic science" rather than a professional scientist, "Mrs Rotenberg is well fitted to discuss the various ways in which the clever woman transforms her house into a home" ("An Interesting Week for Women Listeners" 1940).

An overview of CBC talks for women running at the end of 1942 highlighted six separate series for women, including *Youth in Wartime*, featuring a series of child guidance experts dealing "with problems peculiar to youth in these war years" and which were "designed for the general listener as well as parents, teachers, and youth workers and will have special value to Women's Clubs or Home Listening Circles, for group listening and discussion" with transcripts being published and distributed at no cost by the National Committee on Mental Hygiene. Other programs included Ethelwyn Hobbes's weekly commentaries on *Wartime Shopping*, a dramatized series on *Nutrition as Part of Canada's All-Out War Effort* and two series on women and work: Elise Bercovitch interviewing "factory women, teachers, clerks, nurses, army, navy and air women, as well as housewives and part-time voluntary workers in community projects" and Mattie Rotenberg on *Women Workers Today* in which she presented the "latest information on women in industry in various countries in Europe" ("CBC Talks for Women" 1942). Thus, CBC's wartime broadcasts emphasized women's work outside the home, a focus that became more problematic during the postwar era when paid work became more prevalent for women but also was depicted in tension with women's domestic roles.

An article titled "Housekeeping Plus: Mrs Rotenberg's Multi-Sided Career" in January 1950 in the *CBC Times* highlighted the performance required to manage the multiple demands of work, career development, domestic chores, and family responsibility simultaneously. These multiple demands were often mentioned in the profiles of other CBC commentators, for example Joan Marshall, described as a "CBC commentator and Maritime homemaker," was the first speaker on "'Our Summer Holiday', a new radio series in which mothers of eighteen countries will tell how they and their families spend vacations" in 1947. This description gave her access to the national scale in her work as a "commentator," yet she was understood to be pinned to a regional identity in her domestic role as a "home-maker" ("Speaks Wednesday" 1947). The 1950 article describing Rotenberg's daily routine highlighted the multiplicity and fragmentation of this gendered subject most starkly. Rotenberg, while appearing as "a chic little grey-haired woman with warm brown eyes and a quick, bright smile," according to her family was "really several persons rolled into one":

> Every morning she's Mrs Meyer Rotenberg, wife of a Toronto barrister and mother of four lively sons and a daughter. She does her own cooking and housekeeping—her big sons get a kick out of watching their five-feet-one inch mother tackle a sink-full of dishes and wield a broom! ...
>
> With her house shining and her family fed and off to work or school, she hurries down to the University of Toronto early in the afternoon. There she dons a little white coat and becomes Dr Mattie Rotenberg, demonstrator in the physics department.
>
> She stays there all afternoon, explaining to students the mysteries of gravity and sound and other phenomena of the universe. Then she hurries home, puts the kettle on before taking her hat off, and when her family comes in from work and school she has a tempting meal ready for them.
>
> After the dishes, she's Mattie Rotenberg, writer, philanthropist, and club woman. She is a member of the national council of Hadassah [the Women's

Zionist Organisation], and writes articles on education and welfare for religious and community organizations and magazines.

In her "spare" time in the last ten years Mrs Rotenberg has been a radio commentator, and she has become familiar to listeners across Canada through her broadcast talks on social and economic subjects of particular interest to women. ("Housekeeping Plus: Mrs Rotenberg's Multi-Sided Career" 1950)

This profile of Rotenberg's depicts an impossible array of roles, which had to be juggled and swapped to allow for her occupation of the public sphere. Like other female media workers of the mid-twentieth century, Rotenberg's gendered labor included yet another form of work: the labor of self-representation of domesticity (Wang 2018: 67–69).

The topics covered in Rotenberg's broadcasts provide an index to the increasingly global scale that she introduced into talks about domestic activities and Canadian women during the war, eventually leaving them behind altogether in a focus on international political events. Rotenberg's personal files at the Canadian National Archives record her "Talks" career starting in November 1940, with "Forgotten Women: A Housewife in Crete" and ending on January 23, 1964, with "Disarmament Conference at Geneva" and January 28, 1964, "France and China" (Rotenberg 11/1940–1964). In early 1949 she gave a series of talks under the banner *World Housekeeping*, which framed social issues through a domestic frame, but also surpassed it, with individual talks including "Who to plan for," "Health for all," "How to budget," "Food for all," "Education for all," and "No more wars" (Rotenberg 1949). Other talks recorded during 1949 as part of a series entitled *Fighting Pioneers* about women social reformers were "distributed round the world in twenty-eight languages by UNESCO" ("'Mr Prime Minister' New Women's Series [*Our Country Women*]" 1950) and in the late 1940s and early 1950s she reported for the CBC from the UN Conferences at Lake Success, NY (Long 1950).

At exactly the same time as the portrayal of Rotenberg as working long hours outside the home, while still being responsible for feeding her family a "tempting meal," she focused almost entirely on discussion of world events after the end of the 1940s, covering topics such as the cold war, visits to Israel, women in science, UN Status of Women Commissions, "World Refugee Year," and "Daughters of the American Revolution vs the UN" in 1954. Additionally, her talks from the mid-1950s onwards were not flagged as talks specifically for women (after a 1954 series on *Modern Woman*).

Behind the scenes: Elizabeth Long

In the background of these programs and guiding their development was the formidable figure of Elizabeth Long. Long was the director of Women's Interests at the CBC for eighteen years from 1938 until 1956 (Freeman 2011: 10). The body of work produced under her directorship was incredibly diverse and was of such a volume that it is hard to draw out patterns from the content, but the programs described above give a sense of the innovative approaches that Long's directorship encouraged. Starting as assistant supervisor in charge of Women's Interests in August 1938, after she was hired by Donald Buchanan, CBC's supervisor of talks from 1936 to 1939, Long "was the first woman hired in an executive capacity" at the CBC "and from the outset held a relatively high degree of autonomy and authority" (Taylor 1985: 63–64). Within the Talks and Public Affairs Department, Long mentored a group of women broadcasters who were experts on national and international current affairs, such as the later chair of the Royal Commission on the Status of Women, Ann Francis ("Ottawa Woman to Talk in Daily Commentary" 1947; Campbell 2009: 53), which became known as "Bessie's Stable" (Bruce 1981–1982: 14).

As early as 1942, Long developed connections with community organizations to bolster listenership for CBC women's programming. As reported in June of that year, the Federation of Canadian Home and School Clubs (Ontario Board) had found in a survey of member's responses to CBC Women's Service programmes "that under the direction of Elizabeth Long the programmes were very popular, with just over forty percent of the members of Home and School Clubs ... tuned in to the afternoon programmes developed for women listeners, five days a week at 4.05 EDT, 5.30 ADT" ("Popular" 1942). Long also drew on her connections nationally and internationally, as a member of the International Council of Women (ICW), and in 1947 she was elected as convener of the Radio and Television Committee of the ICW (Long 1960), where she aimed "to create better international understanding through person to person broadcasts, with regular women's programmes including news and views of women of other countries" (Long quoted in Freeman 2011: 117). While not explicitly acknowledging that Long had gained this role, the *CBC Times* described her at the time as having a "firm belief that women can help build peace through international understanding" and quoted her as saying: "All women have something in common ... and I think that through women speaking to other women, by means of radio, we can show that boundary lines and oceans are no barrier to understanding" ("Personality of the Week in Radio—Elizabeth Long, CBC Women's Interests" 1947).

At the time of her formal retirement in 1953, while still an adviser to the CBC, she endorsed and helped bring to fruition the introduction of CBC radio's *Trans-Canada Matinee* (TCM), a program that would later take an overtly liberal-feminist approach in its coverage of Canada's Royal Commission on the Status of Women during 1968 (see, for example, Patterson and Reid 1968a, b; Casselman et al. 1968). In a 1976 program to mark "The First Forty" years of CBC as a broadcaster, Helen James, Long's successor as director of Women's Interests and initiator of TCM, described Long as recognizing "that life was circumscribed by being at home" and that "TCM [was] a first for both subject matter and language" for the ways it refused to "protect women" from debate and explored "strange types of programming" (Christie and MacDonald 1976).

Together with colleague Marjorie McEnaney—who according to her visa application for a visit to Soviet Union in 1955 as part of a Canadian Women's Press Club delegation held the position of "Organiser of Programs for the National Networks of the CBC in the Dept of Talks and Public Affairs" (McEnaney 1955)—James developed an approach to intimate life that was portrayed in the poem held in McEnaney's personal files that heads this chapter as "mental health on a national scale." In her application for the Russian visit, McEnaney described her "main interests [for the visit as] in observing welfare projects: car [*sic*] of old people, very young children and mental health services." McEnaney filmed this visit for CBC Television's *Newsmagazine* program, and while footage of welfare projects is conspicuous by its absence, the voice-over provided by McEnaney gives a positive commentary on life in the USSR, noting the holiday trips for workers to health spas provided by trade unions and the lack of obvious discrimination against women in the range of occupations open to them (CBC Online 1955). Shortly after Long's final departure from the CBC, in 1957, talks on women's health by obstetrician and gynaecologist Dr Marion Hilliard produced for TCM continued this project by canvassing topics such as the need for men to share housework, female sexuality, depression and anxiety, menopause, and menstruation (Hilliard 1959a, b, c, d). These talks were so popular, perhaps because they addressed topics not explored elsewhere, that they were repeated several times and published in the progressive women's magazine *Chatelaine* and as a book (Hilliard 1957; Korinek 1996: 115; Mendes 2010).

This project of national "mental health" was yet to make its claims through an explicitly politicized intimate voice, one that would fundamentally question the separation of private and public spheres and work to go beyond individual experience, but the challenge to established formats of women's programming developed during Long's reign over "her own little empire" of women's talks (McEnaney quoted in Cayley 1986: n.p.) indicated that this possibility was on the horizon.

Conclusion

The industrial situation of women at the CBC was later exposed as highly problematic and eventually led to an inquiry into employment for women in the Canadian media as part of the 1967 Royal Commission (Cox 1966; Freeman 2011: 119). As Crean wrote in 1987, looking back over the original programming produced by the CBC women's producers:

> It does seem clear that CBC radio functioned as an oasis of opportunity for women in an otherwise arid broadcasting environment. It is equally evident that this was not the result of any conscious corporate policy, but of the efforts of the women themselves, with a little help (or at least non-intervention) from their male colleagues. (Crean 1987: 98)

Described in the staff poem as one of the two "formidable teamsters," Long together with James sought to enlarge "women's window on the world" (Cayley 1986: n.p.). James, in an interview included in David Cayley's retrospective documentary for the CBC's fiftieth anniversary in 1986, describes in concrete detail who she was broadcasting for in these programs:

> The woman on the farm, the woman in the small town who saw her kids off to school and her husband off to work, and then what did she have? She had this radio program that she listened to for an hour every day, and that made me feel very, very responsible that we brought her some real meat. *I struck up a friendship with a woman from the Magdalen Islands, a British war bride, who said that she couldn't live without this program.* She was English-speaking woman, married a French-speaking fisherman from the Magdalen Islands, and went to live with her in-laws. *Had to speak French ... learned to speak French, and felt very isolated, of course, in that community. No libraries. But she listened to this program, and this was her link with the world,* and this, I'm sure, was true in many communities across Canada. This program brought the world in. (James quoted in Carley 1986: n.p., emphasis mine)

This vision consistent with a 1954 article that described the radio women of the CBC as the "Eyes, Ears and Legs" of the "lonely Housewife" depicts the vision embodied in "the nation-wide service rendered by the CBC's regional morning commentators." Authors of the article Helen James and Catherine McIver, writing as Long's deputies in the "Women's Interests Department," quoted from listener letters that gave testament to the role of radio in forging a connection with listeners:

> Sometimes it's a letter that starts like this:
>> Dear Jane Weston
>> Your broadcasts are always interesting and enjoyable, especially to those of us who live outside the city. I sometimes think I know more about what goes on in Toronto now than I did when I lived and worked there, but was not able to listen to interviews and talks such as yours …
>
> or this
>> Dear Miss Hinds
>> I live on a farm 50 miles from the nearest town, and often during the winter weeks go by without hearing another woman's voice, except for the radio. So you see how important your program is to me. Now I'm going to ask you a favour since I don't know anyone else in the city …
>
> or this
>> Dear Eileen Laurie
>> I always look forward to your morning visit. It's not only that I like hearing what you tell us; I like to think of all the other women listening at the same time. It's like belonging to a club …. (James and MacIver 1954)

James and MacIver reported:

> The thing that makes it all so fascinating [to work in women's talks department] is that, since their voices as well as their words go daily into thousands of homes, they form a personal bond with their audience … it's a two-way friendship in which the broadcaster is always learning more and more about the people she's serving.

This formation of a "personal bond" between audience and institution was fundamental to the intimate geographies developed by the CBC programming canvassed in this chapter. The overview of the groundbreaking work of the women given above indicates that the medium of radio provided way of networking homes through the figure of the personality broadcaster, as well as a set of metaphors for understanding the new transparency of domestic space in consumer culture. Speaking to the listener as "the best-dressed woman" as well as a "world housekeeper" gives an impression of endless possibilities, yet these possibilities were constrained for the very women who spoke about them at the time.

Rather than a clear division between public and private, it is apparent that the potential of radio as imagined by these women at the CBC in this atmosphere of benign neglect, and at times active discrimination, did pluralize public and private spheres and thus move beyond the public-private distinction as a "set of imageries and metaphors, more or less coherent, more or less prone to conscious manipulation, designed to organize … thinking according to recurrent, value-laden patterns" (Klare 1982: 1358–1359, quoted in Rossiter 2002: 54). As Rossiter has argued, moving beyond this distinction is dependent on recognizing the multiplicity of the private and the public, and how it is embedded in a range of "material spaces, metaphoric stories, institutional structures, juridical and political categories and discursive contexts," which are not coextensive with each other (2002: 55). This multiplicity was materially enacted and embodied by the forms of the public service broadcasting project. The daytime radio imaginaries described here constructed and intertwined the public and private in ways that signified a new kind of gendered space, yet promised that it would not be contained by any single formation of institution and audience. As the case of the CBC women's programs and their unique recognition of a female audience shows, daytime programming before the second wave could be relational, diverse, and complex in its address to women, a potential that I explore in the next chapter as emerging more fully at the BBC in the postwar era.

Listening to the Listener: Constructing
Woman's Hour at the BBC, 1946–1955

Here, with my hand on the latch, I am two persons.
I am the woman with the basket, the passer-by in the street,
Unnoticed, anonymous, an infinitesimal part
Of a great multitude that, with purposeful feet
Plodding the pavements, streams on perpetually
Into the abyss of time past.
One person: I have only to push the gate open,
And, in a step, I shall be wholly that other;
For here, where so small a plot contains a world,
I have a face, a name; I am wife and mother,
Blessedly beloved. The stored years wait in the house,
And as I cross the threshold, their warm sweet breath
Will welcome me again into that happy bondage
Intangible as the hearth smoke, and stronger than death.
With familiar incompetent click the gate half-closes behind me,
I have all things, I am myself, I have come home.
Mrs Vera M. Prince, The Oast, Spot Lane, Bearsted, Near Maidstone, Kent (Prince,
"The Gate," Poem written to BBC *Woman's Hour*, 07/27 1956)

An article in the British national tabloid *Daily Mirror* in January 1944 noted that
the BBC's "Irish-born, Oxford graduate" talks assistant Miss Janet Quigley was
to receive an M.B.E. Quigley had been nominated for her work at the BBC since
1936 within a "special department [to] find out what talks appealed to women
listeners" ("Ordinary Men and Women (910 of You) Honoured: Talks Expert"
(1944)). Quigley's central role in wartime broadcasting represents a decisive shift
in the BBC's ongoing interest in gendered programming. From its first days the
BBC explicitly included programs addressing a gendered audience, with a "Men's
Hour" and a "Women's Hour" from London on 2LO during 1923, as outlined
in Chapter 2. In contrast to the other broadcasters documented in this book,

this kind of programming continues today on the BBC, with *Woman's Hour* on BBC Radio 4. And from 2010 to 2015, Radio 5 Live, the BBC network's rolling news and sports service, ran a "Men's Hour"—described as "the men's magazine for the modern man" (BBC 2015). This chapter explores the consolidation and institutionalization of gendered programming on the BBC through the work of Quigley and others on *Woman's Hour* during the first decade of its existence. This chapter also aims to map these new connections as imbricated with new kinds of relationships between the home and the state, and the role of public service broadcasting as a mediator of these relations.

Quigley's career parallels the BBC's intricate role within British postwar society as independent from government influence yet closely connected to the ideological project of the welfare state. She joined its Foreign Department in 1930 on the recommendation of her university friend Isa Benzie, who was later to become foreign director from 1933 to 1938 (Murphy 2016: 158, 178). The "special department" mentioned in the *Daily Mirror* report was the Talks Department, which Quigley joined in August 1936. While it was not, as the paper reported, solely tasked with finding out "what talks appealed to women listeners," daytime talks for women were certainly central. As part of Talks, Quigley was also a driving force behind several programs aimed at both a male and a general audience. During the late 1930s, she worked on several "high-profile evening programs including *Men Talking* and … *Towards National Health*" (Murphy 2014: 213). The Talks Department did specifically target a female audience during this period, with gendered programming including *Five O'Clock, Tea Time Talks, This Week in Westminster, Other Women's Lives, Sickness in the House*, and a series entitled *Housewives and Careers for Girls*, all worked on by Quigley and broadcast on the BBC's National Service (Murphy 2014: 216).

The BBC's prewar women's programming, a foreshadowing of its wartime efflorescence, is exemplified by an item in the "Radionews" column of the *Gloucester Journal* during March 1939, which advertised (presumably drawing closely on BBC publicity material) that

> Janet Quigley, of the BBC Talks Department, has prepared some interesting new daytime talks, including series on cookery, to be broadcast in the April to June quarter. Entitled "Foreign Fare" these talks will be given each Tuesday and will deal with everyday dishes from various countries, such America, France, Germany and Spain. The speakers will either be natives of those countries or people with first-hand experience in the preparation and consumption of the recipes they describe. (Wellington 1939)

After the outbreak of war, these cosmopolitan nuances would be replaced by more patriotic subject matter. During the early 1940s, Quigley worked on wartime women's programming for the Home Service, including *The Kitchen Front* ("a talk about what to eat and where to get it"), *Calling All Women* ("a five-minute talk on matters of urgent concern to women behind the fighting line"), *Your Health in Wartime* ("topical notes on wartime health, mainly by doctors"), and *Talking It Over* (weekly afternoon talks on topics related to living during wartime) (see Murphy 2014: 216–217; taglines from various listings in *Radio Times* 1939–1942). This body of work represented the female-targeted element of what Nicholas has called the "home front propaganda" of the wartime BBC (Nicholas 1996). Like the BBC's early experiments during the 1920s with informational talks for women, these programs were the direct antecedents of the postwar *Woman's Hour*. *Woman's Hour* was a spoken-word fixture of the popular music-heavy BBC Light Programme from 1946 until 1967 (when the Light Programme was rebranded as Radio 2) and a flagship program on the more highbrow BBC Radio 4 since 1973 (Leman 1996; Rewinkel 2013). While the programs Quigley worked on were originally envisioned as primarily educational, and marked by a highly didactic form of address, the way that they were reformulated over time by their producers, presenters, editorial, and technical staff drew on and promoted new ways of talking about social issues within the frame of personal experience. Taken as whole, this programming went well beyond the original model of "service talks" for women.

This "shifting register of broadcasting strategies" (Cardiff 1980: 29) toward a more informal address to audiences within radio was broadly institutionalized within the BBC in the 1970s. Whether BBC executives were aware of it or not, this register had been long-established in women's programming. It was only when it was manifest as an editorial directive in general programming that it emerged as a conspicuous style of public intimacy. Hendy describes a "therapeutic sensibility" permeating the BBC at this time, a tone of address and structure of feeling that was most prominent (and contested) in the first decade of BBC Radio 4 (Hendy 2007: 227). In the vision of Tony Whitby, Radio 4 controller during the early 1970s, the station was to become a place to make "programmes about people's human situation and emotions as opposed to their political and purely social problems" (Whitby quoted in Hendy 2007: 227).[1] Hendy argues that once this vision was made into policy with the appointment of Whitby in 1974,

What remained to be worked out [by the staff of the broadcaster] was how on earth therapy could be offered in public without the airwaves being filled with a torrent of dark secrets, self-indulgence and exhibitionism—characteristics that seemed not just uncomfortable to witness, but somewhat ill-becoming for a public service broadcaster. They were the kinds of questions that would only be resolved by more than a decade of experimentation and dispute. (Hendy 2007: 227)

According to Hendy, this shift from the BBC's long-defended role of heroically uplifting the masses—associated with its first director general, John Reith— to listening more closely to the intimate lives of the British public provoked widespread alarm among Radio 4 staff. This deliberate shift to representing everyday experience in the public sphere was foretold by its opponents as a descent into a mirrored hall of mediated narcissism, in which the audience potentially was to be given free range for emotional outbursts and traumatic repetition. I argue that this apprehension needs to be understood as having a history, as it rests on a separation of spheres that attempts to keep politics and emotion apart in a gendered binary. The model of *Woman's Hour* during the late 1940s and early 1950s, and the proto-feminist politics it embodied during its first decade, demonstrates that there were already existing modes of public discourse that spoke directly of human experience in ways that were neither "self-indulgent" nor "exhibitionistic," but rather signaled new and salient connections between private experience and public issues.

Woman's Hour's collective project during the late 1940s and 1950s to give voice to intimate lives was not a radically new one, as it was drawing on minor modes of expression already circulating for some time in popular media such as women's magazines (Duffy 2013; Forster 2015; Johnson and Lloyd 2004; Leman 1980). These media forms had not thus far been destructive of rational discourse but had drawn different trajectories between gendered subjectivities and the public sphere than the "cultural uplift" model promulgated by public service broadcasting. Indeed, these minor modes have been argued to create imagined communities that challenge racialized and gendered forms of oppression (Landes 1984: 29; Lake 1990; Weir 2013). These intimate modes of disclosure have been able to articulate issues that were marginalized in contemporary mainstream cultural production, for example in nineteenth-century African-American women's magazines, which sought to construct black women as a group through explicit tabling of emotion for political purposes (Rooks 2004). The kind of role envisaged by Whitby for Radio 4 in the early 1970s, in which a monopoly public service broadcaster would forge a public discourse based on the everyday experience of ordinary people, had already been practiced by the *Woman's Hour* for nearly a quarter of a century and in other gendered forms of public address for much longer.

This chapter traces how these explicitly gendered programs became the space that this particular mode of engagement with the listener would emerge at the BBC. The first section of the chapter gives an account of the initial experiments with gendered broadcasting undertaken at the BBC between the two world wars. The chapter then focuses on the work of Quigley and other radio producers as they negotiated the boundaries of what was considered acceptable for broadcast and to what extent the program should challenge existing norms of public discourse. Finally, the chapter gives an account of some key moments in this transformation, which help understand what was at stake in these new ways of hearing and speaking in public that *Woman's Hour* exemplified. Hendy notes that *Woman's Hour*, on its transfer to Radio 4 in 1967, had "established a reputation for breaking many broadcasting taboos": "It operated, so to speak, under cover of daytime, when few senior BBC managers bothered to listen" (Hendy 2007: 332). Hiding in plain sight (or earshot), female BBC producers such as Quigley, as well as others such as Olive Shapley (Shapley and Hart 1996), helped shape a role for radio as a means to address personal and interpersonal concerns within a public medium. The aftereffects, as well as the promises, of these intimate geographies are still with us today.

Women's Hour and after

As noted in Chapter 2, the BBC inaugurated its *Women's Hour* in its first days of broadcasting, with a member of the British royal family, HRH Princess Alice, Duchess of Athlon, giving an afternoon talk on the "Adoption of Babies" on May 2, 1923, followed by another lady peer, fashion designer Lucile, introduced by the BBC by her more stately title Lady Duff-Gordon, speaking on "Fashions." Regional stations (at that time broadcasting in Birmingham, Manchester, Newcastle-upon-Tyne, Cardiff, and Glasgow) also ran their own "Women's Hours," although like the London version, their programs lasted "for half this period":

> The composition of [the regional programmes] varied slightly, but in the main it consisted of music and talk, the music in the Provinces generally consisting of piano solos by the Station accompanist and occasionally as singer; but in London there would more frequently be a minor concert artist, either instrumental

or a singer. The talks material was syndicated to the various Stations from [Head Office], the manuscripts being typed in London and sent round to the provinces. In London, the practice would often be to put the name of the talk in the *Radio Times*, but in the provinces more generally the talk was selected at the last moment and was usually read by the chief "aunt" or some other woman. ("Women's and Household Talks," n.d.: 1)

This pattern is evident in the first issue of the *Radio Times*, which advertised the London version of *Women's Hour* as the first evening radio program at 5 p.m. (following a four-and-a-half-hour break in transmission after the broadcast of a "Morning Concert" from 11.30 a.m. to 12.30 p.m.). On Monday October 1, 1923, the first day that listings were printed and included in the inaugural edition of the *Radio Times*, 2LO featured "Ariel's Society Gossip" and "Mrs C.S. Peel's Kitchen Conversation," followed by "Children's Stories: *Little Black Sambo*" at 5.30 p.m. The regional stations' pattern of programming for women followed immediately by children's broadcasts was broadly similar with the BBC's Birmingham station advertising "Ladies' Corner" at 5.30 until 6 p.m., followed by "Kiddies' Corner"; Manchester with "Mainly Feminine" at 5, also followed by "Kiddies' Corner," with a "Farmer's Weather Report" in between; Cardiff with the "Women's Hour" and "Children's Stories"; Glasgow with "A Talk to Women" and "The Children's Corner"; and finally Newcastle hosting the rather technical-sounding "Women's Transmission" at 4.45 p.m., followed, inevitably, by the "Children's Transmission."

This construction of women's interests, and its close connection with supervision of children's listening, was not taken as given by its audience, however, even in this early incarnation of the BBC. From the beginning of her role as Central Organizer of *Women's Hour* (Murphy 2016: 195), Fitzgerald was charged with putting together "Women's National Advisory Committee ... who could make useful suggestions with regard to speakers, subjects, timing of programmes" and they met for the first time in January 1924 ("Women's and Household Talks," n.d.: 1). This group quickly contested the limited agenda of such programming and sought listener feedback on what should be the program's content, as well as its timing: "Following a suggestion [from Fitzgerald, see Murphy 2016: 197] made at the first meeting, a debate was staged by two of the members and broadcast early in February on the subject of the *Women's Hour*, listeners being invited to send in their opinions as to the most suitable matter and timing for this period":

As a result it was found that 75% of listeners wanted talks on general topics, and the remaining 25% wanted talks concerning the home, but not cookery hints or housekeeping wrinkles. The time most favoured was 3.30 to 4.30pm, instead of the 5pm which had obtained hitherto. The *Hour* was therefore modified on these lines.

By February 1924, the Advisory Committee had gone further to recommend that the program name, *Women's Hour*, itself should be dropped, "although the talks given should deal mainly with topics which would particularly interest women." On March 24 the title was indeed dropped, "and the two talks usual to this period were incorporated into the afternoon concert, from 4 to 4.30pm."

Further changes came in 1930s, aimed at centralizing control over content, when in the summer of 1930 morning talks for women from 5XX (the medium-wave program broadcast nationally) and 2LO from London were relayed to regional stations. In early 1932 a brief "experiment was tried of giving some of the morning talks at 1.45pm, which was thought to be more convenient to many people than the earlier morning ones, but it only lasted for a few months." This change in timing was conveyed to the BBC audience via the *Radio Times* in January 1932 ("Hints from Other Cooks" 1932) and perhaps reflects what Hilmes has identified as a decline in the importance of BBC women's programming within talks after the departure of former MI5 operative and the BBC's first director of talks (Hunter 2012), Hilda Matheson, in late 1931 (Hilmes 2006: 9). The BBC certainly was moving away from Matheson's vision of all its listeners as "citizens of the world" (Cardiff 1980: 31) and devised the timing of this new programming to fit with what the producers imagined to be the flow of domestic life: "The time [of] 10.45am [for women's talks] was [eventually] chosen with the idea in mind that many women would turn on their sets for the weather forecast and morning service and leave them running while they were busy about the house" ("Women's and Household Talks," n.d.: 2). The example of programming content given here seemed to further enmesh women in the routines of housework, concluding, with a somewhat circular logic, that women at home listening to the BBC "would therefore be edified by a discussion on, e.g. paint-washing."

The question of the BBC's vision for women's programming was revisited in April 1936, when an "all-day" Women's Conference was held. An agenda for the meeting records that groups invited included a range of post-suffrage middle-class and working-class women's organizations:

The National Federation of Women's Institutes, the National Union of Guilds for Citizenship, the British Legion (Women's Section), the Women's Freedom League, the National Citizens' Association, the Open Door Council, the Women's Gas Council, the National Adult School Union, the Electrical Association for

Women, The Association of Maternity and Child Welfare Centres, the T[rade] U[nion] C[ouncil] Women's Committee. (BBC 03/26 1936: 1)

The organizations considered the BBC's role in reaching a gendered audience as very important, with some of the organizations "sending at least four delegates … [and] a strong contingent is coming from the North of England." "Representative women journalists and others not specifically attached to any organization" were also invited. The items for discussion on the day revisited, yet again, the question of "the timing of talks" and specifically whether 10.45 a.m. was a convenient time for "housewives who do their own work" or whether the unnamed "critics" of this timing had in mind an "alternative hour *in the morning*" (emphasis in the original). The committee was also asked whether "talks for women [would] be appreciated between 4.00 and 5.00 pm?" and if so,

> should they follow the lines of the present morning programmes, that is, include practical talks on cookery and welfare, etc., as well as matters of general interest?
> Is the audience for afternoon talks likely to be drawn from the same public as those for the morning talks?

In the absence of a Listener Research Department at the BBC, which was not established until October 1936, the committee sought to find out the preferences of women listeners in an indirect way by gathering together these women's organizations and other public figures such as journalists. Apart from fine-tuning the timing of talks, the meeting was to discuss questions of content such as "Do listeners like regular talks on current affairs?" and ways of increasing audience share and engagement such as "Can the Organizations suggest any special methods for encouraging their own Members to make more use of broadcast talks? For instance, by circulating advance information to their own Members, or by arranging regular meetings to discuss talks recently heard?" (BBC 03/26 1936: 2). This engagement with the audience was to be a hallmark of women's programming at the BBC, and while the suggestions from committees such as this one were not always enacted, the intent, begun by Fitzgerald, to involve the audience as much as possible was to develop in new and interesting ways in the following decades.

A question of genre

As in both the Australian and Canadian cases, profound social changes following the Second World War created new institutional and discursive possibilities for women's self-representation in the public sphere. During the war, radio had been entrenched in its new role as a modernizing force in the home, and women had been directly addressed as workers in the war effort, whether in industry, active service, or domestic work and care. Following on from this new visibility of women, and in some part as an attempt to manage the reconfiguration of gender roles at the end of the war, gendered programming on the BBC was revisited in the immediate postwar period. Quigley's own career trajectory mirrors this shift. Leaving the BBC in October 1945 when she married Irish author and broadcaster Kevin Fitzgerald, she returned to the broadcaster as editor of *Woman's Hour* in June 1950, taking over from Evelyn Gibbs, who was retiring ("*Woman's Hour* Editor: Miss Janet Quigley Returns to BBC" 1950).

The arrival of Norman Collins as controller of the Light Programme in November 1945 prompted discussions between Collins and the BBC's postwar director-general, William Haley, about a *Woman's Hour*-type program. The idea of a women's magazine radio program had been suggested immediately after the war in late 1945 by BBC staff with experience of a similar program in commercial radio (Skoog 2014: 103), possibly Radio Luxembourg (Mattelart 1986: 64).[2] In March 1946 a listener from Rochdale, near Manchester, wrote to the BBC's "Listener Research Director" about her ideas for such a program. She included with her letter a printed page of readers' responses to a call from "a little monthly paper called *Housewife*," which had asked its readers to write in with designs for their own radio programs (Schofield 1946: 1). The listener felt that she spoke on behalf of "a great many middle-class educated women, who have perforce to spend much time in their homes doing their own chores, and who feel that their brains are in danger of becoming thoroughly mouldy":

> It is [for] women such as us that I appeal for a *Woman's Hour*, on the radio, at a time—preferably between 2 & 3 each afternoon—when we can relax & listen to something really interesting. The various letters in the enclosed will give you some very good expectations for items of interest. You did start a woman's magazine at 4.30 but I see that this has fizzled out[3]—I don't think it was a very good time.
>
> Now *The World and His Wife*[4] is broadcast and is very interesting, but what a hopeless time, 6.30[pm]. Most women to whom it would appeal are either washing up after a meal or preparing one, or putting the children to bed.
>
> In view of the fact that the BBC pays large sums to dance bands & crooners, I think they might engage a woman with the right personality to run a *Woman's Hour* on the lines I have suggested. I am sure the right type of person would

make a big success of it & would be appreciated by a very deserving part of the community who have not had much consideration of late. I hope you will be able to do something about this. (Schofield 1946: 2)

Collins's program proposal to Hayley described a format that drew on the new genre that so engaged this listener, the magazine program. Although he did not name it as such, his suggestions to Hayley clearly envision the program as a daily "magazine," with mix of more or less serious and entertaining items, hosted by a regular presenter ("Points for Discussion with D.G. 15th March" 1946).

The question of timing of such a program, as it had in the 1920s and 1930s, created much interest in the gendered organization of domestic time. A Listener Research Department report in April 1946 gave the results of a survey of over 600 "local correspondents," which found that for "housewives ... with babies" 2–3 p.m. and 7–8 p.m. were the most popular times (both 16 percent) (Listener Research Department 04/1946: 1). For all other groups ("with children preschool age," "7–12 years," "12–16 years," and "without children"), "11am-2pm and 4-7pm were relatively unsuitable" and that "housewives without children are alone in finding 8-9am reasonably acceptable and their best time appears to be 9-10am." The report found that "on the whole, the housewife's day has some degree of flexibility, that her time-table can be adjusted within moderate limits and that a quarter of an hour's difference during the mid-morning or mid-afternoon periods is neither here nor there." When asked about preferred days of the week for the program, the report found that for "every group, Tuesday wins ... while Friday is generally and decisively rejected as a suitable day for housewives" (Listener Research Department 04/1946: 2).

Envisaged as running daily from 4 to 5 p.m. and beginning on the first day of June 1946, Collins thought that the hour-long program should be structured around a daily serial, *The Robinson Family*. Described in the *Radio Times* as the "day-to-day history of an ordinary family," *The Robinson Family* had been embedded in the afternoon schedule of the Light Programme since its first broadcasts and was merely the latest incarnation of a very popular serial that had been running since 1937 as *The English Family Robinson* on the National Programme, and during the war was recast as *Front Line Family* on the North American and Overseas Services (Hilmes 2006: 14–16; "The Robinson Family," 1945). While this plan to include the serial within *Woman's Hour* did not eventuate, Collins's assumption of a natural affinity between *The Robinson Family* and an afternoon women's program is telling, given the work that Hilmes has done to uncover the "contentious negotiations around notions of national cultural production, class, gender and broadcast practices" that surrounded this serial's various incarnations (2006: 24). As Hilmes outlines, the serial was closely linked to growing anxieties of the Americanization and feminization of the BBC, and as such the introduction of the serial threatened the perceived status of the BBC as a Reithian bulwark against popular culture.

The remaining three-quarters of an hour of the new program was imagined by Collins as ballast for such populist fare, anchored by two five-minute daily talks, each on the half- and final quarter-hour. Potential sources for these talks included "Radio Doctor, Psychologist … Padre or school teacher speaking to parents, Houghton-equivalent [a reference to Douglas Houghton, host of *Can I Help You?*, a wartime evening BBC program responding to listeners' problems] and Godfrey Winn [relationship advice columnist for British tabloid papers such as the *Daily Mirror* and the *Sunday Express* and regular wartime women's programme commentator] (all at 4.30); and talks on clothes, cooking, household management, beauty culture, gardening (all at 4.45)." The proposal underscored the need for direct engagement with the potential audience's concerns in "*daily 3–5 minutes of letters probably at 4.15*" (emphasis in the original) and the "remainder of period to be filled with overflow [musical] requests from 9.10–10 am 'Housewives' Choice'." The proposal also proposed a direct link between its representatives of its audience and program staff, without the earlier mediating influence of women's organizations, recommending a "Housewives' Committee of say six persons, drawn from the public."

The list of items covered by the proposal sets the structure for a new kind of program, one that was very different from the topic-based talks that the BBC had earlier focused on and much closer to the example of the ABC *Women's Sessions*. As mid-twentieth-century cultural forms, print magazines, popular films, and radio programs aimed at women, rather than simply "giving voice" to the housewife—as Johnson and I have argued elsewhere—both constructed the figure of the woman listener-at-home and allowed for challenges to and contestations of this figure (Johnson and Lloyd 2004). Despite the sexist stereotypes and gendered assumptions of invisible and unpaid domestic labor baked into the women's programming format, Skoog's recent work on *Woman's Hour*'s relationship to the wider women's movement of the 1940s and 1950s has shown that both "broadcasters and the female audience [were able] to shape broadcasting content and practices" and that the staff of *Woman's Hour* "without a doubt created a programme that ought to be seen as an early example of feminist media" (Skoog 2010: 137, 2017). In this aspect, the program as envisaged by Collins, and actualized by production staff including the program's first organiser, Nest Bradney, drew on models from commercial radio as well as the success of BBC wartime women's programming (Skoog 2010: 130–131, 2014: 102–103).

The program, like its wartime BBC precursors *The Kitchen Front* and *Woman's Page*, pioneered the magazine format (Forster 2015: 209–211; Hendy 2007: 80–83; Nicholas 1996: 70–107; Skoog 2010: 182). Such a format was well suited to the intense production cycle of an hour-long program that had to be filled with new content every weekday. The format allowed staff time to be used as effectively as possible because individual producers would work on separate items to their own timelines. As these items were completed, the regular presenter would combine all these disparate elements into a smooth sequence at the same time every day. Because the magazine format allowed for such routinized novelty, it would become dominant in the talk-heavy "block"-driven public service broadcasting radio schedules during the 1970s, in contrast to the music-based "flow" formats of commercial FM radio emerging at the time. In the early Radio 4 examples examined in detail by Hendy (*You and Yours, Woman's Hour,* and the long-format current affairs model represented by programs such as *PM*),

> the overall "shape" of each programme would be familiar enough to regular listeners, but the content ever-changing, each "item" a self-contained three or four minutes that could be placed in almost any part of the running order, or dropped altogether if a better story came along close to transmission. Magazines allowed more to be covered in less time, and could be produced in something approaching an "assembly-line" style, where well-oiled routines ensured no programme had to be built entirely from scratch every day. (Hendy 2007: 80)

Apart from being a format that could discipline unpredictable factual content for tightly regulated radio broadcast schedule, and thereby choreograph an audience by inviting them to integrate such programs into their daily activities, the magazine format has long been associated with an openness to nonprofessional broadcasters. Early versions of women's radio programming in the United States in the 1920s were built on print-based "true confession" tabloid magazine properties, which in turn had deliberately mined the personal lives of their readers for the most sensational content, resulting in a unique genre that connected individual experiences with social critique (Hilmes 1997: 99–102). Thus, this complex of print and broadcast media institutions, production staff, and audience actively sought out gendered experiences that had not previously been able to be heard and represented and circulated them within public discourse. The next section of this chapter looks at the struggles at the BBC around the creation of such media.

Defining *Woman's Hour*

Woman's Hour went on the air at 2 p.m. on Monday October 7, 1946, replacing a regular "Songtime" slot of "your favourite singers on gramophone records" ("*Woman's Hour*: 7 October" 1946). Advertised in the *Radio Times* as a "daily programme of music, advice, and entertainment for the home," the first edition featured Alan Ivimey introducing "Mary Manton on 'Mother's Midday Meal' and Kay Beattie on 'Putting Your Best Face Forward." Rather than starting with *The Robinson Family* as suggested by Collins,[5] the program finished with a daily reading of a serial story, in this case "Stanley Weyman's 'Under the Red Robe." The program included a repeat of the morning's "*Housewives' Choice* of gramophone records" from the same station. Even with the repeat of *Housewives' Choice*, the first *Woman's Hour* was an island of speech in the Light Programme's music-based afternoon lineup, lapped at its shores by popular classics. On its first day, it could be heard at 2 p.m. following the daily *Bandstand* program—performed by the "Central Band of the Royal Air [*sic*]" at 1.30 p.m.— then followed at 3 p.m. by Spike Hughes presenting highlights from "'Rigoletto', Verdi's famous opera." Another factual magazine-type program would not be heard on the station until the next morning when a *Current Affairs* program came on the air at 10.45 for fifteen minutes, before the station's staple music programming again took over.

For this "*Woman's Hour* Inaugural Program" the producers designed a "listener panel" that would be recorded and broadcast the next day, and on October 2, Collins requested approval from BBC management "for a luncheon party for six people" for this group (Collins 10/02 1946). The invited guests included Margaret Bondfield, feminist, trade unionist, and the Labour Party's Minister for Labour in the second MacDonald ministry from 1929 to 1931, Deborah Kerr, British film and stage actress, and also a woman Collins only described in his request for a catering budget as "a North Country housewife." Also present at the lunch would be the "home team, Mr Rendall [Controller, Talks], Mr Holland-Bennett [BBC producer and interviewer of the panel] and myself [Collins]." The second edition of *Woman's Hour* on Tuesday October 8 did indeed include a recording of this panel giving their reactions to the first program, and Collins's "North Country housewife" was revealed as "Mrs Elsie May Crump, butcher's wife of Chorlton cum-Hardy" ("*Woman's Hour*: 8 October" 1946). This inclusion of and address to an archetypal "ordinary" female listener within the program—here in the person of Crump—was a hallmark of the program from its earliest beginnings.

Yet this distinction between experts and ordinary people was contested by the mainly female producers and BBC management (represented in the figure of Collins). Peggy Barker, talks producer, reported in early October:

> I have had a word with AA [admin. assistant] (Talks) and he is quite agreeable to our choosing *Woman's Hour* experts on whom we can draw for information. I think the best thing is to pay them a sum down (say 10 guineas) for the privilege of calling them experts and of calling upon them at any odd time. They will of course broadcast talks from time to time, for which they will be paid the usual fee.

The speakers that Barker had in mind were drawn from the world of women's publishing and consumer advice:

> Helen Burke ... Household subjects (well-known broadcaster and writer on these subjects); Jeanne Heal ... Furnishing; colour; making do generally with what equipment one has; Jean Cleland ... beauty (beauty editress of *Woman's Journal* and *Evening Standard*); Sophie Somers ... washing (head of Port Sunlight Washability Bureau); Guilfoyle Williams ... fabrics (care of, etc.) (John Lewis' Laboratory).

However, a handwritten note from Norman Collins at bottom of this memo indicates that while he agreed with this list, he felt that an emphasis on traditional "service talks" was still needed: "[shouldn't] Ruth Drew [author of a 1964 collection of her BBC talks entitled *The Happy Housewife*] have [been] added? I understand that she has already been roped in for this kind of job" (Barker 10/02 1946). Shortly after this exchange, Collins wrote to program organizer Nest Bradney, decrying the representation of speakers as "experts" on such subjects: "Would you, by the way, please be especially careful to see that the fatal word 'expert' does not creep back into *Woman's Hour* in contexts where such a thing as an expert cannot possibly exist" (BBC WAC quoted in BBC Four 2015).

Collins also sought to shape interactions between the BBC as public service broadcaster and *Woman's Hour*'s potential audience, as, according to a memo sent to BBC staff in August 1946, he was keen to keep the program clearly defined as a medium for proper, rational discussion of social problems, rather than a site of melodramatic confessions:

As I have previously warned, Light Programme will be starting a daily Monday to Friday inclusive feature entitled *WOMAN'S HOUR* in the second week of October. There will be two talks on matters of general women's interest, e.g. household management and care of children, each day and additionally there will be a period of approximately 5 minutes daily in which listeners' letters dealing with general points of women's interest will be answered. It will be made abundantly clear on the air that the BBC is not an Advice Bureau and therefore cannot undertake to answer either at the microphone or through the post all the letters which are sent in; in particular it will be emphasised that purely personal points (e.g. "my husband left me" will not be answered at all). (Collins 08/28 1946)

With climbing audience figures in its first few weeks of broadcasting, Collins wrote the *Radio Times* editor on October 28 asking for a greater profile for the program in the publication:

Despite what one of the Radio critics had to say about us we have scored a very big success indeed and have converted a listening figure of round about 4 between 2 and 3pm to a listening figure of round about 13. I am very anxious indeed that we should continue to keep this running in a really big way and any help that you could give would be enormously appreciated. Knowing all the difficulties about the position in which *Woman's Hour* might come on the page, may I still ask if you could bring the maximum possible collective ingenuity to bear on and see if we could show *Woman's Hour* in the Light Programme page as a daily *box*? (Collins 10/28 1946, emphasis in the original)

The figure of 13 represents 13 percent of the "available audience," a category derived by BBC Listener Research from the "estimated percentage of the adult civilian population of Great Britain ... estimated to be approximately 35m" (BBC Listener Research Department 1946).[6] Approximately three and half million more listeners were tuning in to the BBC's Light Programme each day to hear *Woman's Hour*, or one in ten of all adults, including men and women, regardless of whether they were working in paid or unpaid work and were at home to listen to the program. As Collins wrote a few days later to the BBC's director general, asking for more resources for the program, the LRD reports showed "moreover ... an average Appreciation Index of 55 which is the average appreciation figure for [all] magazine talks programmes in Light Programmes" (Collins 10/30 1946: 1). Collins stressed the need for full-time editor, as well as more staff to work with him so as to maintain a "Light Programme" approach while concentrating on Talks. Collins also envisaged that *Woman's Hour* should not be restricted to speakers in studio, but make use of the possibilities of outside broadcasting, which would require further skilled staff and technical resources. *Woman's Hour* soon acquired a full-time editor, Nest Bradney, which became an ongoing position, as Bradney was succeeded in the summer of 1947 by Eileen Molony. Molony in turn was replaced in 1948 by Evelyn Gibbs, who handed over to Janet Quigley in 1950 (Briggs 1979: 52). A weekly contribution from the "BBC Mobile Units" to *Woman's Hour* appeared within two months of the program being on air ("*Woman's Hour*: 6 December" 1946).

Collins's direction on topics for the program, and his attitude toward current affairs in particular, echoes similar struggles for editorial autonomy at the ABC discussed in the previous chapter (see also Skoog 2014 for detailed discussion of Benzie and Molony's responses to and critiques of the problematic management of *Woman's Hour* during this period). While Collins's vision for *Woman's Hour* was clearly paternalistic and he was to clash with several producers over material he thought was not "feminine" enough, he believed in *Woman's Hour*'s unique role as a flagship for the "Light Programme," and he took the overwhelmingly positive initial response from its audience as sign of its potential:

> I do not want the words "Light Programme" approach to be misconstrued. I am not (pace certain of the critics) asking that LP should be exclusively frivolous. On the contrary where I have intervened it has been precisely because important topics of the day have in the absence of a resident editor, been in danger of being ignored. On the other hand, *Woman's Hour* must cater for all tastes and the Editor must be as aware of the interest aroused by the Mountbatten wedding in Romsey Abbey as by Basil Henriques' [Children's Court Magistrate and child welfare advocate] remarks on Juvenile Delinquency.
>
> *We should at the outset recognise the magnitude of the task. At the moment more than a thousand letters a week are coming into* Woman's Hour. *These require analysis and in some cases action—though I have said that I do not feel that formal reply is necessary in the majority of cases.* (Collins 10/30 1946: 2, emphasis mine)

A few weeks later, *Woman's Hour* producer Leslie Perowne wrote to Collins that the first four weeks of his role had "inevitably been a period of much trial and considerable error, but my views on the programme have now crystallised and I offer them to you for what they are worth" (Perowne 11/11 1946). He reminded Collins that his first impression of the program as its producer "a month ago, was that it was *dull*, at least *as a programme*. Individually, it had interesting and absorbing items, but as an hour's entertaining listening it simply didn't ring even a muffled bell" (emphasis in the original). While he acknowledged that his and

Collins's "ideas of a *Woman's Hour* … [we]re fundamentally opposed," in that Collins wanted *Woman's Hour* "to instruct rather than to entertain in a broader sense," he hoped he had "carried out [Collins'] wishes so far as regards [his] broad policy."

While Perowne's approach "so far been to tighten up the presentation of the material handed to me on a plate by Talks Department, and to a lesser extent, Recorded Programmes" and he had given the presenter, Alan Ivimey, "a certain amount of encouragement to lighten his approach (albeit with occasional dire results)" he felt that given "the present framework and with the present material … we cannot go much further." Rather than changing the presenter or the material, Perowne's suggested solution, however, was to change the program's name:

> The title *Woman's Hour* surely leads the listener to expect an hour's entertainment for all types of women from duchesses to charladies. From the most sophisticated subjects to "woodworm in the kitchen chairs." I suggest that a more honest title for our present series would be, *HOUSEWIVES' HOUR*, an hour's information and instruction for The Woman in the Home. Is it too late to alter the name of the programme? (Perowne 11/11 1946, emphasis in the original)

Whether as a result of such comments on his presentation style or not, Ivimey only lasted three months, and a new female presenter, Joan Griffiths, made her appearance on New Year's Day 1947, in an edition that continued what Perowne saw as a dull focus on domesticity, including talks by James Laver on "Why do men dress like that," Ruth Drew, Jeanne Heal, and Guilfoyle Williams "Answering Your Household Problems," and the return of Mrs Crump with "What I think of *Woman's Hour* after three months" ("*Woman's Hour*: 1 January [1947]" 1946). A serialized reading by Nesta Sawyer from Monica Dickens's nursing memoir *One Pair of Feet* closed Griffiths's first show.

Later in that month, talks producer Archie Gordon wrote a report to the acting controller talks, outlining Collins's vision of current affairs within *Woman's Hour* (Skoog 2010: 156–157). He reported that Collins

> visualises these talks as being normally of direct interest to women, and as up to the minute news talks whenever possible. He is willing to break the normal planning of *Woman's Hour* in order to get the CA talk in on a day other than Friday if this is in the interests of topicality.
>
> If no direct women's subject presents itself, the talk should be introduced by way of some topical event of interest to women—for example: the arrival of lemons in the shops might be the peg to hang a talk about trade relations with,

and the general situation in citrus-growing countries. I think this second class of talk is likely to be the normal for this period …

He seems definitely to rule out from *Woman's Hour* in general, any talk—no matter what its subject—which does not in some way accept the conception of a special audience of women in the home. *Any subject which does not come under a recognised "women's interest" must be hung on a suitably beribboned peg.* (Gordon 01/17 1947, emphasis mine)

In late October of 1947 the BBC Glasgow acting talks producer wrote to the *Woman's Hour* editor with a set of "Suggestions for *Woman's Hour*" from a potential local contributor: "Mrs Whitley of Newark Manse, Port Glasgow— who has incidentally a first class broadcasting voice and writes quite a lot for the *Glasgow Herald*." Mrs Whitley thought that the program should take a very different direction from the one endorsed by Collins:

1) Housewives are most consistent women listeners (except invalids) as they are most consistently housebound. What they surely need is a total change from cooking, housekeeping, and the rest. Something solid, and not too snippity. For example: Woman to woman the world over: international parliament (chaired by Mrs Aaron) …

2) Taking your share of government (talks on being a town councillor, member of parliament etc) …

4) "10 Minutes for men," a helpful (or frankly malicious) burlesque of the usual cosy, chatty little women's Playtime corner. (Acting Talks Producer 10/31 1947)

This suggestion for a "total change" from domestic service talks was not taken up within *Woman's Hour*, but the role of current affairs material within the program remained a source of contention during the late 1940s. Within the steady stream of instructional talks—London-based professional ratcatcher Bill Dalton on "Getting Rid of Mice" ("*Woman's Hour*: 28 November" 1947), medical doctor and fashion historian Willett Cunnington on "The Use of Gloves" ("*Woman's Hour*: 5 December" 1947), and a hospital dietician on "Nice Puddings for Diabetic People" ("*Woman's Hour*: 12 December" 1947)—more explicitly political content emerged. The June 6 edition included a discussion from Northern Ireland between "Elizabeth Boyle and Kay McMeekin on 'Can a Woman Make a Success of Marriage and a Career?,' with Jeanne Cooper Foster in the chair" ("*Woman's Hour*: 6 June" 1947) and in the September 29 edition BBC German specialist and left-leaning BBC producer Trevor Blewitt (Burke 2014: 189) speaking on "Sharing Your Income" ("*Woman's Hour*: 29 September" 1947), as well as a series on "What's Going On—'Spotlight on Current Affairs'" ("*Woman's*

Hour: 10 October" 1947; "*Woman's Hour*: 17 October" 1947). The program's first "Birthday number" included "birthday greetings" from the Countess of Albemarle, Chairman of the National Federation of Women's Institutes, The Lady Hiliingdon, D.B.E. Vice-Chairman of the Women's Voluntary Services, Miss Joan M. Loring, Chairman of the National Union of the Townswomen's Guilds, and a "Housewives' quiz from Scottish, Welsh, Northern Ireland, North, Midland and West Regions" ("*Woman's Hour*: 7 October" 1947). The mix of "celebrity" and "ordinary" established in the listener panel from the program's launch edition was continued with an account of "What I think about *Woman's Hour*" by stage and screen actress Flora Robson alongside a report "from the Listeners' End" provided by "two housewives—Trixie Sparrow and Kate d'Arch Smith."

A memo in April 1948 from Tom Chalmers, acting controller, Light Programme, to George Barnes, director of Spoken Word, who in that role was responsible for both radio and television, tried to give an estimate of the "ratio of service talks to current affairs" in *Woman's Hour* (Chalmers 04/16 1948). Chalmers noted that this calculation was a difficult process "as we put in a fair amount of unbilled last minute material of a topical nature" but "our *regular* output" (emphasis in the original) included:

Service talks
Cookery
Gardens, animals as pets or for profit, bees, poultry etc.
Household repairs, etc.
Fashion
Answers to listeners' household problems
Grandma Buggins
(a mixture of service and entertainment—she always includes at least one recipe)

Current affairs
What's going on? Spotlight on current affairs
What's your worry? a talk explaining current social legislation (at the moment concerned with national insurance) (Chalmers 04/16 1948)

Chalmers reported that while "total number of billed talks per week is 20," Barnes would "see that there is a good deal of ad hoc material which may or may not be related to current affairs," with "cushion space every day to allow an extra five minutes space for topicalities." His analysis concluded that "the ratio is 32:16 (minutes), i.e. 2:1, but my guess is that with the additional ad hoc talks the ratio increases in favour of service talks." He thought the "division of *Woman's*

Hour into Service talks and Current Affairs is too rigid" and asked Barnes the question "What would you call a talk on the Ideal Homes Exhibition? Or the serial reading?"

Collins's departure to BBC Television in late 1948 appears to have been connected with a shift toward nondomestic topics in the program, with Chalmers taking up the role of Light Programme controller (Briggs 1979: 74). Olive Shapley's tenure as *Woman's Hour* host from 1949 to 1953 also coincided with a new era of experimentation in documentary features using portable recording equipment. Such technologies contributed to a shift away from scripted studio talks. One of Shapley's first programs included a featured "Farming Exchange," which was "a description of a recent visit to farms in France by three [British] women agriculturists: Mary Day, Jean Gardner, and Gladys Stuckey" ("*Woman's Hour*: 28 February" 1949). Shapley later wrote that "*Woman's Hour* was at that time unique among radio shows"[7]:

> Though it certainly tried to lighten the household chores and give listeners a new interest, albeit an appropriately feminine one, it also tried to open a window on the world outside, in a way which listeners themselves might not have had the time or opportunity to do so. So, the programme items were always wide ranging, in both subject matter and format: live discussions and interviews, news digests, straight talks, book reviews, and, of course, the daily serial. (Shapley 2000: 37)

Beginning in 1947, the program regularly included "contributions from the BBC's Mobile Units." The first mention of the location of Mobile Unit recording broadcast in *Women's Hour* was a visit to "the new radio-equipped maternity unit at the West Norfolk General Hospital, King's Lynn," which appeared in a Shapley-hosted edition in August 1949 ("*Woman's Hour*: 17 August" 1949).

The relative emphasis of "domestic" and "public" in the program, and the "balance" between them decreed by BBC management, shifted again during the 1950s, when, in echoes of Collins's "suitably beribboned peg," the need for "a public affairs element" in *Woman's Hour* was debated inside and outside the BBC. In September 1953, Mary Somerville, controller of talks, requested a report from the *Woman's Hour* deputy editor, Joanna Scott-Moncrieff, on talks planned for the rest of the year, after a report in *Broadcasting News* suggested "that the Public Affairs element was missing from the program" (Scott-Moncrieff 09/08 1953: 2). In response, Scott-Moncrieff listed upcoming talks such as "For Your Information," "a series of talks placed at irregular intervals to explain new legislation affecting the housewife," "Health Education," by a professor of dentistry on "the development and care of teeth" with the object of "dissipat[ing] the ignorance which leads to personal inefficiency and suffering and to needless national expenditure," as well as a series on "Economics," explained as "in which the development of the prices of a) a tomato, b) a pair of nylon stockings, c) a baking tin will be traced through from grower or manufacturer to consumer." A handwritten note from Somerville, dated September 8, gave her endorsement of this approach as a "ground plan" for the rest of the year (Scott-Moncrieff 09/08 1953).

While the range of topics to be discussed in *Woman's Hour* continued to be monitored for their appropriate gendering, while ensuring relevance to the interests of the state, it was the status of professional and nonexpert knowledge that would arise as another point of struggle and highlight issues of class and gender. The next section of this chapter explores this tension between recognizing the everyday realities of listeners and their existing agency and skills in managing their own lives, and the BBC's self-image as a social institution that would bring a new rationality to domestic life.

The middle-class *Woman's Hour*?

Joan Mollinson, a loyal West London listener who wrote to *Woman's Hour* in July 1947 with several suggestions for topics to cover, reserved her "greatest criticism" of *Woman's Hour* for its upper-middle-class agenda:

> It seems to be directed very much to the (fortunate) woman who a) has a house to herself & b) enjoys an income which places her in the middle-class. Now we who married during the war and are making do in rooms with perhaps no sink and very little money—we are quite numerous & that little chat on how to take care of one's curtains riled a little. I take my one pair down wash 'em & put 'em straight up. And that effort about bottling peaches—we daren't look at fruit with the price it is! (Mollinson 07/29 1947)

Similarly, a letter from deputy editor Mary Hill to a Miss KM Healey of Birmingham in August 1948 about her suggestion for a "Talk on Refrigerators Etc" declined the possibility of covering the topic because it would alienate working-class listeners:

> Thank you for putting this forward. I don't think, however, we can use it because we have to face the fact that the very large majority of our audience have no such helpful appliances as vacuum cleaners and refrigerators, and listeners'

correspondence show that they are intensely irritated by such reminders of comforts beyond their reach. (Hill 08/19 1948)

On a letter to *Woman's Hour* from "Clarice Herret (Mrs.)," a listener from Nottingham who wrote asking for the program's "Radio Doctor" to "please settle some arguments for us, over the air—small points among ourselves about our three year old son (on November 11) [who is] rather delicate," Benzie included her own handwritten notes, commenting on the author's perplexing child-rearing techniques such as the listener's question "Should he feed himself now (I still feed him every spoonful, nearly 2hrs a meal)?" (various listeners 08/14 1947). Benzie included an exclamation mark in pen in margin next to this point and explained in her cover letter that this type of maternal behavior should be a justification for *Woman's Hour* covering modern, and presumably less time-consuming, processes of child-raising: "attached for general information on the high degree of stupidity common, apparently, about children in better off households."

As these discussions show, the production staff of *Woman's Hour* were very interested in the class composition of their audience and asked the LRD to assist with a systematic study. In May 1948, Joe Trenaman of the LRD reported to Evelyn Gibbs that the *Woman's Hour* audience included "a rather greater proportion of lower middle class and of working class people than upper middle class" noting that "the former are, of course, much more numerous and that is why they cover 97% of the total audience" (Trenaman 05/05 1948: 1). He also noted that "*Woman's Hour* evidently attracts rather more listeners over 30 than under 30 (both proportionately and in numbers)." The reach of the program is the most striking aspect of the report:

> One of the most interesting figures is the 22% of women listeners. *If you are getting one-fifth of the country's women listening to your programme every day— and that means that you are really drawing on a much larger proportion since not everybody listens every day—you are surely not doing too badly.* (emphasis mine)

The report also records that the preceding program (during 1948, usually a variety musical program or band concert) attracted only 3 percent of the same population, which demonstrated that "listeners have obviously formed the habit of switching on for *Woman's Hour* at 2.00 pm, and off again at 3.00" (Trenaman 05/05 1948: 2).

The London listener who wrote the previous year with her critique of the middle-class bias of the program had also offered her own "suggestions for programmes," which she thought "would fill a long-felt want!":

First how to budget on say a four-pound a week housekeeping when one is not experienced enough to know which of the cheaper foods provide the same food value as the more expensive fruit and vegetables. I've learnt the hard way but I'm sure lots of people would be grateful for tips from an expert. Secondly any washing expert telling me the best way to wash babies' clothes & napkins in congested space with no sink (lots of use to new mothers in this position). (Mollinson 07/29 1947)

This listener not only wanted to hear about these practical concerns but also contested the privatization of experience that the program took for granted in its address to the figure of the woman at home:

Now another side of women's lives—*instead of these little intimate chats about the wives of film stars what about getting a few women who fought to get every avenue opened to their sex to talk to us.* The story of women's suffrage is not only a heroic one but darned exciting and I'm sure the political inertia of women would go if some of the older suffragettes and the leading feminists of today could talk to the housewife who is perforce slightly cut-off from the outside world. They could explain that we can never conquer war, poverty and get a happy world for our own and all our fellow women's children until we all take part in the fight and use our vote won so hardly by those very fine women.

The listener concluded that she had felt that these suggestions would be welcomed because of the program's imaginary dialogue with its audience:

I hope this long letter being inflicted on you isn't too tiresome but *I've a feeling that behind Woman's Hour there is a very real interest in knowing what the listener does want so I'm hoping you'll use some of these suggestions,* I should thank you for the enjoyment and hints I've already got from the programme. (Mollinson 07/29 1947, emphasis mine)

As the discussions over the separation of "ordinary" knowledge from "expert" knowledge canvassed earlier showed, inside *Woman's Hour* itself, these discussions of the BBC's class-based assumptions of women's lives signaled ongoing contestations over the ideology of separate spheres. The program's regular segment "Housewife Exchange," described as "tips and hints from housewives" around the regions (see "*Woman's Hour*: 28 October" 1947), seemed to be the most volatile in this regard, as it attracted attention to the way that knowledge was imagined to circulate between public and private domains, and from the BBC's regional outposts to its metropolitan center. In late 1947, Molony wrote to a "Miss Healey, Birmingham," a producer for that local BBC station, urging her not to withdraw from regular contributions to the segment, which was one of the established means by which regional voices were heard in the program:

> Having worked in the regions myself I am more than sympathetic about the staff problem, but I do ask you to think seriously before withdrawing from *Woman's Hour*, and its audience of some three to four million listeners, because it does seem such a grand opportunity of putting over local colour. (Molony 09/10 1947)

However, it would be *Woman's Hour*'s treatment of issues of women's role in the family as responsible for childcare that would be the most revealing of the particular set of intimate geographies that were emerging at the time.

Something about children

Housewife meets expert

At the end of *Woman's Hour*'s first year, Benzie wrote to Eileen Molony, *Woman's Hour* editor, with a set of suggestions, "partly my own and partly requests from listeners' letters." She prefaced her list with a paragraph that gives a sense of both Collins's conservative vision for *Woman's Hour* and Benzie's more feminist appropriation of it:

> First, to recall; the Ante-Natal Clinic was ordered by Mr Collins, the weekly children's-psychology was ordered by him when *Woman's Hour* first began and the "something about children" on Thursdays I took over a while ago by agreement with Miss Barker in order that these talks should be rather less flimsy than they had previously been. (Benzie 08/14 1947: 1)

Unfortunately, copies of every letter to *Woman's Hour* have not been kept, but the final pages of Benzie's memo records over forty questions from listeners, some representing multiple queries on the same topic, which Benzie thought showed "incontrovertibly ... the kind of thing over which listeners consistently need help and which they are deeply interested" (Benzie 08/14 1947: 5). These questions included:

> "Am I safe from pregnancy at my age" (very frequently asked) ...
> Ghastly results on child of strict father—"what can I do?" (quite common) ...
> "Please tell us about cancer" ...

"What can have caused me to be afraid to go out at all—what can I do about it?" (astonishing number of similar letters, some attached) …

"Why do I do everything with tense muscles and unnecessary vigour—from cleaning my face to sweeping the floor—so that often my teeth are literally clenched?"

"Could you give a short talk on depression?" (Benzie 08/14 1947: 5–7, notes in brackets added by hand by Benzie)

Many of these questions were picked up and answered in the program, but maternal responsibility emerges as a crucial trope for both Benzie and her letter writers in this memo. *Woman's Hour* as a potential means of popular education for the great mass of women at home made mother-and-child psychological topics rise to the top of Benzie's list and thus echoed a broader postwar "anxiety to maintain the family" (Riley 1979: 102). Benzie's "Favourite Suggestion"— although she didn't say whether it was hers or a listener's—was indeed "How to Treat Children: An Education in Child Psychology," which was to be "done by reading passages from literature in which the artist gives out of his own wonderful insight, and [sic] intensely felt experience, imaginary or otherwise, a demonstration of a universal truth of child-psychology" (p. 1).

In March 1947 the Listener Research Department had proposed their in-house researchers would work with Benzie and Dr Elliot Jacques, a Canadian psychoanalyst and future management psychologist who was a founding member of the Tavistock Institute for Human Relations and had been trained by child development specialist and psychoanalyst Melanie Klein. Both Jacques and Benzie had an interest in understanding audience reactions to psychological talks in the program. The application of medical expertise to home life, and the formative role of women as mothers in bringing up "well-adjusted" children, was to become another central concern of *Woman's Hour*. In this aspect *Woman's Hour* had a key role in shaping what Shapira has called a shift from "collective wartime citizenship toward a postwar domestic citizenship" as *Woman's Hour*, under the direction of Quigley and Benzie, included psychoanalysts and child psychologists as regular speakers (Shapira 2013: 135).

Following second-wave feminist work on the gendered dimensions of attachment psychology in postwar British society, notoriously embodied in the figure of Tavistock Clinic member John Bowlby, Mathew Thomson has described the rise of "Bowlbyism" as "helping to bring a social and democratic model of relations into everyday lives" (Thomson 2013: 82; see also Riley 1979: 106). The prominence of developmental psychology in discourses around maladapted individuals placed the housewife at the center of postwar reconstruction, giving rise to a political phenomenon and mode of psychosocial action described by Foucauldian historical sociologists Peter Miller and Nikolas Rose as the "Tavistock effect" (1988: 178). The BBC's expertise in program production and its role as a pillar of postwar reconstruction here assumed the home as the factory for a new kind of nation, and it devoted its resources in listener research to furthering a potentially transformative dialogue between the program and its listeners. Here, daytime radio lent itself to the "talking cure," although not exactly in the way imagined by Freud.

Described as the *Woman's Hour* psychiatrist "when *Woman's Hour* is on the air," Jacques anonymously gave "a weekly talk on Fridays, endeavouring to illuminate some simple point of behavioural problems" not only of children but also of women themselves (Listener Research Department 03/17 1947). The titles of talks published in the *Woman's Hour* listings in the *Radio Times* indicate that the topics explored by Jacques highlighted everyday domestic mishaps and conflicts and what they might mean for women on an individual, psychological level, for example with a talk in January 1947 on "Breaking Dishes" ("*Woman's Hour*: January 31" 1947). A one-line excerpt from a talk by "A Psychiatrist" (presumably by Jacques because of the date of the broadcast) published in *The Listener* under the title "Another Thought from *Woman's Hour*" asked an assumed female listener "If you keep forgetting that you have set the potatoes on to cook so that you're frequently burning the dinner, don't take memory exercises, but ask yourself: 'Now, why don't I like to cook?'" (A Psychiatrist 1947). Because of this psychological paradigm operating within these talks and women's programming more generally, the answer to the question was anticipated as an individualized response to a purely personal problem. Other answers, which might provoke further questioning of the gendered division of labor, were not anticipated by this kind of therapeutic inquiry.

Yet the talks, because of their presence in a society-wide broadcast medium, proved difficult to leave at the metaphorical doorstep of the individual listener's home. After Jacques's broadcasts generated "occasionally definitely unpleasant letters" in early 1947 (Benzie 03/04 1947, quoted in Karpf 2014: 96), the LRD was asked to help tease out the reasons behind the strong audience reaction to such content.

A specific talk was singled out from Jacques's contributions as in need of investigation. Entitled "Your Health Problems," the talk had been "the most popular [talk amongst the Panel] in the week October 7th–11th, as seen in

LR/6420" (Listener Research Department 03/17 1947). Perhaps because the broadcasting encounter lacked immediate feedback, Jacques was seeking a more direct encounter with the embodied listener to continue the virtual process of psychoanalysis via radio. Jacques was reported as wanting to "get some meaningful reaction to his talks," as he was especially concerned "that in an endeavour to do good he is only stirring up antagonism and hostility" (Listener Research Department 03/17 1947). Whether the panel seeking reactions to this particular program took place is not evident from the files, but during late 1948, Jacques employer, the Tavistock Institute of Human Relations, hosted a series of focus-group-style meetings of women listeners on their preference for current affairs within *Woman's Hour* to complement consultations on the same topic with women's groups such as the National Federation of Women's Institutes, the National Union of Townswomen's Guilds, and the Social Service Clubs of the National Council for Social Service (Skoog 2010: 176–177, 2017: 958).

Other collaborations with psychologists include the highly popular talks by pediatrician Douglas Winnicott during the late 1940s and early 1950s within *Woman's Hour* in a series entitled "The Ordinary Devoted Mother and Her Baby" (Karpf 2014; Shapira 2013: 134–135; Winnicott 1939–1968). Benzie and Quigley were instrumental in getting Winnicott's talks on the air and he cited Quigley's influence in molding his radio persona and helping craft the talks as effectively as possible (Winnicott 1939–1968). Quigley was also vigilant in editing his scripts and giving him guidance in what she saw as his role as an expert to interpret rather than diagnose the maternal experience. This collaboration is understood to have resulted in Winnicott's talks emphasizing the agency and expertise of women in childrearing, rather than pathologizing the mother–child relationship and thereby countering some of the mother-blaming tendencies of Bowlby (Karpf 2014: 90–91).

Woman's Hour's collaborations with the LRD and these medico-psychological professionals took place alongside a wider societal impulse to utilize expert social scientific knowledge for the management of the self within everyday life (Miller and Rose 1988). This impulse found both institutional purchase and a time and space for action within daytime radio programming for women. As a spoken-word program on a monopoly broadcaster such as the BBC, *Woman's Hour* had privileged access to its audience and constructed the figure of the mother-in-need-of-instruction as an entrée point to the proper regulation of the modern nuclear family. Thus, *Woman's Hour* sought to investigate the potential for using radio to listen to women's everyday emotional lives in a therapeutic sense. While the full text of these experiments in the form of the actual scripts put to air are not recorded, there was much discussion of their impact and influence between the staff of the *Woman's Hour* and the wider BBC.

During this period *Woman's Hour* consolidated its agenda as a proponent of social democracy from a standpoint on everyday life. This agenda is most apparent in the way the BBC saw the program's value in creating links between scientific knowledge and the conduct of everyday life. Yet the medium of radio inevitably led to the interrogation of expert knowledge itself. This critical shift emerges very clearly in a memo from Molony in August 1947, in which she suggested a series of talks titled "The Housewife and the Expert":

> A little while ago we had a very successful 8 minute interchange between Rosetta Desbrow, an economist [later public relations officer for the UK Council of Industrial Design], and a housewife. The fact of the housewife being present in the studio kept her down to earth, and the housewife was also able to follow up her questions by subsidiary questions. I think this idea could be developed. (Molony 08/28 1947)

Molony pointed to "a recent public opinion report" in which nearly two-thirds of people surveyed "said that they knew nothing about the Marshall Plan." She thought that "too often newspaper articles and the BBC talks take for granted the fact that people in this country are familiar with ideas and phrases which they bandy about easily but which have never been explained simply to the rest of the public":

> If we could cross-examine some of these alleged experts it would help housewives when they came to read their daily papers. I am sure we could find one or two sensible but not widely read housewives who could examine economists, political correspondents, sociologists, doctors, anthropologists etc in this way. (Molony 08/28 1947)

In October the program did indeed introduce a regular "Housewife Meets Expert" fixture, "a new series in which the housewife puts some searching questions on current affairs to politicians, economists, sociologists, and journalists" ("*Woman's Hour*: 24 October" 1947; "*Woman's Hour*: 28 October" 1947; "*Woman's Hour*: 31 October" 1947).

This meeting between the national scale and the ordinary, while part of a newly intimate polity, meant that women's public participation continued to be bracketed by the domestic. Anchoring political discussions in "the woman's angle" tacitly reproduced the separation of spheres. Even when women's paid work was discussed, the program's remit predetermined such representations as being framed by an essentialized responsibility of women for unpaid domestic labor. Benzie made clear how these ideological tenets played out within program policy when she wrote in September 1947 that she thought it

> would be awfully interesting to have rather a special issue of HE [Housewives' Exchange] in which the housewives were, for example: [composer] Elizabeth Lutyens, [poet] Anne Ridler, [sculptor] Dora Gordine and [medical researcher] Annis Gillie—one of the most distinguished general practitioners in London— or another woman doctor or ["psychiatrist" crossed out and replaced with "scientist"] with a family. These ladies all either have several children and/or are remarkably good cooks and/or have special problems as: a doctor's house must be pretty clean looking; and Dora Gordine has to clean the great sort of washtubs in which she slaps the clay about, and makes you take off your shoes at the front door, and wear a pair of bedroom slippers provided—with which you polish her floors! (Benzie 09/19 1947)

It would be difficult to imagine that Benjamin Britten, T.S. Eliot, Henry Moore, and Alexander Fleming would have been asked to speak on the same topics, if they had been guests on the program. The brief notes made by Benzie for this segment also elide any other kinds of caring work or domestic labor that the proposed guests may have had paid for to enable their professional role. Yet Benzie's intention with this segment, to profile women's working lives while exploring their solutions for cutting down on housework, did challenge existing notions of women's interests as centered on home life to the exclusion of paid work or creative practice. The next section explores the implications of this shift, as it emerged in a new focus on the public circulation of gendered experience in ways that highlighted the patriarchial and heteronormative hierarchies of knowledge that structured the BBC and the public service broadcasting project at the time.

Making space for listening

Benzie's 1947 memo also included the possibility of "Listeners Reading their own Letters sent in response to broadcasts, e.g. the attached from Mrs Patricia George, referring to 'A Holiday in Hospital.' A thing to do only as and when we have a really good letter." (Benzie 08/14 1947). The idea of listeners speaking on air in their own voice demonstrates the potential that Benzie and others felt existed to capitalize on and deepen the existing connection between its listenership and the program. *Woman's Hour's* relationship to its audience was evolving in response to the fact that the program had from its first days elicited an enormous upwelling of concerns and worries from its listeners. The act of gathering and tabling so many isolated experiences into the public sphere energized the program during the late 1940s, and its producers would channel these first steps of listening to their listeners into an explicitly gendered editorial agenda during the 1950s. As Olive Shapley was to write in her autobiography some forty years after her work on the program:

> Psychology and human relationships were still largely uncharted territory even in ordinary private conversation, and into this area *Woman's Hour* again leapt fearlessly. I chaired a discussion in 1952 called "Women without Men" between five women, including myself: three "spinsters," as I called them, a divorcee, and myself, a widow. Issues which are commonly explored now on radio and television and in magazines, like women's self-image and role in society, loneliness, deprivation of sex or children, and old age, were ranged over with a good deal of frankness for that time. And, as ever, we found that despite male apprehensions these were definitely not taboo topics for our listeners, who welcomed them. (Shapley 2000: 39)

Benzie's comments on the letters attached to her 1947 memo to Molony signal her desire to open up a new space for discussion of issues relating to women's lives that had previously been marginalized or ignored. Some topics—varying from varicose veins, "staying in" complex (agrophobia), "change of life," painful menstruation, care of children ("3yr old child will not eat," "5yr old nailbites," "9mth old won't take bottle but prefers breast"), "17 yr old daughter afraid of male strangers"—were outlined by listeners in detail and included requests for help and advice, accompanied by moving accounts of having exhausted all other possibilities when coming up against a dismissive medical system. In response to these letters, Benzie also identified a series of

> subjects [that] very badly want discussing: Feeding difficulties in children (Letter attached from Mrs Gimlett, West Wickham. This is a horrifyingly wide-spread trouble in the better-off classes) ... several things to do with child-birth ... To be helpful we should explain and explain and explain the mere physiology of child-birth. The depths of ignorance are exemplified by the enquiry "I suppose you take the cod-liver oil to grease the baby." Similar can be collected from any ante-natal centre.

A letter from a "regular listener" addressed to "The *Woman's Hour* Producer" in September of the same year had also made suggestions about the program about the way it covered childbirth, urging the program to highlight current medical practice and alleviate women's anxiety about birth:

> In this series may I also suggest that the doctor spares one talk to reassure the prospective mother about the actual process of birth. I have a six months old daughter and was really frightened before hand having read realistic novels & heard old wives tales. I do not think it can be too much emphasised that given help by the gas & air apparatus and trained midwives it is not a thing to be dreaded as it is by so many women even now. Analgesia in childbirth could also be discussed in *Woman's Hour*—this is a most important topic. (Mollinson 07/29 1947, emphasis in the original)

Here, by tabling such first-hand accounts, Benzie was building *Woman's Hour*'s role as a platform for articulating personal experience with the ongoing medicalization of everyday life. In this aspect, such discussions on *Woman's Hour* prefigured organized feminist pressure on male-dominated institutions such as medicine during the second wave. Yet the treatment of these topics on *Woman's Hour*, and the BBC management's response to "women's troubles," also made clear that there were limits to the performance of intimacy and what could be heard in the mediated public sphere of daytime radio.

Benzie had annotated all the letters to emphasize her points to Molony about what *Woman's Hour* should be covering from its listeners' perspective. For example, a nineteen-year-old listener from Newquay wrote (assuming that the letter's recipient would be male) asking for help from the program and recounting her experience of debilitating period pain, including indifference from her local doctor:

> Dear Sir,
>
> I listen to your programmes on the wireless quite regularly and am wondering if you can help me.
>
> I am nineteen years of age and quite healthy, and have seen very regular menstruation since the age of eleven but always accompanied by severe pain. When I say severe I mean it is really very bad, sometimes almost more than I can bear. My mother took me once to see my local doctor, and I have been again quite recently, though candidly speaking I don't think takes the matter very seriously. I have fainted several times at the office, and at the end of the period I look as if I have been very ill.

I hope you do not think I am making a great deal of fuss about nothing, and I don't mind putting up with it, but I would like to know if it is natural. In every medical book I read it usually states "accompanied by slight discomfiture" or something similar, but I can assure you, being unable to stand up at times is more than "a slight discomfiture."

The majority of my friends never feel any difference.

I would appreciate it very much if you could help me and I enclose a stamped envelope for your reply.

I am always in pain for the first two days and usually the third, keeping me awake most of the night.

Yours faithfully,

Margaret Ellacott (Miss) (various listeners 08/14 1947)

The phrase from this letter "I don't think [my local doctor] takes the matter very seriously" was underlined in pen by Benzie and "exactly!" written in the margin. Although it seems to have had a tick against it on Benzie's list, the topic of "menstruation" was later crossed out, and another note from Benzie indicated that apart from this particular listener's letter, it had been a controversial topic in general, with a note to Molony "as already discussed with you" (p. 3). Any discussion of menstruation, according to both these BBC files and listings in the *Radio Times*, was indeed not covered until 1961 ("*Woman's Hour*" 1961).

One topic that did receive a tick from Molony on Benzie's list was "menopause":

"The Change," which has already been approved by Mr Collins to be billed as "Getting Past 40," but I should welcome guidance on whether only a single talk is wanted, or more. This has very often been asked for and there is a great deal of re-assuring which can be done. Characteristic letter from Mrs Harvey, SE11, attached. (Benzie 08/14 1947: 3, emphasis in the original)

This particular proposal from Benzie, via listeners' letters, was eventually produced in early 1948 as a series of talks on "The Older Woman" by "a woman gynaecologist" (see "*Woman's Hour*: 9 January" 1948 and "*Woman's Hour*: 27 February" 1948). This series generated a set of correspondence between John McMillan, chief assistant to the Light Programme, and T.W. (Tom) Chalmers, acting controller of the Light Programme, during March 1948 about what was suitable for broadcast in *Woman's Hour* as a daytime program. McMillan had already "queried the wisdom of the talk ... with [assistant head Talks Department] Newton and [talks producer] Boyd" but had been "assured that it was in line with current practice [so] I didn't exercise our editorial right to censor" (McMillan 03/16 1948). Despite this advice, he did believe that the inclusion of such a talk represents a lowering of broadcasting standards. It is acutely embarrassing to hear about "hot flushes," diseases of the ovaries, the possibility of womb removal and so on being transmitted on 376 kilowatts at 2 o'clock in the afternoon. This view is shared by the female staff of our department.

Chalmers's reply of March 16 is recorded handwritten in pen at the bottom of this memo, and while he disagreed with McMillan that this sort of talk does represent "a lowering of broadcast standards," he felt that "nevertheless, I would myself have been embarrassed, if listening at home, to have heard such intimate physiological details described" and asked his superior, presumably assistant controller of Talks Mary Somerville, "Is it 'in line with current practice?'" (McMillan 03/16 1948)

A few days later Somerville responded to Chalmers defending *Woman's Hour*'s editorial decision to broadcast the talks as she interpreted it as in line with the BBC's stance on other, non-gendered medical topics:

> We met with the same kind of objection years ago when we broadcast talks to Mothers about bed-wetting, and masturbation in young children. The then Permanent Secretary of the Ministry of Health wrote to the then DG [(Reith!) written in pen in margin] complaining of these on much the same grounds as Mr McMillan. The DG replied, I remember, the effect that the BBC's medical advisers had assured them that there was a need for courageous plain-speaking, and he was glad and proud that the BBC had reared up a public that could take it.
>
> I think I would give the same kind of answer here—if the facts permit. Presumably we have been advised that this kind of talk is needed. I don't know what the statistical picture is, but we certainly don't want to emulate the USA commercials, some of which have the effect of making people overanxious about their health, leading normally healthy people to expect the worst as a matter of course. Granted, however, that we have been properly advised, I should expect the section of the public who would normally listen to *Woman's Hour* can take it. (Somerville 03/21 1948, emphasis in the original)

Somerville argued in her response that there was, "or ought to be, nothing intrinsically more embarrassing in this subject than 'Constipation and its consequences'—about which the Radio doctor goes in for a lot of very plain speaking indeed":

> In short, once we have committed ourselves to Health education, it is very difficult to draw the line. We can only see to it that the plain speaking is in

itself seemly, and I don't see anything to complain of in this script on that score, though I would be inclined to question the stress laid upon the possibility of disease.

Her solution was not to eliminate this kind of "women's health" topic from the program but that "periodical talks of this 'embarrassing' kind" could be included

at the end instead of the beginning of the body of the programme so that listeners who do not need to listen could switch off, c.f. the position of "Recipes for Housewives" in the *Listener*. I daresay this would be regarded as undesirable for other reasons, but if there is any considerable body of complaint it might be worth considering. (Somerville 03/21 1948)

Somerville's support of *Woman's Hour*'s inclusion of this material, perceived to be too "embarrassing," too "feminine," and therefore troubling to male listeners (and the unnamed female staff in the Light Department's executive office mentioned by Chalmers), was a milestone in the crafting of new articulations of public and private spheres through radio. As Sally Feldman later recollected, *Woman's Hour* was the first BBC program to discuss prostitution in 1956, and in the same year "when it first broadcast a talk about cancer, there was a warning that some people might wish to switch off … [as did] Olive Shapley in 1967 [when introducing] an interview with a couple who had chosen to live together without being married" (Feldman 2000: 67). In an interview recorded in June 1976, Shapley, then in her mid-1960s, described *Woman's Hour* as a "great pioneer program" for the way it was "putting out all sorts of medical programs, that were not covered by magazines" (BBC 1976). She described this 1948 series of talks by "Joan Malleson, a medico" and the gynaecologist behind "The Older Woman" series as "most beautiful … very consoling" and noted that the program "had hundreds of letters, from ladies who thought that they were suffering alone." However, the topic was still considered too shocking for male technical staff to hear during production: "We had to have all woman engineers that day, I remember because it was considered not quite nice."

This and other topics on the list of listeners' questions that Benzie had gathered canvassed the concerns with a sexist medical establishment that would be the foundation of the later feminist health movement. This implicit discussion of personal experiences of discrimination and oppression echoes women's liberationist techniques of consciousness-raising. The listeners' direct questions and the program-makers' active curiosity and openness to listening to them via their written letters contrast here with a passive vision of postwar femininity, perhaps best epitomized by a melodramatic title, presumably devised by the architect himself, included by Benzie for a talk by male architect and promoter of British "New Towns" Bertram Clough Williams-Ellis. Evoking housewives as victims of modern planning, the title used the architect's motto, "Too many homes are built on a foundation of crushed women." Benzie was not convinced by this depiction and confirmed that she had a "script by him in hand, but need[ed] a total rewrite—too thin" (Benzie 08/14 1947: 8). It was the combination of agency and empathy that the program fostered, and in doing so, contributed to reshaping women's culture, alongside other media such as women's magazines and television. However, *Woman's Hour*'s staff did not place listeners' experiences in the public sphere in an unmediated way and exercised editorial control over the material in a dialogue that had class and gender implications. They also came up against much more impermeable boundaries between public and private experience, especially in discussions of sexuality that were to be deemed unlistenable on the BBC, despite *Woman's Hour*'s transgressive agenda during the 1950s.

The limits of listening

Benzie continued to advocate for including topics suggested by listeners in the programme and for presenting the voices of listeners as directly as possible through the early 1950s. She tried to expand the scope of topics that could be discussed when she wrote to *Woman's Hour*'s deputy editor on November 5, 1954, with a suggestion for the program to feature "Our Anonymous Letters." She attached one from a "former mental patient," which "impresses me as much as it clearly does you, and I feel that to broadcast it would be a public service" (Benzie 11/05 1954). Benzie further appealed to the BBC's public service remit in that "we are, after all, one of the few agencies in the country exposed to the receipt of confessions like these … and we are not proposing to put them out because they are admissions of self-induced suffering … but because they are pleas to the world for charity."

A second letter, described by Benzie as "requiring sub-editing, [but] would it not be a splendid one to think of putting out?", was a heartfelt two-page testimonial from a young gay man. The letter-writer did not describe himself as "gay" but rather as a "male listener" who experienced "inversion." He wrote that while he had come to recognize that his "impulses" were "not a disease," he was still "condemned to eternal solitude" because he had been denied the "moral right to found a home, to embrace a child of my own [due to] the opinion of society ... based upon ignorance, stupidity and ill-nature." He ended his letter with a postscript apologizing for not including his name and address, but with the "hope [that] my letter may be the means by which a lot of mothers will understand their children a little better" (p. 2). Quigley wrote back to Benzie on November 16 via a handwritten note in the margin of the same memo, "It is an interesting suggestion," but the rest of her note is unreadable, and this and other letters were not read out on air (Andrews 2012a: 120). Despite Quigley's stated "policy of bringing hush-hush topics into the open" (Quigley quoted in Feldman 2000: 67), during the 1950s the program was still circumscribed by notions of public and private, and would not explore questions of gender and sexuality in any explicit discussion of gay experience outside a medical model within the medium of radio until after her departure from the program in 1956.

While "*Woman's Hour* was certainly one of the earliest programs to address its listeners intimately and directly and respond to their questions and needs," as claimed by Sally Feldman, herself a *Woman's Hour* editor during the late 1980s and early 1990s, I have not been able to find the 1955 edition of the program that Feldman cites in her chapter on *Woman's Hour*'s history for the book *Women and Radio: Airing Differences*, which she says "was the first to mention homosexuality" (Feldman 2000: 1967). The first time the topic appears in the daily listings for *Woman's Hour* in *Radio Times* was on July 4, 1958, under the heading "You Ask For It: A doctor speaking about the nature of homosexuality" ("*Woman's Hour*: July 10" 1958). Other programs on the topic of sexuality around this time were broadcast late at night, for example, a panel program titled "The Homosexual Condition," on the Home Service at 10 p.m. on a Thursday night in July 1957. Described in the *Radio Times* as "A study of a social problem," the program anticipated the impending release of the Report of the Departmental Committee on Homosexual Offences and Prostitution, better known as the Wolfenden Report ("The Homosexual Condition" 1957). The Committee, which had been set up in 1954, had heard testimony from high-profile gay men about their treatment under British law, which at the time criminalized homosexuality and was charged with making suggestions for law reform. The panel discussion was moderated by former London City policeman and journalist C. R. Hewitt, and featured Kenneth Walker, "surgeon and sexologist," and Claud Mullins, "former Metropolitan

Magistrate, a psychiatrist, and prison medical officer." This program articulated the two dominant discourses framing gay people in Britain at the time, medical and criminological, as it aimed to discuss the "homosexual as a patient and, in the present situation as lawbreaker" ("The Homosexual Condition" 1957). The following year, Hewitt, as C. R. Rolph, together with Walker, would become founding members of the Homosexual Law Reform society (Cook 2004: 202), and in 1967 male homosexuality would be decriminalized in Britain.

Thus, *Woman's Hour*'s desire to create new publics, provoked and prodded by its audience, remained constrained by notions of gender that placed such experience within a pathology of disease during the 1950s. The program may have been the starting point for discussions of these topics, but media representations of gay liberation, on the BBC at least, had to wait for substantial political change and resulting change to law and policy. For now, these personal revelations were to remain on the individual level in a confessional mode.

Conclusion: Gender, time, and labor

"The Gate," the poem written by a listener to *Woman's Hour* in 1956 that prefaces this chapter, speaks of women's occupation of separate spheres. The author of the poem highlights the sense of two parallel lives, one as anonymous citizen-consumer and the other as a person with a "face, a name," secure in her role as "wife and mother/Blessedly beloved" (Prince 07/27 1956). The poem, whether the author intended it to be or not, says much about the role of radio as a transit between the homely world of belonging and the anonymous modern street, between the spheres of everyday life and public institutions such as the law, the state, and its agencies. *Woman's Hour* as a program was to act as a "gate" between these two worlds, but also drew these worlds into different patterns and thereby transformed the possibility of keeping them separate. Alongside decades of feminist activism before and after the period covered in this book, the program enabled a tabling of important and complex issues relegated to the private sphere. Thus, both the producers and listeners of *Woman's Hour* reconfigured mediated geographies in such a way that the separation of intimacy and public life could no longer be so tightly held. The rhythms of everyday life were changing, and radio as a domestic technology was adapting to and shaping these rhythms.

When Mollinson, the listener who suggested talks to alleviate women's anxieties about giving birth, commented on the timing of *Woman's Hour's* talks directed at working women who were pregnant, she very rightly pointed out that *Woman's Hour* was unable to reach parts of its audience because of the BBC's assumption that all women would be listening during the day, even if they were in paid work: " … re the 'ante-natal' talks [i.e.] the one addressed to the pregnant woman keeping on her job—the subject matter was no doubt excellent but would the women in a job be at home to listen at 2pm?" This issue was to recur at the BBC during the 1950s when Mary Hill, writing to the *Woman's Hour* editor, reported that when she

> recently attended the Broadcasting Sub-Committee of the National Council of Women, I was unhappily impressed with their feelings of—I think I can truthfully say—"looking down" on *Woman's Hour*. This was not, I am quite sure, because of the programme content. It was quite clear that the members had neither the time nor the inclination to listen at that time of day and I had a very strong feeling that, were the *Woman's Hour* to have a time, even once a week, either at the weekend or in the evening, its prestige among women who do not necessarily spend all their time at home, would be greatly enhanced. I think that not only could we get a good figure in the evening or at the weekend, but I think it might well be that the prestige value would add to our daily listening figure. (Hill 03/29 1951: 1)

Hill continued that it was

> not at all clear to me on what basis the various requests for a *Woman's Hour* at the weekend are refused. At meetings with CLP [Controller of Light Programme, Norman Collins] a year or more ago he said that he could not afford his listening figures to drop over the weekend, but I have just been looking at the last week's figures available on the green sheets [for] February 15-21st and some very interesting facts come to light.

Hill's analysis compared the audience figures for the Saturday schedule of the Light Programme—afternoon programs such as *Rhumba Orchestra, Band Life Guards,* and *Theatre Organ*—with *Woman's Hour* figures on weekdays for the same period. She also cited the figures for the *Woman's Hour* summer replacement program *Light Orchestra,* comparing it with *Woman's Hour's* figures when it returned at the end of summer in August 1950 and concluded that "it seems reasonable to assume that a *Woman's Hour* on a Saturday afternoon or evening would show a better figure than any of these programmes" (Hill 03/29 1951: 2).

Hill also noted that she "was unaware, until I examined this week's figures, how very high the *Woman's Hour* figure of 9 is in relation to any other Talks programme" on both the Light Programme and the Home Service. She concluded that while these were "only figures taken at random" she thought that the *Woman's Hour* editor "might find them interesting and useful to have by you, because my own feeling is that there is very, very strong case to have a *Woman's Hour*, or half and hour, at the weekend or in the evening and I think it would be of all round benefit." A weekend version of *Woman's Hour* did indeed start in 1953, with *Home for the Day* being broadcast for the first time on March 29 at 9.10 a.m. on the Light Programs, following a news bulletin after a monthly program "reflecting on life in the country" entitled *The Countryside in March* and before a broadcast of *Stories from the Ballet "Coppelia."* With Elizabeth Webb as "hostess," the program was advertised as "a supplement to *Woman's Hour* for those who are out at work during the week" and the April 5 editions included "Ambrose Heath making a hard-boiled egg," "Bernard Werthenall advising on a 'job for the day,'" "Ruth Drew on polishing shoes," "Wynn Griffith thinking about being a grandfather," "Nancy Spain with more news and views," and a book reading from Sybille Bedford's *The Sudden View* ("Home for the Day: 29 March" 1953). A new sense of flows between media and everyday life was being delineated at this time, as depicted by Hill in her analysis of the potential for a weekend edition of *Woman's Hour*.

In 1956, Quigley was promoted out of the *Woman's Hour* role and gendered programming more broadly to become the BBC's chief assistant of Talks (Sound) ("Janet Quigley [Obituary]" 1987). Both Benzie and Quigley had been part of the development of a new culture of listening while working on the program during the late 1940s and early 1950s. Quigley and Benzie continued their partnership by going on to develop the BBC's breakfast current affairs program, *Today*. *Today* began in October 1957 "as a light-hearted morning miscellany for busy 'people on the move'" (latter quote from Ronald Lewin, head of Home Service planning, *Radio Times*, October 1957 cited in Donovan 2004). Benzie was the first editor of *Today*, and her embrace of the audience demonstrates the lessons she had learnt on *Woman's Hour*. She wrote to Quigley in May 1957:

> I should like the job of organising this programme. I can't see how it goes on the
> air without an organiser. It wants lots and lots of fresh ideas … *The audience, to*

me, is typically on its feet, dressing, making packed lunches, cooking and eating—certainly before I am. Everything must exploit the virtues of brevity. (BBC WAC, cited in Donovan 2004, emphasis mine)

This depiction of the *Today* audience is not explicitly gendered as female by Benzie, but the listener she imagines here could be an audience member of *Woman's Hour* ten years before, now in paid employment and ready to head out the door to work.

6

The Long Legacies of Women's Programming

Having recently acquired the status of housewife, I can now understand why
my mother never allowed us to bother her while she listened to Trans-Canada
Matinee. I have found your program stimulating and informative—in fact
I thoroughly enjoy the majority of the programs offered by the CBC here in
Montreal.—Mrs R.B.M., Dorval, Que.
Dorval [Letter "To the Editor ... " published in *CBC Times*] 12/26 1964

When Adam delved and Eve spun
Unisex had not begun
But now in fashionable places
We grease the car: you air the graces
You think that Women's Lib's a fuss;
But see yourselves as you judge us.
We've fashioned it to your design
Our sweet and sour Valentine
Knowles [*Woman's Hour* presents "A Radio Valentine to Men"]
12/20 1971

It is now impossible to make the claim, as Anne Karpf quite accurately did so in 1980, that while "academics and women's groups have been diligently monitoring television, cinema, and the press: decoding signs of sexism, uncovering masculinist ideology, and promoting feminist alternatives ... radio, the medium which permeates women's lives more than any other, has been largely ignored" (Karpf 1980: 41). The work of feminist media researchers and historians, including Karpf herself, has overturned this absence (Baker 2017; Carter 2004; Crean 1987; Hilmes 1997, 2006, 2013; Horne 2017; Johnson 1988; Karpf 1980, 1987, 1996, 2014; MacLennan 2008; Smulyan 1993; Veerkamp 2014; Wang 2002). This book has sought to contribute to this feminist project of recuperating radio as a "forgotten medium." It also goes beyond received understandings of radio as a gendered medium to look at the configuration of intimacy and publicity in radio during the twentieth century. This story is integral to the changing cultural forms and structures of gender embodied in contemporary online and digital media. As scholars have mapped out since the 1990s, we are now inhabiting a new kind of mediated public sphere based on a rapidly circulated, politicized intimate voice (Allen and Light eds 2015; Duffy 2013; Eckert and Steiner 2016; McLean and Maalsen 2013). Yet as Matthews (2007) and others (e.g., Thompson 1995) have pointed out, this mediated public sphere is not entirely new, but rather an intensification of patterns that has been emergent throughout the history of mass media.

Yet as Alice Goldfarb Marquis recorded in a brilliant article on the early radio published in 1984, from its beginnings broadcast radio offered something "extra." Radio evoked a particularly "intimate relationship with the listener, perhaps because the receiver was part of the furniture in his home, perhaps its disembodied voice made the listener feel that it was speaking directly to him" (Marquis 1984: 395). One listener letter she singles out from reports of fan mail sent to US radio network NBC during the 1930s captures "one of radio's major appeals" in this regard (Marquis 1984: 396). Writing to NBC about their live coverage of the 1931 London Naval Conference, a male listener had extolled "an enterprise that permits ordinary men to button up their underwear to the accompaniment of an address by a European monarch" (Lumley, "Fan Mail," *Literary Digest* (May 22, 1937), quoted in Marquis 1984: 396). As this listener realized, his "presence" "at a news event … was radio's most remarkable contribution to journalism. Previously, even the most detailed printed account was filtered through the mentality and the words of the reporter" (Marquis 1984: 396).

Marquis characterizes radio in the United States from 1937 onwards as marked by the Era of Maturity, when radio found "a large and growing audience for serious cultural offerings, both music and drama" and developed "coverage of current events of a fairness, depth and sophistication that rightfully alarmed newspapers, and [a widespread] acceptance" (Marquis 1984: 412). As the survey of women's programming in the three countries covered in this book suggests, we could add to this periodization by designating the late 1940s until the mid-1950s as radio's Era of Intimacy. During this period, against the looming presence of both television and the music-heavy formats of FM radio, gendered spoken-word programming drew new connections between the audience and broadcast institution, navigating between what was considered un-hearable due to its personal nature and what was considered to be of public interest. As noted in Chapter 5, this form of address became "mainstreamed" in the late 1960s and 1970s, developing a new "therapeutic sensibility" for broadcast media. Thus, the current negotiations around the role of mediations of public and private in the rise of podcasting and its remediation of women's and feminist broadcast forms (Veerkamp 2014), as well as neoliberal tensions over public broadcasting, are themselves imprinted by this intimate turn (Berry, Harbord and Moore 2013; Dawes 2017). This concluding chapter explores the afterlife of gendered programming. First, I examine the changes to such programming during the late twentieth century within the broadcasters covered in this book, then I highlight some high-profile forays by media organizations into female-targeted media during the twenty-first century.

The cold case of the disappearance of women's programming

In September 1970, Kathleen Abbott wrote to the editor of the *Canberra Times* about a recent discussion on the ABC's morning program, *Ellis Blain's Guest,* which ran from 9.30 to 10.30 a.m. Her letter approved in principle of the regular guests on the program as their "accomplishments, talents and experience are of general interest" (Abbott 1970). The writer thought that the program itself was "a little more thought-provoking for the average listener at this time than the never-ending top pops etc, of the alternative programmes." However, she found criticism of Blain and the nature of the program made by one of his recent guests, religious broadcaster and Liberal member of parliament in the Gorton Ministry and also a figure associated with the international conservative Christian movement, Moral Rearmament, Dr Malcolm Mackay, to be "impertinent." The writer voiced a critique of Mackay's "interest in the media and morality" as evidence of an "old pattern of repression [within] the Gorton Government in the absence of constructive policy" in education and media reforms. The reforms that she particularly wanted to see were regulation of cigarette advertising on commercial radio and television and the introduction of an publicly funded educational television channel rather than awarding more licenses to commercial players. This letter, while not directly on the topic of gendered programming, sparked an exchange about the status of programs for women on the ABC between Abbott and highly incensed Mrs O'Hanlon of Ainslie, and gradually drew in other readers of the *Canberra Times*.

Responding to Abbott via the letters page, O'Hanlon wrote that her own reaction to Mackay's criticism of the program was opposite to that of Abbott's. O'Hanlon reported that her letters to the ABC and Post-master General had no effect so far on the "decadent content of either the Ellis Blain Show or the replacement programme on the other ABC station, *Morning Call, of what used to be the women's session, whose demise I very much regret*":

> Dr Mackay's condemnation of a particularly offensive remark gave me a return of confidence in the Government that we, after all, elected to intervene for us when the structure of our society is threatened by negative and unwholesome forces.
>
> It is a pity that the Postmaster-General, who has the portfolio of the ABC, does not use the power of Parliament to once again give the people a say in the programming of the ABC which at the moment we are subsidising for a mischievous minority. (O'Hanlon 1970a, emphasis mine)

Patricia Skeates, of Curtin, joined in the debate about *Women's Sessions* by endorsing O'Hanlon's "proposal that the ABC change its ideas about women" and return to dedicated gendered program: she didn't want to be entertained by ABC women's programs but to hear "something to keep us mentally occupied while doing housework":

> Are there any other women who would like to learn a language, listen to a series of lectures on child psychology, or a talk by an expert on first aid, home nursing, buying a house etc—not a five minute segment interrupted by the prattle of an interviewer, but a talk that goes on long enough to make it worthwhile listening.
>
> Maura O'Hanlon hasn't had much success on her own. Perhaps, if all those interested write to the ABC, we might get somewhere. (Skeates 1970)

Keeping the focus on the decline of women's programming, O'Hanlon wrote again the editor of the *Canberra Times*, responding in turn to Skeates's letter with worries that the disrespect to women signaled by changes to the ABC *Women's Sessions* would result in the forced marriage and enslavement of Australian women:

> Patricia Skeates (Letters, September 30) misread my letter criticising the ABC for the decadent content of [*At Home This Morning with Elizabeth Bond*] their new morning programme replacing the women's session (Letters, September 25) insofar as the entertainment angle was not worrying me so much as that the new programme was derogatory to women.

The twice-weekly poetry leadings of Professor May rob women of the nobility and dignity they are entitled to equally with men, and the occasional flippant comments on women's role in society by the otherwise excellent compere show she is not aware of the danger into which lessened community respect for women can place our women of the future in Western society.

The enslavement of women in other societies in the form of concubinage, harems, etc highlights this danger, and is most blatantly shown in a news item on Zanzibar telling of 14-year-old girls forced to marry already married men of the Revolutionary Council (Zanzibar Government) [,] their fathers having been whipped and gaoled for having attempted to protect them. (*The Canberra Times,* September 29)

O'Hanlon concluded that because women's "sense of responsibility toward their children makes them vulnerable, so society, and especially other women, must protect their interests," a "women's session organised by responsible, mature women, and containing constructive features such as those suggested by ... Skeates, should be restored by the ABC thus keeping women's true position in focus for the community" (O'Hanlon 1970b).

A letter from O'Hanlon along the same lines appeared in December 1975. Speaking as an ABC "shareholder," she began by agreeing with a recent letter criticizing "indecent ABC programming," for example *GTK* (*Get to Know*, an early evening pop music television program aimed at teenagers) and an edition of *Young World*, "a replacement program for the *Children's Session*," which "gave a list of where contraceptives could be obtained":

Over the past few years programs of general interest—*Women's Session, Children's Session, Hospital Hour*, all professionally produced—have been replaced by amateur dilettantes with narrow doctrinaire subjects, larrikins, indulging in horseplay and local topics of narrow interest, to the exclusion of nation-wide folk music and stories, and knowledge of our rural producers and families and their special activities.

The replacement of women's programming on the ABC with gender-neutral programs such as *Morning Call, At Home This Morning with Elizabeth Bond,* and *Ellis Blain's Guest* challenged definitions of women's interests, and to this letter-writer at least, this move seemed to signal a sense of vulnerability to countercultural forces and eventual social collapse. Well into the 1950s, the ABC *Women's Sessions'* resident medical broadcaster Dr Clair Isbister promulgated a highly maternalist view of the role of Australian women, including in her talks on "The Tired Housewife" the claim that such "tiredness, head-aches, pains-in-the-back, sore feet and chapped hands, as well as the general feeling of dis-satisfaction and restlessness (known as 'the psychosomatic housewives' illness') … is a particular kind of overstrain from which the career-woman turned housewife is especially likely to suffer" ("Health Hints for Harassed Housewives" 1954; see also "Women's Interests of the Air: Housewives Are Now Labelled Psychosomatic" 1954). She perhaps created most controversy when she advocated four-child families to "add to the population" ("Families of Four Urged by Doctor" 1954). The Communist Party-sponsored *Tribune* was far from convinced by Dr. Isbister's claim that "the average working class family could easily afford to have four children" because they would "save enough by not being able to go out to feed and clothe the new baby" and included her ideas on the matter in its "Krazy Capitalism" column (09/15 1954). Isbister would later be known as a founding member of the Festival of Light, a lobby group that was explicitly formed to counteract second-wave feminist's perceived attacks on the family ("[Advertisement] Stand up—Be Counted, Hyde Park, April 7" 1974) and that she described in an oral history interview as "a family foundation to provide information [on] home management and family counselling [based on a] Judeo-Christian ethic" (Isbister 1975).

The story of women's programming on public service broadcasters after the 1950s is entangled with a range of wider factors, including the history of each state's openness to progressive civil society organizations as well as internal pressures stemming from female employees for an improvement in their industrial situation, both in terms of equal pay and in the choice of jobs available to them. On the ABC the *Women's Sessions* continued until 1965 when they were replaced by *Morning Call* at the same time of 10.30–11 a.m. on the ABC's Second (capital city) and Third (regional) Networks (Inglis 1983: 240, 320; Marriott 1969). The changes that Mrs O'Hanlon railed against were the result of a new regime at the public broadcaster, which paralleled the rise of new social movements linked to identity politics, feminism, civil rights, and youth culture. The changes to names and program philosophies recorded in this rather hysterical correspondence were a result of such movements as well as a new generation of staff putting pressures on media institutions as frontline operations in a cultural revolution. At the same time, these social movements were instrumental in bringing an extended period of conservative government to an end in Australia, where the Liberal Party had held government for thirty-three years from 1949 until 1972. Several figures instrumental in the demise of the *Women's Sessions* at the ABC and the move to non-gendered programming were directly involved with these new programs that so upset the *Canberra Times* letter writers, including Alan Ashbolt, controversial producer and leader of a unit, Special Projects Radio, set up in 1969 to marginalize his tendentious influence on the ABC, and one of his protégées, Marius Webb, described as "a hairy and lively young male producer" by official ABC historian, Ken Inglis (1983: 320).

After internal ABC criticisms of *Morning Call* as "stodgy," it was replaced with *At Home This Morning ...* hosted by Elizabeth Bond in late April 1970. These changes to women's programs at the ABC during the late 1960s and early 1970s were positively received by most critics, with Heather Chapman, radio critic for Sydney tabloid *The Daily Mirror*, saying of *At Home This Morning ...*: "It has been so bright ... that there have been times when I could hardly believe that it was an ABC radio programme" (Chapman quoted in Inglis 1983: 320). The program was taken off the air in late 1970, after increasing complaints about frank discussions of sex, as well as challenges to the Australian government's censorship of books and films voiced by regular guest Frederick May, professor of Italian at the University of Sydney (May 1970). Bond herself remembers an on-air debate about racialized violence as the final step in the program's demise (Nicholson and Nattrass 2003). Replaced on the ABC's capital city network in 1971 by *The Peter Young Show*, reportedly described officially as a "programme of non-controversial interviews and music" and on the regional stations by *Sounds Easy*, a "programme of music and current affairs for country people," explicitly gendered programming seemed to have been definitively discontinued at the ABC (Inglis 1983: 320).

The replacement of the Gorton Liberal government by the Whitlam Labor government in December 1972, however, allowed for a new set of social actors to energize the ABC. The Whitlam government actively courted the women's liberation movement and was responsive to media activism growing around issues of sexuality, race, and class (Baker and Lloyd 2016), as well as youth and music cultures, all of which culminated in the appointment of Australia's first-ever Minister for the Media in December 1972. These changes resulted in the establishment of a network of community and ethnic broadcasting stations and a new ABC youth music-based station, 2JJ in Sydney in 1975.

At the ABC in the early 1970s, pressure was growing from women working within the organization to be able to move out of female-designated positions such as typing and secretarial work and access career paths as journalists and producers. These women formed the Australian Women's Broadcasting Collective (AWBC), a pressure group of activist women within ABC, provoked by a suggestion of one-day only International Women's Day broadcast in 1974. Believing this kind of inclusion to be "total and absolute tokenism," they sought to give female broadcasters editorial control over women's programming (Inglis 1983: 365). The program that resulted from their actions, both within and outside the ABC, resulted in a new weekly women's program *The Coming Out Ready or Not Show* going to air on IWD 1975, known as *Coming Out* and eventually changed to *The Coming Out Show* (Inglis 1983: 364–365). Imagined as broadcasting *for* and *by* women, rather simply broadcasting *for*, as the *Women's Sessions* had done, the *Coming Out Show* ran for the next twenty years until it was retitled *Women Out Loud* in 1995 and eventually dropped altogether in 1998 (Henderson 2006; Inglis 2006: 358).

In 1983 Irene Greenwood wrote in her diary about the Women's Christian Temperance movement, which had radicalized her mother's generation:

> So it was they who worked for women's rights in its truest sense and formulated the women's movement, which had its roots in the emancipation of slavery and general social justice. Young feminists don't seem to realise this. They think they invented feminism, ala the *Coming Out Show*. (Greenwood quoted in Murray 2002: 50)

The revolutionary historical narrative that Greenwood referred to, reproduced by the AWBC in its moment in the mid-1970s and later retellings of AWBC achievements, ignores the backstory of women's programming told in this book. What emerges from this study's focus on the pre–second wave period is an alternative history of women's programming, for example in Greenwood's reimagination of gendered norms of separate spheres. When I started this project, I was fascinated by the question of the AWBC's relationship to the *Women's Sessions* (Lloyd 2004). My original questions revolved around this absence: Why and how had the AWBC left out the past fifty years of ABC's *Women's Sessions*? What had actually been happening during this period? How had feminist broadcasting been able to overlook how its particular agency came from—even if purely as a resistance against, as it did for women such as Greenwood—such unique programming that imagined a specifically female audience?

The story rethought in this book is not intended to paper over the fact that women speaking on and working for these broadcasters experienced sexism and discrimination throughout the twentieth century. For example, the first foray into television during 1964 by Anne Deveson, journalist and filmmaker, contributor to the *Women's Sessions* during the 1960s, and later a leading figure in the Whitlam-sponsored and feminist-inspired Commission of Inquiry into Human Relationships (Arrow 2016), drew attention for her transition from women's programming into primetime ("ABC Features: *Impact* Will Delve into Personalities" 1964). *The Canberra Times'* television reviewer John Howard panned Deveson's interviewing style on *Impact* and trivialized daytime programming for women by describing her technique of asking one-word questions "which the subject is supposed to give his reaction to … " as producing the effect of subjects "interviewing themselves" (Howard 1964). He thought that this might be "all right at ten-thirty in the morning while making beds, but it is dreadful television."

The ABWC's 1977 *Women in the ABC* report found systemic discrimination against women in the organization, a pattern that Kylie Andrews has argued needs to be seen against "continuations of the gendered workplace conventions firmly entrenched in the 1950s and 1960s" (Andrews 2016). Similar studies at the CBC (Crean 1987: 32) and BBC (Murphy 2016: 262–263) found depressingly familiar patterns of women being trapped in pink-collar jobs and active exclusion from skilled or highly visible roles such as executive production or reading the news. However, despite the invidious similarities, gendered programming had manifested on each broadcaster quite differently as I have shown here.

In the case of the ABC, the demise of women's programming during the 1960s had provoked a decidedly feminist response ten years later. In the case of the CBC, gendered programming had not been politicized to the same extent, perhaps because programs such as *Trans-Canada Matinee* were not exclusively pitched to women in their domestic role from their beginnings in the 1960s. Further, the autonomy of women's programming within the CBC had made the broadcasts overall much more open to feminism in the postwar period and thus had more naturally evolved along with the second wave into general programming. The case of the BBC seems the most startling: a continual focus on women as an audience with a specific set of needs and interests throughout the nearly 100 years of its history and the continuation of *Woman's Hour* well into the twenty-first century.

Feminists' Hour or *Woman's Hour*

While the BBC has been singled out for the feminist-leaning approach of *Woman's Hour*, it would be hard to argue that the program contains the seeds of a revolution in contemporary gender roles. Lauded by Peter Forster, the British conservative magazine *The Spectator*'s arts and media critic, in 1961 as the only BBC radio magazine program to "increase its audience after the advent of television," as discussed in the previous chapter, *Woman's Hour* entrenched itself in the schedule of Radio 2 during the late 1960s (Forster, "A Look at Sound" 01/13 1961: 4 in "[Cutting from *Spectator*]" 01/13 1961). The program was relaunched in late 1971, reportedly "aimed at disproving accusations that it [was] too middle class" and needing to "attract more younger listeners", with a special 25th anniversary edition "devoted to people around the 25 year age bracket" ("BBC *Woman's Hour* Seeks a New Image" 1971). Moving to Radio 4 in the summer of 1973, where it was seen to fit with the personable yet intellectual atmosphere cultivated by Radio 4 controller Whitby (Hendy 2007: 62), the 28 June edition of the *Radio Times* covered the arrival of the program on the station under the headline "A New Hour Strikes" ("A New Hour Strikes" 1973). The program did indeed thrive in this new environment, as noted by Whitby himself in August 1973 when he commented in a memo headed "New Radio 4 Pattern" that the program had "made its transfer from Radio 2 with no loss of audience— if anything a slight increase" (Whitby 08/30 1973). It further consolidated its position as a BBC stalwart throughout the 1970s, as has been covered in detail elsewhere (Elmes 2008; Feldman 2000, 2007; Karpf 1996; Knowles and Evans 1981; Minic 2008; Murray 2006).

Signs of a shift in its audience and a resulting sense of crisis emerge though in a BBC Broadcasting Research report from January 1982. While many female listeners reported that their listening habits had been shaped by their own mothers' attention to the program, and then when they themselves stopped work to raise children and were at home during the day rediscovered it on Radio 4, its 14 percent of male listeners came across it by chance, and wished for a change of title so that they could feel less "embarrassed" at listening (BBC Broadcasting Research 01/1982: 3). Non-listeners reported that the "Radio 4 image" was a barrier, as the program was seen as "high-brow" and "middle-class" (BBC Broadcasting Research 01/1982: 4). Even the categories of "female listener" and "male listener" reflect a changing understanding of audience, with the former defined as someone "who currently listens 'at least once a week'" and the latter as someone who had "ever listened 'within last year' and 'available' to listen to the radio between 2.00 and 3.00pm most weekdays" (BBC Broadcasting Research 01/1982: 6). There was a decline in audience share, down from its reported peak of 5 million (Segal 1952) and well over 10 percent of the British population in the late 1940s to around 700 thousand people and 1.4 percent of the population in the first quarter of 1981 (BBC Broadcasting Research 01/1982: 1). This decline was furthered during the 1980s, with BBC Radio steadily losing its market share to independent commercial radio from 1988 onwards (Brown 1991).

Radio 4 controller Michael Green announced in December 1990 "that the programme was to be moved from its 2pm slot to 10.30am, to address the substantial mid-morning drop in Radio 4's audience" (Henry 09/02 1991). Immediately after this announcement, as *The Guardian* reported in September 1991, thousands of "letters of protest ... dropped on his desk, and MPs ... signed a condemnatory Commons motion" (Henry 09/02 1991). *The Independent* asked on January 23, 1991, "Can BBC Radio Four's *Woman's Hour* Survive a Move to a New Morning Slot?" and reported that the proposed changes had indeed been limited by the letter-writing campaign:

> It is proof positive that letters of protest have an effect. The BBC, inundated with complaints from furious listeners reacting to the news that *Woman's Hour* was to move its time slot and change its name, has relented on one point at least. The name—the dear, old-fashioned, sexist, wartime name—will not change after all. *Woman's Hour* it has been for the past 47 years, and *Woman's Hour* it will remain ....
>
> Anna Massey, the actress, who has appeared on the programme many times, summed up listeners' feelings wittily when she said: "To lose the 2pm slot could be counted as a misfortune, but to lose the title as well must be counted as carelessness." Tony Benn had previously raised the issue in *Any Questions?* and a motion deploring the move was even tabled in the House of Commons, which has attracted 42 signatures so far. (Lambert 1991)

In November *The Times* reported:

> *Woman's Hour*, which has always aspired to be the voice of British women, has increased the proportion of its male listeners by 6% to 36%, and men are baring their souls and innermost feelings to Jenni Murray, the show's presenter, more often. "I am amazed how frankly they talk about personal problems and emotions," said Sally Feldman, joint editor of the programme with Clare Selerie-Grey. "They open up on air to a woman in a way they never would if they were being interviewed by another man." (Wittstock 1991)

However, these shifts in gender norms touched some nerves, and an article headed "'Feminists' Hour' under Fire from Listeners: *Woman's Hour*," which appeared in *The Sunday Times* in December 1992, signaled the opening of a new line of attack, with a report that the program was "attracting complaints from traditional listeners who have branded it 'Feminists' Hour', suitable for women who are more at home with *Spare Rib* than *Good Housekeeping*" (Dixon 1992). The article cited comments made by BBC listeners on *Feedback*, Radio 4's "own forum for listeners" as evidence of a backlash against the supposed radicalization of *Woman's Hour*, casting such listeners as "defenders" of the program, "the BBC's post-war cultural institution," against the "hardline feminism" of presenter Jenny Murray:

> After 46 years as a mirror to middle-class Home Counties zeitgeist neither exclusively female, nor afraid of gently tackling taboo subjects the daily magazine programme faces grumbles that it has become a platform for hardline feminism …
>
> Enough is enough, [have] argued defenders of the BBC's post-war cultural institution [on the forum]. "Last week I accidentally tuned into *Woman's Hour* and instantly received a grim reminder of why I gave it up," said one listener from Salisbury, Wiltshire. "'As we all know, feminism is fun!' Jenni Murray was saying, with all the steely jocularity of a nanny telling a child that spinach is delicious. Feminism is neither fun nor delicious, however good for us it may be."
>
> Another, Amanda Beale, of northwest London, had a suggestion: "Can a nice late-night slot be found for Jenni Murray's 'Feminists' Hour,' and can we have *Woman's Hour* back please?" (Dixon 1992)

The *Times* singled out for derision recent topics covered on the program such as "anti-pornography legislation in the United States, and older women and environmental protests in Canada" and focused on the feelings of "Elizabeth Mumford, vice-president of the Mothers' Union in Winchester and a fan for 25 years" who "longed for the days of Jean Metcalfe when it was associated more with jam-making and knitting," quoting her as saying: "It has become stridently feminist in the last year. A lot of it is down to the presenter Jenni Murray" (Dixon 1992). Conservative MPs were also interviewed. Tony Marlow, Tory MP for Northampton North, who had tabled a motion in the House of Commons "demanding Murray be removed" as presenter was quoted as saying: "Feminism is as political as being Labour, Conservative or anything else and many people would be deeply concerned if *Woman's Hour* was influenced in a feminist direction." The justification for demanding Murray's removal was that she had expressed her personal opinion of marriage as "an insult"—and quoting Mary Wollestonecraft, as "legalized prostitution" (Feldman 2000: 71)—in an article for *Options*, a short-lived women's magazine aimed at 25- to 35-year-old

British women. The article concluded with a quote from Rosie Boycott, founding editor of *Spare Rib*, then editor of *Esquire*, which confirmed the paper's worst suspicions: "It is rather wonderful that they have become more radical. There's a real ballsiness about *Woman's Hour* at the moment" (Dixon 1992).

A few days later *The Guardian* visited the *Woman's Hour* studio, noting that during the same period singled out for such complaints the program had also covered "sauces and gravies, Chanel and chapped lips" and evoked criticisms of the program from the Quigley era:

> Murray and her producer, Sally Feldman, are all too aware of the publicity their programme creates. It is a sitting duck, an easy lampoon, a great joke for the buffoons. ... The producer quotes another report which charged the programme with being [both] laughably obsessed with domestic detail and too radical for popular tastes. The report was published in the 1950s. Dismaying it may be but *Woman's Hour* is stamped with a very specific stereotype which lingers long in the memories of many. (Moir 1992)

A February 1993 report, also in *The Times*, claimed that still "haunted by the trauma of moving from the afternoon to the morning, *Woman's Hour* is being threatened anew," and "Rewind Productions, an independent production house," was proposing its own woman's program for commercial stations in direct competition. To be aimed at 18- to 32-year-olds and broadcast on "17 independent local radio stations," the article quoted an industry source as saying the new programme would have

> far more fashion and beauty than *Woman's Hour* and far more direct access to sex and relationships. The problem with *Woman's Hour* is that it is BBC types talking to BBC types. It has no basis in what most people are actually interested in. ("Diary: Sick of Sex: Rewind Productions Competes with the BBC" 1993)

The proposal for this postfeminist program was followed closely by the announcement in July 1995 of the UK's first women's radio station, *Viva! 963AM*, which was to "eschew strident feminism and feature a regular programme aimed at male listeners":

> Lynne Franks, chairwoman of *Viva! 963AM* ... said yesterday the station aimed to attract intelligent career women "who do not want to be patronised with bland, old-style knitting patterns and cooking recipes."
>
> She said: "We want men to listen—we are men-friendly. Magazines like *Cosmopolitan* have a large male readership, and if men want the inside track on relationships with women, *Viva!* is the station they must listen to." (Culf 1995)

By mid-1996, media critic Maggie Brown reported that the ailing *Viva!* was under new ownership and that the new owners, Liberty Radio, wanted "to abandon the all-women format, in favour of interesting programmes which anyone will want to turn to":

> The basic problem with *Viva!* is that the concept is wrong. I'm the first to pick up glossy women's magazines when time allows, but it has never been clear that this impulse to browse could translate into enjoyable talk-based radio for female achievers. I often listen to *Woman's Hour* on Radio 4 but it is an honourable exception. To aim a station at women, especially professional women, is daft: we are too diverse and busy to build a commercial radio brand upon: it does not meet a desperate need. When busy women get into the car, or mooch around on Sundays, we just might want to tune into the mainstream. (Brown 1996)

With innovations such as the "all-women" format now looking decidedly stale, *Woman's Hour*'s fiftieth anniversary in October 1996 provoked a round of examination of the relevance of gendered programming (Daly 1996; Karpf 1996; Midgley 1996).

Conclusion: Whisky and wives

A column by *Herald Scotland*'s "Urban Voltaire," Jack MacLean in May 1997 compared the recent marketing of BBC Scotland to "younger people and women" to trying to sell whisky to the same groups: "The notion that women and young people will take to whisky is daft enough but dafter still is that proper radio programmes should become, I quote, 'younger and more female-friendly'. Why? For God's sake why?" The author found this angling of content to such listeners "patronizing" to its desired audience and "insulting" to its entire audience, because it was based on the outdated and irrelevant model of *Woman's Hour*:

> I don't know how the BBC Scotland radio people are going to "attract" new listeners by being more so-called female-friendly but if it means being like *Woman's Hour* on Radio 4 and endlessly telling us about breast cancer and how bad things are for lesbians in the armed forces it will not attract women for a start. And why should it?
>
> Women aren't halfwits whose only concern in life is how to start a yogurt culture while installing a new Aga or how to deal with post-pregnancy depression. Most women don't have any of these things, especially not an Aga, and most women are perfectly capable of dealing with such thorny brain difficulties like

for instance the news, or literature, or society or most things normal people can somehow manage to think about …

Young people and the notion of women which Beeb Scotus is thinking of will not tune in to the radio anyway, at least not the kind of radio which the BBC at its best can provide. (MacLean 1997)

The *New Statesman* asked in 2007 "What is it that makes *Woman's Hour* so appealing to male listeners?," describing its newly found demographic of under- and unemployed young men, "half-listening" at home while doing household chores:

"*Woman's Hour*? I live by that programme." That was the surprising, but not uncommon, reaction of one male friend when I told him I would be reviewing one of Radio 4's most venerable institutions. Think of it, and you immediately think of the cuddly-but-scarily-tough persona of its main presenter, Jenni Murray, who has been with the show since 1987. Well, now you can also think of legions of semi-employed young men tuning in as they stand, with Marigolds on, in front of a sink full of dirty dishes. The BBC press office folk are being coy; they won't tell me what proportion of the *Woman's Hour* audience is male, but a 2004 article in the *Independent* claimed about a third. (Trilling 2007)

The decline of the breadwinner role, signified here in the presence of men at home during the day, as well as the decline of full-time employment more generally, has seen a changing gender dynamics of broadcast media use. In the years since, a rise in websites and social media targeted at women, exemplified by Salon.com, Slate.com, and PoliticsDaily.com's forays into female-targeted subsites and blogs during the early 2000s, triggered a similar debate about the marginalizing effect of a "new [online] gender apartheid" (Rosen 2010). When the Australian Fairfax press launched a new women's news portal in early 2012, entitled *Daily Life* (Hicks 2012), the Institute of Public Affairs' Lydia Bevege, writing in the newsletter of the free-market think tank, saw its arrival as "the most piteous" of "all the warning signs that have signalled the steady decline of the Fairfax media empire" (Bevege 2013: 17).

Reportedly targeted at 30 to 45-year-old women who "take an active interest in the news of the day as well as enjoying fashion, food, intelligent commentary and debate," the site generated a welter of online comment, including the user "bm"'s comment on an otherwise overwhelmingly public relations-orchestrated announcement on a media industry blog: "Awesome a site for women—I had such trouble reading the big words on other sites" (Hicks 2012). A welter of other online comment about the site appeared shortly after, ironically referencing the site via the hashtag #dailywife (Hills 2012). In 2017, the presence of the portal was downplayed and eventually subsumed under the "lifestyle section" of the main Fairfax site.

Pressures on public service broadcasters seem to have provoked a new focus on gender issues at the same time as providing fodder for attack on public funding of media. For example, an editorial in March 2017 in the Murdoch-owned national broadsheet *The Australian* asked its readers on International Women's Day, it is "Women's ABC Today but When Will It Be Your ABC?" While approving of ex-Google chief executive Michelle Guthrie's policy of "doing more with less" at the ABC, the editorial excoriated the "national broadcaster's preoccupation with the issues and attitudes of the inner-city green-left rather than the daily concerns of suburban and regional Australians." As the AWBC had in 1974, the *Australian* saw a recent International Women's Day broadcast that handed "all hosting places to women" as tokenistic, describing it as a "cute stunt" and a "distraction" from the organization's lack of "diversity in political or ideological opinion":

> [As] an organisation charged with reflecting the plurality of Australia [the ABC] projects an endless run of green-left perspectives. … There is a dearth of conservative or mainstream presenters. There can be no doubt this skews coverage of climate change, border protection, tax reform and even the rise of Donald Trump in a way that puts the ABC out of touch with swaths of the public. It also tends to undercut the considerable output of the many ABC content producers who strive for objectivity. The ABC could not be politically savvy and relevant by employing a stable of ideological eunuchs—even if they did exist. So it must provide diversity and plurality: not of gender but of world view. ("Editorial: Women's ABC Today but When Will It Be Your ABC?" 2017)

Thus, the newspaper echoed fears about the political transformation traced in this book. Like these earlier fears, such concerns were expressed in terms of the over-running of clear boundaries between rationality and emotion, of explicit attention to gender as complicating "objectivity." In this afterlife of gendered programming, explicit attention to the kinds of relations being created between social change, space, and collectives in media forms is key to moving beyond this opposition.

Notes

Chapter 1

1   Fraser says that the phrase "has been used by many feminists to refer to everything that is outside the domestic or familial sphere. Thus, 'the public sphere' in this usage conflates at least three analytically distinct things: the state, the official-economy of paid employment, and arenas of public discourse" (1990: 57).

Chapter 2

1   Despite the rise of mass production, the costs of buying a set were still prohibitive for most people, and therefore having a radio at home would have been only available to middle- or upper-middle-class families. In the Australian case, for example, in 1924 a radio license had to be bought for each set, so the combined cost of a low-priced basic radio receiver and its license was around two and half times the average weekly male wage (equivalent to $12,840 in 2015, adjusted for inflation, see Commonwealth Bureau of Census and Statistics 1924): 35 shillings (equivalent to $136 in 2015) for the license and £6 s6 ($490 in 2015) for a "one-valve amplifier" to attach to a crystal set, boosting its reception range to around 100 kilometers (Listening-Insect 1924). More powerful ready-made two-valve models that could pick up interstate stations began at more than double that price and would have therefore represented an outlay of five times the average weekly wage.

Tellingly, the radio columnist for the *Australian Woman's Mirror*, writing to give advice to busy mothers who might be interested in purchasing a radio, emphasized the relative value of a radio in terms of conspicuous consumption: "The cheapest ready-made two-valve set I have seen costs 16 guineas ... Sixteen guineas is only relatively a lot of money. It would, for instance, be a lot of money for me (or anybody) to expend on a second-hand Ford car, whereas it would not be a lot of money for Eve to spend on a new dress, provided that dress earned the envy of her neighbours to a satisfactory degree" (Listening-Insect 1924).

2   The Association's program ran daily from 10.40 to 11 a.m. Regular segments, all presented by Varley, ranged from "Madam, do you know?" ("Every Friday for ten minutes Miss Varley tells the housewife numerous hints on home-craft—many of them are introduced from America, and are much appreciated, judging by the letters

that hundreds of women send to their secretary, Miss Varley.") to "Tennis Coaching"
("Make up your mind to master a weakness during your holiday play … urges
their tennis enthusiast who has been the means of enrolling over 500 women in the
ABC women's tennis clubs"). Twice a week at 6.45 p.m., a "Younger Set Session,"
also presented by Varley, invited school-age girls to undertake social and physical
activity. For example, the "Younger Set" program on Thursday January 8 advertised
as a "Girls' Radio Club Session" conveys Varley's enthusiasm for sports and talent
for organizing: "For this week Miss Varley will conduct [the session] … alone. It will
take her the full twenty minutes to put up various and new schemes she has in her
mind for the Girl's Radio Club members. The formation of a GRC committee, on
which two delegates of every club will sit, is one of her schemes. A picnic during the
school holidays, and a younger set tennis competition, etc., etc., are among her many
schemes" ("ABC Women's Association Session" 1930).

3   Knight was a journalist associated with conservative politics as the wife of the antisocialist
and protectionist politician John William Leckie and in 1920 became the mother-in-
law of future Prime Minister Robert Menzies when her stepdaughter Pattie Mae Leckie
married the then barrister. She had worked for *Punch* in the 1910s and the *Sydney Sun*
until her marriage in 1917, then rejoining the *Melbourne Sun* in the early 1920s.

No details of the content of the programs that Knight broadcast on the 3LO
exist, apart from titles such as "Shopping in Bourke Street" (August 24, 1929),
"Women's Interests at the Show" (September 14, 1929), "Choosing My Cup Dresses"
(September 28, 1929), and "Baby Health Centre" (October 5, 1929).

Her print journalism, however, gives the flavor of her political stance. For
example, her feature "The Shades Discuss Sex Equality: Famous Women of the
Past Are Critical of the Independent Modern Miss," published in *The Argus'*
"Weekend Magazine," in September 1938 fancifully brings together Queen Elizabeth,
Catharine the Great, Nell Gwynn, and Cleopatra, as well as other famous female
characters from theatre and literature, for tea in "Shadowland" (Knight 1938). As
the "Conservative Society of Shades," the women discuss these "quaint moderns,"
young women "who are running round getting all excited about sex equality, and
being gloriously Independent by buying their own buns and tea," as "stupid and
ridiculous." The women decide that "women are unsuited for politics," except when
Portia, the female heroine of *The Merchant of Venice*, says to Queen Elizabeth I:

> There are many exceptions naturally. You [Queen Elizabeth], Madame, for
> example, are one of the most brilliant exceptions. You had your work thrust
> upon you, and you shouldered It courageously. But you were not a feminist.
> You were not defiantly anti-man. You were a ruler, and you used men and
> made them do your work for you, never Insisting upon leading the regiment
> personally or anything like that …

Ultimately the discussion concludes that

If men did not challenge them, did not differentiate and emphasise that they were women, but accepted them as citizens ... There would be very few wanting to be JP's and all those dull things ... And they would probably all go home and do their knitting ... And there would be an immediate improvement in the birth rate.

4 This incident must have taken place early in the program's existence during the mid-1940s, as Charlton left ABC Perth in mid-1947. See "Transfer of ABC Manager— Conrad Charlton for Melbourne" (1947) *Kalgoorlie Miner*, Wednesday April 2: 4.

Chapter 3

1 Firth cites as evidence the trumping of women's equal pay within the Australian Federal government's employment policies in the postwar period, which emphasized male full employment at the expense of equal pay (2004: 503–504).

2 While the letter was written on behalf of the "WCRU," 14 Aberdeen Street was the headquarters of the Women's Christian Temperance Union (whose initials would be WCTU, not WCRU), and at the time that the letter was written in 1940, the "State corresponding secretary" was actually Greenwood's mother, Mrs Mary Driver. This letter was also published word-for-word on October 16 in the *Daily News*, signed "Secretary" (1940).

3 As the representative of the Women's Service Guilds, Greenwood gave evidence to a Australian Broadcasting Commission hearing in Perth during May 1944 "in support of its application that the women's session be reinstated in the ABC programme ... as a result of which hopes run high for the resumption of the sessions ... particularly on cultural lines for the women in the outback and rural areas" ("ABC Women's Session" 1944).

4 In 1949 press reports noted the new career of former ABC *Women's Sessions'* director Clare Mitchell as part of an article on a "touring photographic team of two," when, together with Ursula Powys, an English society photographer, she travelled in an ex-Army Dodge command car through isolated communities across rural NSW and Victoria:

Next week the two will open an exhibition of pictures at David Jones art gallery, the best of their output over the last eighteen months ... Clare, prior to her job with the ABC, was a cooking demonstrator with the Department of Agriculture, and on her falls the providoring and cooking as well as the accountancy side of the business. With headquarters (for developing and printing) in Sydney, the two make sortees [*sic*] inland for three to four weeks, taking pictures of country homes and, families on their way. ("Girls Take Camera Caravan to Record Life in the Country" 1949)

The remarkable photographs resulting from this journey, now out of copyright, can be seen online in the State Library of Victoria's collection (see Powys-Lybbe 1948–1987).

5 It is unclear from the report whether by "them" Heaven meant the women's lack of interest in politics was a reflection on the women themselves, the politicians or the actual broadcasts.

6 On November 28, 1956, *Women's World* opened ABC Sydney TV station ABN's daily broadcasting from 3.30 to 4 p.m., followed by a one and a half-hour close, then "Film" 5.3–6, and another hour-long close before "News" at 7 p.m.

Chapter 4

1 CBC also bought many commercial US programs for daytime broadcasting, including from the CBS, NBC, and Blue networks during the 1930s and 1940s. These included music programs such as *The Hitmakers* and "dramatic sketches" or serials such as *Life and Love of Dr Susan* and *Big Sister*. *The Happy Gang*, a half-hour variety lunchtime program, was the flagship of CBC-produced radio emanating from Toronto (see Maclennan 2001: 386).

2 By 1950, Mugan was working for the BBC (McEnaney 1950) and was a presenter on *Woman's Hour* ("*Woman's Hour*: 15 June" 1950).

Chapter 5

1 The moment of this step-change in the vision of the BBC, as proposed by Whitby, took place on the eve of the BBC losing its exclusive rights to the airwaves in 1973 with commercial radio about to be licensed in the UK.

2 Neither program and station were directly referenced in the staff suggestion, but Radio Luxembourg did broadcast *L'heure des dames et des demoiselles* from 1935, which translates as "The Hour for Women (Miss and Mrs)" and Mattelart describes as "a feminine byword" until it was taken off the air in the mid-1960s (1986: 64). Thanks to Virginia Madsen for the translation of the program title.

3 Possibly a reference to *Let-Up*, a "magazine program for busy people who could do with twenty minutes' break for tea and talk," broadcast at 4.25 p.m. on the Home Service from July to November 1945. The October 22 edition featured "Vicra Warr on Australia," future *Woman's Hour* inaugural presenter "Alan Ivimey on what you can see from nowhere else but an aeroplane," and "Antonia Ridge on anything at all" ("Let-Up" 1945).

4 It began in January 1946 on the Light Programme and was described as a "new magazine programme: hobbies, fashion, true stories of adventure, popular science, queer characters, sport, flying, and the men behind the movies" presented by Peter Watson ("The World and His Wife" 1946).

5 *The Robinson Family* kept its 4–4.15 p.m. slot until the end of 1947, although it was renamed *The Robinsons* in March of that year. Its main scriptwriter during 1947, Jonquil Antony, also worked on serialized adaptations of short stories and novels for *Woman's Hour* during that year, then switched to writing for *The Robinsons'* replacement, *Mrs Dale's Diary*, when it began in a 4.15 p.m. timeslot in early 1948 and, after Radio 2 replaced the Light Programme in 1967, continued until the end of 1969 (Skoog 2013).

6 If a "listening figure" of 1 represented 350 thousand listeners from this potential audience, as calculated by LRD daily surveys of "a random sample of about 3,000 adult civilians" multiplied by "available audience" (BBC Listener Research Department 1946), then against LRD reports of "the listening figure of 3 which was previously earned by light music at this time" (Collins 10/28 1946), a jump of ten points represented more than a fourfold increase in audience numbers.

7 Presumably, Shapley meant only BBC radio programs, as commercial radio did not start in the UK until the early 1970s.

Bibliography

Books and articles

Allen, D. S. and Light, J. S. (eds) (2015), *From Voice to Influence: Understanding Citizenship in a Digital Age*, Chicago: University of Chicago Press.

Andrews, K. (2016), "Don't Tell Them I Can Type: Negotiating Women's Work in Production in the Post-War ABC," *Media International Australia*, 161 (1): 28–37.

Andrews, M. (2012a), *Domesticating the Airwaves: Broadcasting, Domesticity and Femininity*, London; New York: Continuum.

Andrews, M. (2012b), "Homes Both Sides of the Microphone: The Wireless and Domestic Space in Inter-War Britain," *Women's History Review*, 21 (4): 605–621.

Andrews, M. and Lomas, J. (2017), "Home Fronts: Gender, War and Conflict," *Women's History Review*, 25 (4): 523–527.

Ariès, P. (1962), *Centuries of Childhood: A Social History of Family Life*, New York: Alfred A. Knopf.

Arrow, M. (2016), "'Everyone Needs a Holiday from Work, Why Not Mothers?': Motherhood, Feminism and Citizenship at the Australian Royal Commission on Human Relationships, 1974–1977," *Women's History Review*, 25 (2): 320–336.

Arthurs, J. (2003), "*Sex and the City* and Consumer Culture: Remediating Postfeminist Drama," *Feminist Media Studies*, 3 (1): 83–98.

Badenoch, A. (2005), "Making Sunday What It Actually Should Be: Sunday Radio Programming and the Re-Invention of Tradition in Occupied Germany 1945–1949," *Historical Journal of Film, Radio and Television*, 25 (4): 577–598.

Bailey, M. (2009), "The Angel in the Ether: Early Radio and the Constitution of the Household," in Bailey, M. (ed), *Narrating Media History*, 52–65, Abingdon: Routledge.

Baker, J. (2017), "*Woman to Woman*: Australian Feminists' Embrace of Radio Broadcasting, 1930s–1950s," *Australian Feminist Studies*, 32 (193): 292–308.

Baker, J. and Lloyd, J. (2016), "Gendered Labour and Media: Histories and Continuities," *Media International Australia*, 161 (1): 6–17.

Baldock, C. V. (1993), "In Memoriam: Irene Adelaide Greenwood, 1992," *Australian Feminist Studies*, 8 (17): 1–4.

Baudino, J. E. and Kittross, J. M. (2015), "Broadcasting's Oldest Stations: An Examination of Four Claimants," in Godfrey, D. G. and Brinson, S. L. (eds), *Routledge Reader on Electronic Media History*, 45–60, New York: Routledge.

Berlant, L. (1998), "Intimacy: A Special Issue," *Critical Inquiry*, 24 (2): 281–288.

Berlant, L. (ed) (2000), *Intimacy*, Chicago: University of Chicago Press.

Berlant, L. and Warner, M. (1998), "Sex in Public," *Critical Inquiry*, 24 (4): 547–566.

Berry, C., Harbord, J. and Moore, R. (2013), "Introduction," in Berry, C., Harbord, J. and Moore, R. (eds), *Public Space, Media Space*, 1–16, Basingstoke: Palgrave Macmillan.

Betts, P. and Crowley, D. (2005), "Introduction: Domestic Dreamworlds: Notions of Home in Post-1945 Europe," *Journal of Contemporary History*, 40 (2): 213–236.

Bien, A., W8TAY (1941), "YLRL, QRV!," *QST*, October: 32–37, 78

Bijsterveld, K. (2016), "Ethnography and Archival Research in Studying Cultures of Sound," in Papenburg, J. G. and Schulze, H. (eds), *Sound as Popular Culture: A Research Companion*, 99–109, Cambridge, MA: MIT Press.

Birdsall, C. (2012), *Nazi Soundscapes: Sound, Technology and Urban Space in Germany, 1933–1945*, Amsterdam: University of Amsterdam Press.

Blatterer, H. (2010), "Social Networking, Privacy, and the Pursuit of Visibility," in Blatterer, H., Johnson, P. and Markus, M. (eds), *Modern Privacy: Shifting Boundaries, New Forms*, 73–87, New York: Palgrave.

Boardman, A. E. and Vining, A. R. (1996), "Public Service Broadcasting in Canada," *Journal of Media Economics*, 9 (1): 47–61.

Bok, S. (1982), *Secrets: On the Ethics of Concealment and Revelation*, New York: Pantheon Books.

Boris, E. (2004), "Working in the Home: Continuing the Discussion of Women's Labors [Editorial]," *Journal of Women's History*, 16 (2): 66–67.

Briggs, A. (1979), *The History of Broadcasting in the United Kingdom: Volume IV: Sound and Vision*, Oxford: Oxford University Press.

Briggs, A. (1980), "Problems and Possibilities in the Writing of Broadcasting History," *Media, Culture and Society*, 2: 5–13.

Brown, A. (2009), "Public Service Broadcasting in Four Countries: Overview," *Journal of Media Economics*, 9 (11): 77–81.

Bruce, J. (1981–1982), "Women in CBC Radio Talks and Public Affairs," *Oral History Forum d'histoire orale*, 5 (1): 7–18.

Burke, D. (2014), *The Lawn Road Flats: Spies, Writers and Artists*, Woodbridge: Boydell Press.

Calhoun, C. (1992), "Introduction: Habermas and the Public Sphere," in Calhoun, C. (ed), *Habermas and the Public Sphere*, 1–48. Cambridge, MA: MIT Press.

Campbell, G. G. (2009), "'Are We Going to Do the Most Important Things?': Senator Muriel McQueen Fergusson, Feminist Identities, and the Royal Commission on the Status of Women," *Acadiensis*, VIII (2): n.p.

Cardiff, D. (1980), "The Serious and the Popular: Aspects of the Evolution of Style in the Radio Talk, 1928–1939," *Media, Culture and Society*, 2: 29–47.

Carmi, E. (2015), "Taming Noisy Women," *Media History*, 21 (3): 313–327.

Carter, S. (2004), "A Mic of Her Own: Stations, Collectives, and Women's Access to Radio," *Journal of Radio Studies*, 11 (2): 169–183.

Cassidy, M. F. (1998), "Sob Stories, Merriment, and Surprises: The 1950s Audience Participation Show on Network Television and Women's Daytime Reception," *The Velvet Light Trap*, 42 (Fall): 48–61.

Cassidy, M. F. (2005), *What Women Watched: Daytime Television in the 1950s*, Austin: University of Texas Press.

Clampin, D. (2017), "Building the Meaning of the Second World War on the British Home Front in Commercial Press Advertising," *Media History*, 23 (3–4): 469–488.

Cohen, R. and O'Byrne, S. (2013), "'Can You Hear Me Now … Good!': Feminism(s), the Public/Private Divide, and *Citizens United V. FEC*," *UCLA Women's Law Journal*, 20 (1): 39–70.

Coltheart, L. (2005), "Citizens of the World: Jessie Street and International Feminism," *Hecate*, 31 (1): 182–194.

Cook, H. (2004), "Sex and the Doctors: The Medicalisation of Sexuality as a Two-Way Process in Early to Mid-Twentieth Century Britain," in de Blécourt, W. and Usborne, C. (eds), *Cultural Approaches to the History of Medicine: Mediating Medicine in Early Modern and Modern Europe*, 192–211, Basingstoke: Palgrave Macmillan.

Cooke, N. (2003), "Getting the Mix Just Right for the Canadian Home Baker", *Essays On Canadian Writing*, 78: 192–219.

Craig, D. B. (2000), *Fireside Politics: Radio and Political Culture in the United States, 1920–1940*, Baltimore: Johns Hopkins University Press.

Crean, S. M. (1985), *Newsworthy: The Lives of Media Women*, Toronto: Stoddart.

Crean, S. M. (1987), "Women in Broadcast Management: A Case-Study of the Canadian Broadcasting Corporation's Programme of Equal Opportunity," in *Women and Media Decision-Making: The Invisible Barriers*, 95–118. Paris: UNESCO.

Curran, J. (2002), "Media and the Making of British Society, c. 1700–2000," *Media History*, 8 (2): 135–154.

Dahl, H. F. (1994), "The Pursuit of Media History," *Media, Culture and Society*, 16 (4): 551–563.

Davidoff, L., L'Esperance, J. and Newby, H. (1995), "Landscape with Figures: Home and Community in English Society," in Davidoff, L. (ed), *Worlds Between: Historical Perspectives on Gender and Class*, 41–72, New York: Routledge.

Davidson, R. (2006), "The *Homemaker's Program*," in *9XM Talking: WHA Radio and the Wisconsin Idea*, 251–258, Madison: University of Wisconsin Press & Terrace Books.

Dawes, S. (2017), *British Broadcasting and the Public-Private Dichotomy: Neoliberalism, Citizenship and the Public Sphere*, Cham: Palgrave Macmillan.

DiCenzo, M. (2004), "Feminist Media and History: A Response to James Curran," *Media History*, 10 (1): 43–49.

DiCenzo, M., Delap, L. and Ryan, L. (2011), *Feminist Media History: Suffrage, Periodicals and the Public Sphere*, Basingstoke: Macmillan.

Duffy, B. E. (2013), "Making the Magazine: Three Hundred Years in Print," in *Remake, Remodel: Women's Magazines in the Digital Age*, 21–36, Champaign: University of Illinois Press.

Eckert, S. and Steiner, L. (2016), "Feminist Uses of Social Media: Facebook, Twitter, Tumblr, Pinterest, and Instagram," in Novak, A. and El-Burki, I. J. (eds), *Defining Identity and the Changing Scope of Culture in the Digital Age*, 255–277, Hershey, PA: Information Science Reference.

Ehrick, C. (2016), *Radio and the Gendered Soundscape: Women and Broadcasting in Argentina and Uruguay, 1930–1960*, New York: Cambridge University Press.

Elmes, S. (2008), "10.00am: Progress and Protest: *Woman's Hour* and Change," in *And Now on Radio 4: A Celebration of the World's Best Radio Station*, 90–116, London: Arrow.

Elshtain, J. B. (1981), *Public Man, Private Woman: Women in Social and Political Thought*, Oxford: Robertson.

Feldman, S. (2000), "Twin Peaks: The Staying Power of BBC Radio 4's *Woman's Hour*," in Mitchell, C. (ed), *Women and Radio: Airing Differences*, 64–72, London: Routledge.

Feldman, S. (2007), "Desperate Housewives: 60 Years of BBC Radio's *Woman's Hour*," *Feminist Media Studies*, 7 (3): 338–341.

Fell, E. and Wenzel, C. (1995), *The Coming Out Show: Twenty Years of Feminist ABC Radio*, Sydney: ABC Books.

Firth, A. (2004), "The Breadwinner, His Wife and Their Welfare: Identity, Expertise and Economic Security in Australian Post-War Reconstruction," *Australian Journal of Politics and History*, 50 (4): 491–508.

Fisher, C. (2018), "World Citizens: Australian Women's Internationalist Broadcasts, 1930–1939," *Women's History Review*, In Press: 1–19.

Forster, L. (2015), "'Make the Women Feel That They Are Important': Developing the Radio Magazine," in *Magazine Movements: Women's Culture, Feminisms and Media Form*, 185–211, New York: Bloomsbury Academic.

Foucault, M. (1980), "The Eye of Power," in Gordon, C. (ed), *Power/Knowledge*, 146–165, New York: Pantheon Books.

Fraser, N. (1989), *Unruly Practices: Power, Discourse and Gender in Contemporary Social Theory*, Minneapolis: University of Minnesota Press.

Fraser, N. (1990), "Rethinking the Public Sphere: A Contribution to the Critique of Actually Existing Democracy," *Social Text*, (25/26): 56–80.

Freeman, B. (2001), *The Satellite Sex: The Media and Women's Issues in English Canada, 1966–1971*, Waterloo, ON: Wilfrid Laurier University Press.

Freeman, B. (2011), "'We Were Only Women': Elizabeth Long, Equality Feminism and CBC Radio, 1938–1956," in *Beyond Bylines: Media Workers and Women's Rights in Canada*, 93–121, 249–266, Waterloo, ON: Wilfrid Laurier University Press.

Friedman, B., Kitch, C., Lueck, T., et al. (2009), "Stirred, Not Yet Shaken: Integrating Women's History into Media History," *American Journalism*, 26 (Winter): 160–174.

Gabb, J. (2008), "Conceptualisations of Intimacy," in *Researching Intimacy in Families*, 64–98, Houndmills: Palgrave Macmillan.

Ganzert, C. F. (2003), "All-Women's Radio: WHER-AM in Memphis," *Journal of Radio Studies*, 10 (1): 80–92.

Gomery, D. (1991), "Methods for the Study of the History of Broadcasting and Mass Communication," *Film and History*, XXI (2 & 3): 55–63.

Goodman, D. (2007), "Programming in the Public Interest: America's Town Meeting of the Air," in Hilmes, M. (ed), *NBC: America's Network*, 44–60, Berkeley: University of California Press.

Grayzel, S. R. (1999), "Nostalgia, Gender, and the Countryside: Placing the 'Land Girl' in First World War Britain," *Rural History*, 10 (2): 155–170.

Grimshaw, P. (2017), "Transnationalism and the Writing of Australian Women's History," in Rees, A., Clark, A. and Simmonds, A. (eds), *Transnationalism, Nationalism and Australian History*, 69–85, London: Palgrave.

Habermas, J. (1989), *The Structural Transformation of the Public Sphere: An Inquiry into a Category of Bourgeois Society*, Cambridge, MA: MIT Press.

Haring, K. (2003), "The 'Freer Men' of Ham Radio: How a Technical Hobby Provided Social and Spatial Distance," *Technology and Culture*, 44 (4): 734–761.

Haring, K. (2008), *Ham Radio's Technical Culture*, Cambridge, MA: MIT Press.

Hayes, J. E. (2012), "White Noise: Performing the White, Middle-Class Family on 1930s Radio," *Cinema Journal*, 51 (3): 97–118.

Henderson, M. (2006), "The Coming Out Show: Sounding Out the Second and Third Waves," in *Marking Feminist Times: Remembering the Longest Revolution in Australia*, 167–201, Bern: Peter Lang.

Hendy, D. (2007), *Life on Air: A History of Radio Four*, Oxford: Oxford University Press.

Hendy, D. (2012), "Biography and the Emotions as a Missing 'Narrative' in Media History: A Case Study of Lance Sieveking and the Early BBC," *Media History*, 18 (3–4): 361–378.

Hensley, M. A. (2006), "Feminine Virtue and Feminist Fervor: The Impact of the Women's International League for Peace and Freedom in the 1930s," *Affilia: Journal of Women and Social Work*, 21 (2): 146–157.

Higgins, T. E. (1999–2000), "Reviving the Public/Private Distinction in Feminist Theorizing," *Chicago-Kent Law Review*, 75 (3): 847–867.

Hilliard, M. (1957), *A Woman Doctor Looks at Love and Life*, New York: Doubleday.

Hilmes, M. (1997), *Radio Voices: American Broadcasting, 1922–1952*, Minneapolis: University of Minnesota Press.

Hilmes, M. (1999), "Desired and Feared: Women's Voices in Radio History," in Haralovich, M. B. and Rabinowitz, L. (eds), *Television, History, and American Culture: Feminist Critical Essays*, 17–35, Durham, NC: Duke University Press.

Hilmes, M. (2006), "*Front Line Family*: 'Women's Culture' Comes to the BBC," *Media, Culture and Society*, 29 (1): 5–29.

Hilmes, M. (2013), "On a Screen near You: The New Soundwork Industry," *Cinema Journal*, 52 (3): 177–182.

Horne, C. (2017), "Broadcasting the Woman Citizen: Dame Enid Lyons' Macquarie Network Talks", *Lilith: A Feminist History Journal*, 23: 34–46.

Illouz, E. (2007), *Cold Intimacies: The Making of Emotional Capitalism*, Malden, MA: Polity.

Inglis, K. (1983), *This is the ABC: The Australian Broadcasting Commission, 1932–1983*, Carlton, VIC: Melbourne University Press.

Inglis, K. (2006), *Whose ABC?: The Australian Broadcasting Corporation, 1983–2006*, Melbourne: Black Inc.

Jamieson, L. (1998), *Intimacy: Personal Relationships in Modern Societies*, Malden, MA: Polity.

Johnson, L. (1981), "Radio and Everyday Life: The Early Years of Broadcasting in Australia, 1922–1945," *Media, Culture and Society*, 3 (2): 167–178.

Johnson, L. (1983), "The Intimate Voice of Australian Radio," *Historical Journal of Film, Radio and Television*, 3 (1): 43–50.

Johnson, L. (1988), *The Unseen Voice: A Cultural Study of Early Australian Radio*, London: Routledge.

Johnson, L. and Lloyd, J. (2004), "Boredom: The Emotional Slum," in *Sentenced to Everyday Life: Feminism and the Housewife*, Oxford: Berg.

Johnson, P. (2010), "Images of Intimacy in Feminist Discussions over Private/Public Boundaries," in Blatterer, H., Johnson, P. and Markus, M. (eds), *Modern Privacy: Shifting Boundaries, New Forms*, 39–58, New York: Palgrave.

Johnson, R. (1986), "What Is Cultural Studies Anyway?," *Social Text*, 16 (Winter): 38–80.

Karpf, A. (1980), "Women and Radio," *Women's Studies International Quarterly*, 3 (1): 41–54.

Karpf, A. (1987), "Radio Times: Private Women and Public Men," in Davies, K., Dickey, J. and Stratford, T. (eds), *Out of Focus: Writings on Women and the Media*, 168–175, London: Women's Press.

Karpf, A. (2014), "Constructing and Addressing the 'Ordinary Devoted Mother,'" *History Workshop Journal*, 78 (Autumn): 82–106.

Keating, J. (2018), "Piecing Together Suffrage Internationalism: Place, Space, and Connected Histories of Australasian Women's Activism," *History Compass*, 16 (8): 1–15.

Keohane, J. (2018), *Communist Rhetoric and Feminist Voices in Cold War America*, Lanham: Lexington.

Klare, K. E. (1982), "The Public/Private Distinction in Labor Law," *University of Pennsylvania Law Review*, 130: 1358–1422.

Knowles, W. and Evans, K. (eds) (1981), *The Woman's Hour Book*, London: Sidgwick & Jackson with the British Broadcasting Corporation.

Lacey, K. (1994), "From *Plauderei* to Propaganda: On Women's Radio in Germany, 1924–1935," in Mitchell, C. (ed), *Women and Radio: Airing Differences*, 48–63, London: Routledge.

Lacey, K. (1996), *Feminine Frequencies: Gender, German Radio, and the Public Sphere, 1923–1945*, Ann Arbor: University of Michigan Press.

Lake, M. (1990), "Female Desires: The Meaning of World War II," *Australian Historical Studies*, 24 (195): 267–284.

Landes, J. B. (1984), "Women and the Public Sphere: A Modern Perspective," *Social Analysis: The International Journal of Social and Cultural Practice*, 15: 20–31.

Landes, J. B. (1995), "The Public and the Private Sphere: A Feminist Reconsideration," in Meehan, J. (ed), *Feminists Read Habermas: Gendering the Subject of Discourse*, 91–116, New York: Routledge.

Lang, M. L. (1999), *Women Who Made the News: Female Journalists in Canada, 1880–1945*, Montreal: McGill-Queen's University Press.

Leman, J. (1980), "'The Advice of a Real Friend': Codes of Intimacy and Oppression in Women's Magazines 1937–1955," *Women's Studies International Quarterly*, 3 (1): 63–78.

Leman, J. (1996), "'Pulling Our Weight in the Call-up of Women': Class and Gender in British Radio in the Second World War," in Gledhill, C. and Swanson, G. (eds), *Nationalising Femininity: Sexuality and Cinema in World War Two Britain*, 109–118, Manchester: Manchester University Press.

Lewis, J. (1979), *On Air: The Story of Catherine King and the ABC Women's Session*, Fremantle: Fremantle Arts Centre Press.

Lloyd, J. (2004), "Gendering Radio Research: The Circuit of Everyday Culture," ANZCA Conference, Sydney: Australia and New Zealand Communications Association: 1–11. Available online: https://www.anzca.net/documents/2004-conf-papers/292-gendering-radio-research-the-circuit-of-everyday-audio-1/file.html.

Lloyd, J. (2014), "Domestic Destinies: Colonial Spatialities, Australian Film and Feminist Cultural Memory Work," *Gender, Place & Culture: A Journal of Feminist Geography*, 4 (1): 1045–1061.

Loviglio, J. (2005), *Radio's Intimate Public: Network Broadcasting and Mass-Mediated Democracy*, Minneapolis: University of Minnesota Press.

MacLennan, A. F. (2008), "Women, Radio Broadcasting and the Depression: A 'Captive' Audience from Household Hints to Story Time and Serials," *Women's Studies*, 37 (6): 616–633.

MacLennan, A. F. (2013), "Learning to Listen: Becoming a Canadian Radio Audience in the 1930s," *Journal of Radio & Audio Media*, 20 (2): 311–326.

Marquis, A. G. (1984), "Written on the Wind: The Impact of Radio during the 1930s," *Journal of Contemporary History*, 19 (3): 385–415.

Mattelart, M. (1986), "Women and the Cultural Industries," in Collins, R. E., Curran, J., Garnham, N., et al. (eds), *Media, Culture and Society: A Critical Reader*, 63–81, London: SAGE.

Matthews, N. (2007), "Confessions to a New Public: Video Nation Shorts," *Media, Culture and Society*, 29 (3): 435–448.

McLaughlin, L. (1993), "Feminism, the Public Sphere, Media and Democracy," *Media, Culture & Society*, 15: 599–620.

McLaughlin, L. (2004), "Feminism and the Political Economy of Transnational Public Space," *Sociological Review*, 52 (1): 156–175.

McLean, J. and Maalsen, S. (2013), "Destroying the Joint and Dying of Shame? A Geography of Revitalised Feminism in Social Media and Beyond," *Geographical Research*, 51 (3): 243–256.

Mendes, K. (2010), "Reading *Chatelaine*: Dr Marion Hilliard and 1950s Women's Health Advice," *Canadian Journal of Communication*, 354 (4): 515–531.

Miller, P. and Rose, N. (1988), "The Tavistock Programme: The Government of Subjectivity and Social Life," *Sociology*, 22 (2): 171–192.

Minic, D. (2008), "What Makes an Issue a *Woman's Hour* Issue?" *Feminist Media Studies*, 8 (3): 301–315.

Mislán, C. (2017), "Claudia Jones Speaks to 'Half the World': Gendering Cold War Politics in the *Daily Worker*, 1950–1953," *Feminist Media Studies*, 17 (2): 281–296.

Moores, S. (1988), "'The Box on the Dresser': Memories of Early Radio and Everyday Life," *Media, Culture and Society*, 10 (1): 23–40.

Moseley, R. and Wheatley, H. (2008), "Is Archiving a Feminist Issue? Historical Research and the Past, Present and Future of Television Studies," *Cinema Journal*, 47 (3): 152–158.

Murphy, K. (2014), "From *Women's Hour* to *Other Women's Lives*: BBC Talks for Women and the Women Who Made Them, 1923–1939," in Andrews, M. and McNamara, S. (eds), *Women and the Media: Feminism and Femininity in Britain, 1900 to the Present*, 31–46, London: Routledge.

Murphy, K. (2016), "'When They Have Their Cup of Tea': Making Programmes for Women," in *Behind the Wireless: A History of Early Women at the BBC*, 189–219, Basingstoke: Palgrave.

Murray, J. (1996), *The Woman's Hour: 50 Years of Women in Britain*, London: BBC Books.

Murray, J. (2006), *Woman's Hour: From Joyce Grenfell to Sharon Osbourne: Celebrating Sixty Years of Women's Lives*, London: John Murray.

Murray, K. (2005), *Voice for Peace: The Spirit of Social Activist Irene Greenwood, 1898–1992*, Bayswater: Kaye Murray Productions.

Nicholas, S. (1996), *The Echo of War: Home Front Propaganda and the Wartime BBC, 1939–45*, Manchester: Manchester University Press.

Oliver, B. and Latter, W. S. (1996), "Spooks, Spies and Subversives! The Wartime Security Service," in Gregory, J. A. (ed), *On the Homefront: Western Australia and World War II*, 176–185, Nedlands, WA: University of Western Australia.

Pain, R. (2015), "Intimate War," *Political Geography*, 44: 64–73.

Pain, R. and Staeheli, L. (2014), "Introduction: Intimacy-Geopolitics and Violence," *Area*, 46 (4): 344–360.

Parkinson, A. M. (2017), "A Sentimental Reeducation: Postwar West Germany's Intimate Geographies," *Emotion, Space and Society*, 25: 95–102.

Pateman, C. (1983), "Feminist Critiques of the Public/Private Dichotomy," in Benn, S. I. and Gaus, G. F. (eds), *Public and Private in Social Life*, 281–303, London: Croom Helm.

Pearce, S. (1995), "*Speaking Personally* and Propaganda: Elizabeth Webb's Wartime Journalism," *Imago*, 7 (2): 47–53.

Plummer, K. (2001), "The Square of Intimate Citizenship: Some Preliminary Proposals," *Citizenship Studies*, 5 (3): 237–253.

Plummer, K. (2003), *Intimate Citizenship: Private Decision and Public Dialogues*, 3–16, Seattle: University of Washington Press.

Potter, S. J. (2012), *Broadcasting Empire: The BBC and the British World, 1922–1970*, Oxford: Oxford University Press.

Povinelli, E. (2006), *The Empire of Love: Toward a Theory of Intimacy, Genealogy, and Carnality*, Durham, NC: Duke University Press.

Pratt, G. and Rosner, V. (2006), "The Global and the Intimate," *Women's Studies Quarterly*, 34 (1/2): 13–24.

Rakow, L. F. (2008), "Feminist Historiography and the Field: Writing New Histories," in Park, D. W. and Pooley, J. (eds), *The History of Media and Communication Research: Contested Memories*, 113–139, New York: Peter Lang.

Razack, S. H. (2018), "A Site/Sight We Cannot Bear: The Racial/Spatial Politics of Banning the Muslim Woman's Niqab", *Canadian Journal of Women and the Law*, 30 (1): 169–189.

Razlogova, E. (2006), "True Crime Radio and Listener Disenchantment with Network Broadcasting, 1935–1946," *American Quarterly*, 58 (1): 137–158.

Razlogova, E. (2011), *The Listener's Voice: Early Radio and the American Public*, Philadelphia: University of Pennsylvania Press.

Reekie, G. (1985), "War, Sexuality and Feminism: Perth Women's Organisations, 1938–1945," *Historical Studies*, 21 (85): 576–591.

Richardson, J. (1989), "New and Strange Ways: The Radio Broadcasts of Irene Greenwood," *Continuum*, 2 (2): 50–76.

Riley, D. (1979), "War in the Nursery," *Feminist Review*, 2 (1): 82–108.

Robertson, E. (2013), "It is a Real Joy to Get Listening of Any Kind from the Homeland: BBC Radio and Empire Audiences in the 1930s," in Gillespie, M. and Webb, A. (eds), *Diasporas and Diplomacy: Cosmopolitan Contact Zones at the BBC World Service (1932–2012)*, 23–39, London and New York: Routledge.

Rooks, N. M. (2004), *Ladies' Pages: African American Women's Magazines and the Culture That Made Them*, New Brunswick: Rutgers University Press.

Rooney, E. (2002), "A Semiprivate Room," *differences: A Journal of Feminist Cultural Studies*, 13 (1): 128–156.

Rooney, E. (2004), "A Semiprivate Room," in Scott, J. W. and Keates, D. (eds), *Going Public: Feminism and the Shifting Boundaries of the Private Sphere*, 333–358, Urbana and Champaign: University of Illinois Press.

Scales, R. P. (2010), "Subversive Sound: Transnational Radio, Arabic Recordings, and the Dangers of Listening in French Colonial Algeria, 1934–1939," *Comparative Studies in Society and History*, 52 (2): 384–417.

Scales, R. P. (2016), *Radio and the Politics of Sound in Interwar France, 1921–1939*, Cambridge, UK: Cambridge University Press.

Scannell, P. (1979), "The Social Eye of Television, 1946–1955," *Media, Culture and Society*, 1 (1): 97–106.

Scannell, P. (1980), "Broadcasting and the Politics of Unemployment, 1930–1935," *Media, Culture and Society*, 2: 15–28.

Scannell, P. (1989), "Public Service Broadcasting and Modern Public Life," *Media, Culture and Society*, 11: 135–166.

Scannell, P. (1990), "Public Service Broadcasting: The History of a Concept," in Goodwin, A. and Whannel, G. (eds), *Understanding Television*, 11–29, London: Routledge.

Scannell, P. (1995), "For a Phenomenology of Radio and Television," *Journal of Communication*, 45 (3): 4–19.

Scannell, P. (1996), *Radio, Television and Modern Life: A Phenomenological Approach*, Oxford: Blackwell.

Scannell, P. and Cardiff, D. (1991), *A Social History of British Broadcasting: Serving the Nation, 1922–1939*, Cambridge: Basil Blackwell.

Shapira, M. (2013), *The War Inside: Psychoanalysis, Total War, and the Making of the Democratic Self in Postwar Britain*, Cambridge: Cambridge University Press.

Shapley, O. (2000), "Broadcasting a Life," in Mitchell, C. (ed), *Women and Radio: Airing Differences*, 29–40, London: Routledge.

Shapley, O. and Hart, C. (1996), *Broadcasting a Life: The Autobiography of Olive Shapley*, London: Scarlet.

Skoog, K. (2009), "Focus on the Housewife: The BBC and the Post-War Woman, 1945–1955," *Networking Knowledge: Journal of the MeCCSA Post Graduate Network*, 2 (1): 1–12.

Skoog, K. (2011), "Editorial," *Westminster Papers in Communication and Culture*, 8 (3): 1–9.

Skoog, K. (2013), "'They're "Doped" by That Dale Diary': Women's Serial Drama, the BBC and British Post-War Change," in Thornham, H. and Weissman, E. (eds), *Renewing Feminisms: Radical Narratives, Fantasies and Futures in Media Studies*, 124–139. London: I.B. Tauris.

Skoog, K. (2014), "Striving for Editorial Autonomy and Internal Recognition," in Andrews, M. and McNamara, S. (eds), *Women and the Media: Feminism and Femininity in Britain, 1900 to the Present*, 99–112, London: Routledge.

Skoog, K. (2017), "Neither Worker nor Housewife but Citizen: BBC's *Woman's Hour* 1946–1955," *Women's History Review*, 26 (6): 953–974.

Skoog, K. and Badenoch, A. (2016), "Networking Women: The International Association of Women in Radio and Television (IAWRT)," in Medhurst, J., Nicholas, S. and O'Malley, T. (eds), *Broadcasting in the UK and US in the 1950s: Historical Perspectives*, 189–217, Newcastle upon Tyne: Cambridge Scholars Publishing.

Slotten, H. R. (2009), "University Stations, Extension Ideals and Broadcast Practices," in *Radio's Hidden Voice: The Origins of Public Broadcasting in the United States*, 40–78, Urbana: University of Illinois Press.

Smulyan, S. (1993), "Radio Advertising to Women in Twenties America: 'A Latchkey to Every Home'," *Historical Journal of Film, Radio and Television*, 13 (3): 299–314.

Spigel, L. (2013), "Postfeminist Nostalgia for a Prefeminist Future," *Screen*, 54 (2): 270–278.

Steiner, L. (1995), "Would the Real Women's Magazine Please Stand Up … For Women," in Lont, C. M. (ed), *Women and Media: Content, Careers and Criticism*, 99–108, New York: Wadsworth.

Stewart, K. (2003), "The Perfectly Ordinary Life," *The Scholar and the Feminist Online*, 2 (1): 1–11.

Thompson, J. B. (1995), *The Media and Modernity: A Social Theory of the Media*, Cambridge: Polity.

Thomson, M. (2013), "Bowlbyism and the Post-War Settlement," in *Lost Freedom: The Landscape of the Child and the British Post-War Settlement*, 79–104, Oxford: Oxford University Press.

Tinkler, P. and Krasnick Warsh, C. (2008), "Feminine Modernity in Interwar Britain and North America: Corsets, Cars and Cigarettes," *Journal of Women's History*, 20 (3): 113–143.

Valliant, D. W. (2002), "'Your Voice Came in Last Night … But I Thought It Sounded a Little Scared': Rural Radio Listening and 'Talking Back' during the Progressive Era in Wisconsin, 1920–1932," in Hilmes, M. and Loviglio, J. (eds), *Radio Reader: Essays in the Cultural History of Radio*, 63–88, New York: Routledge.

Valliant, D. W. (2013), "Techno-Aesthetic Paradigms in U.S.—French International Broadcasting, 1925–1942," *Technology and Culture*, 54 (4): 888–921.

Veerkamp, H. (2014), "Feminist Frequencies: Why Radio Needs Feminism," *Journal of Radio & Audio Media*, 21 (2): 307–315.

Vipond, M. (1997), "'Please Stand by for That Report': The Historiography of Early Canadian Radio," *Frequency*, 7–8 (Special Issue on Broadcasting's 75th Anniversary): 13–32.

Vipond, M. (2006), "The Canadian Radio Broadcasting Commission in the 1930s: How Canada's First Public Broadcaster Negotiated 'Britishness'," in Buckner, P. and Francis, R. D. (eds), *Canada and the British World: Culture, Migration, and Identity*, 270–287, Vancouver: University of British Columbia Press.

Wang, J. H. (2002), "'The Case of the Radio-Active Housewife': Relocating Radio in the Age of Television," in Hilmes, M. and Loviglio, J. (eds), *Radio Reader: Essays in the Cultural History of Radio*, 343–366, New York: Routledge.

Wang, J. H. (2018), "Producing a Radio Housewife: *Clara, Lu 'N' Em*, Gendered Labor, and the Early Days of Radio," *Feminist Media Histories*, 4 (1): 58–83.

Weir, A. (2013), "Home and Identity: In Memory of Iris Marion Young," in *Identities and Freedom: Feminist Theory between Power and Connection*, 1–22, New York: Oxford University Press.

Wijfjes, H. (2015), "Spellbinding and Crooning: Sound Amplification, Radio, and Political Rhetoric in International Comparative Perspective, 1900–1945," *Technology and Culture*, 55 (1): 148–185.

Wood, H. (2015), "Television—the Housewife's Choice? The 1949 Mass Observation Television Directive, Reluctance and Revision," *Media History*, 21 (3): 342–359.

Zankowicz, K. (2015), "'How to Keep a Husband on Packaged Foods' and Other Lessons: Gendered Education in the Canadian National Exhibition's Women's Division during the Kate Aitken Era, 1920s–1950s," *CuiZine: The Journal of Canadian Food Cultures/Revue des cultures culinaires au Canada*, 6 (2): n.p.

Magazine and newspaper articles

"[Advertisement] Stand up—Be Counted, Hyde Park, April 7" (1974), *Tharunka*. 9.

"[Krazy Capitalism]: Simple" (1954), *Tribune*, 09/15: 8.

"6KY Soon on the Air" (1941), *Mirror*, 20/18: 3.

"6WF" (1936), *Daily News*, 07/30: 12.

"A New Hour Strikes" (1973), *Radio Times*, 06/28 (2590): 6–7.

"ABC Features: *Impact* Will Delve into Personalities" (1964), *Canberra Times*, 08/20: 23.

"ABC: Four Vacancies at Sydney Head-Quarters, to Work in Radio and TV" (1961), *Commonwealth of Australia Gazette*, 01/19 (4): 212–213.

"Advance Programs for the Week" (1925), *Radio Digest*, 10/24 (3): 14.

"An Interesting Week for Women Listeners" (1940), *CBC Program Schedule*, 04/18: 10.

"Announcers at 6KY" (1941), *Westralian Worker*, 20/24: 10.

"BBC *Woman's Hour* Seeks a New Image" (1971), *Birmingham Daily Post*, 20/08: 9.

"Bright and Breezy" (1943), *CBC Program Schedule*, 02/19: 12.

"Broadcasting Programmes" (1933), *The Telegraph*, 04/07: 26.

"Broadcasting Stations: 'A' Class Stations" (1932), *The Argus*, 1/28: 16.

"Broadcasting Today" (1929), *The Labor Daily*, 08/05: 6.

"Broadcasting: Cross Section of Life" (1940), *Sydney Morning Herald*, 01/03: 6.

"Broadcasting: Programmes for to-Day" (1934), *Daily Advertiser*, 08/02: 4.

"Broadcasting: To-Day's Items of Interest" (1940), *The Age*, 1/07: 12.

"Broadcasting: Today's Programmes" (1932), *Examiner*, 07/06: 12.

"Built by Amateur Radio Operator" (1940), *Chicago Tribune*, 04/28: 33.

"CBC Talks for Women" (1942), *CBC Program Schedule*, 11/01.

"Claire Wallace in New Series" (1947), *CBC News Features*, 08/17: 1.

"Countrywomen's Interests: Women Must Contribute to Local Government" (1947), *Farmer and Settler*, 07/11: 18.

"Diary: Sick of Sex: Rewind Productions Competes with the BBC" (1993), *The Times*, 02/9: T.

"Editorial: Women's ABC Today but When Will It Be Your ABC?" (2017), *The Australian*, 03/08: 13.

"Elizabeth Webb" (1940), *Kilmore Free Press*, 20/24: 8.

"Families of Four Urged by Doctor" (1954), *Sydney Morning Herald*, 09/07: 5.

"First Silver Trophy Goes to Alice Bourke, W9DXX, Chicago Ill. For Best Ham Station Photo of the Month" (1938), *Short Wave and Television*, IX (3): 143, 182.

"Flair for Colour and Design" (1943), *Barrier Daily Truth*, 01/20: 4.

"'For You, Madame' ..." (1935), *CRBC Radio News Service*, 10/14: 1.

"Girls Take Camera Caravan to Record Life in the Country" (1949), *The Sun*, 09/21: 23.

"Health Hints for Harassed Housewives" (1954), *The Age*, 02/15: 9.

"Highlights of the ABC: Morning Women's Session" (1940), *Dubbo Liberal and Macquarie Advocate*, 08/08: 5.

"Home for the Day: 29 March" (1953), *Radio Times*, 03/27 (1533): 11.

"The Homosexual Condition" (1957), *Radio Times*, 07/25 (1758): 42.

"Housekeeping Plus: Mrs Rotenberg's Multi-Sided Career" (1950), *CBC Times*, 01/15: 4.

"How a YL Police Reporter Works: The Story of W9DXX—Mrs Alice R. Bourke" (1934), *Radio*, 16 (12): 12–13.

"Interest in Debates on Air Assessed" (1948), *The Mercury*, 01/21: 4.

"International Affairs and Women" (1938), *Daily News*, 10/20: 11.

"Janet Quigley [Obituary]" (1987), *The Stage*, 03/26: 23.

"Kate Aitken Begins New Radio Season" (1949), *CBC Times*, 09/11: 10.

"Kate Aitken" (1954), *CBC Times*, 09/12: 9.

"Listening In" (1934), *Shepparton Advertiser*, 06/07: 4.

"Monica Misses Her Cue" (1942), *CBC Program Schedule*, 03/02: 14.

"New ABC Session: Many Interests Covered" (1944), *West Australian*, 08/30: 3.

"New CBC Talk Series Listed for Women" (1940), *CBC Program Schedule*, 01/09: 7.

"New 'Disk-Jockey' Is Joan Fowler" (1947), *CBC News Features*, 08/03: 1.

"Ordinary Men and Women (910 of You) Honoured: Talks Expert" (1944), *Daily Mirror*, 01/04: 5.

"Ottawa Woman to Talk in Daily Commentary" (1947), *CBC News Features*, 03/02: 1.

"Personality of the Week in Radio" (1947), *CBC News Features*, 01/26: 1.

"Personality of the Week in Radio—Elizabeth Long, CBC Women's Interests" (1947), *CBC News Features*, 11/16: 1.

"Police Raid Communists" (1940), *The Clarion*, May 31: 1.

"Popular" (1942), *CBC Program Schedule*, 06/21: 4.

"'Mr Prime Minister' New Women's Series [*Our Country Women*]" (1950), *CBC Times*, 01/01: 11.

"Radio Broadcasting Stations" (1923), *Radio Digest*, 11/10 (5): 23.

"Radio Items: Women's Session Diary" (1955), *Northern Standard*, 01/06: 6.

"Radio Session Had 14,000 Members" (1953), *News*, 04/22: 20.

"Save Your Husband's Life—with a Salad" (1958), *ABC Weekly*, 04/30: 5.

"School-Bell Sounds for Would-Be Cooks" (1949), *CBC Times*, 03/06: 12.

"Short Waves" (1950), *Truth*, 03/26: 30.

"Speaks Wednesday" (1947), *CBC News Features*, 05/04: 1.

"Stars of the Air: Claire Mitchell to Conduct New National Women's Session" (1946), *Pittsworth Sentinel*, 10/18: 1.

"This Week's Wireless Programmes" (1929), *Weekly Times*, 08/03: 12.

"Turn on the Wireless: Lorna Byrne to Country Women" (1939), *Daily Examiner*, 05/26: 9.

"Woman Broadcaster Leaves A.B.C. after Clash" (1948), *Daily Telegraph*, 01/04: 5.

"*Woman's Hour* Editor: Miss Janet Quigley Returns to BBC" (1950), *Belfast News-Letter*, 04/25: 4.

"*Woman's Hour*: 7 October" (1946), *Radio Times*, 10/04 (1201): 7.

"*Woman's Hour*: 8 October" (1946), *Radio Times*, 10/04 (1201): 11.

"*Woman's Hour*: 6 December" (1946), *Radio Times*, 11/29 (1209): 27.

"*Woman's Hour*: 1 January [1947]" (1946), *Radio Times*, 12/27 (1213): 19.

"*Woman's Hour*: 6 June" (1947), *Radio Times*, 05/30 (1233): 23.

"*Woman's Hour*: 29 September" (1947), *Radio Times*, 09/26 (1250): 13.

"*Woman's Hour*: 7 October" (1947), *Radio Times*, 10/03 (1251): 15.

"*Woman's Hour*: 10 October" (1947), *Radio Times*, 10/03 (1251): 27.

"*Woman's Hour*: 17 October" (1947), *Radio Times*, 10/10 (1252): 23.

"*Woman's Hour*: 24 October" (1947), *Radio Times*, 10/17 (1253): 23.

"*Woman's Hour*: 28 October" (1947), *Radio Times*, 10/24 (1254): 11.

"*Woman's Hour*: 31 October" (1947), *Radio Times*, 10/24 (1254): 23.

"*Woman's Hour*: 28 November" (1947), *Radio Times*, 11/21 (1258): 23.

"*Woman's Hour*: 12 December" (1947), *Radio Times*, 12/05 (1260): 23.

"*Woman's Hour*: 9 January" (1948), *Radio Times*, 01/02 (1264): 19.

"*Woman's Hour*: 27 February" (1948), *Radio Times*, 02/20 (1271): 19.

"*Woman's Hour*: 17 August" (1949), *Radio Times*, 08/12 (1348): 21.

"Woman's Place Is the World!" (1939), *The Workers' Star*, 03/17: 4.

"Women Broadcasters" (1940), *West Australian*, 11/01: 6.

"Women Discuss Growing Up" (1948), *CBC News Features*, 06/04: 1.

"Women Seek Time on Air" (1944), *Examiner*, 04/28: 4.

"Women Workers" (1942), *CBC Program Schedule*, 09/25: 13.

"Women's Affairs" (1942), *CRBC Radio News Service?*, 11/01: 16.

"Women's Hour" (1923), *Radio Times*, 10/01: 1.

"Women's Interests on the Air: Hebrides Flying Doctor" (1953), 06/18: 5.

"Women's Interests of the Air: Housewives Are Now Labelled Psychosomatic" (1954), *Sydney Morning Herald*, 12/02: 9.

"Women's News and Gossip: New Guinea Women 'Alert' Says Broadcaster" (1954), *The Sun*, 11/17: 43.

"Women's Programs to Feature Kate Aiken [Sic]" (1948), *CBC Times*, 09/12: 11.

"Your Radio" (1939), *The Daily News [Perth, WA]*, 11/11: 22.

A Psychiatrist (1947), "Another Thought from '*Woman's Hour*;" *The Listener (London, England)*, 01/30 (1942): 188.

Abbott, K. (1970), "Politics and Education [Letter to the Editor]," *Canberra Times*, 09/22: 2.

Alpen, A. (1939), "Europe through Australian Eyes," *Daily Advertiser (Wagga Wagga, NSW)*, 12/27: 5.

Bevege, L. (2013), "Feminists and Freedom," *IPA Review*, (1): 16–21.

Bourke, A. R. (1922), "O Woe! Radio," *Radio Broadcast*, (1): 107–110.

Brown, M. (1991), "BBC Loses Radio Listeners to Commercial Stations," *The Independent*, 20/10: 5.

Brown, M. (1996), "Media: Niche Radio Needs to Follow the BBC's Fab Five Example," *PR Week*, 005/10: 6.

Bruce, M. G. (1940), "Tuning In," *ABC Weekly*, 10/12: 48.

Carroll, D. (2011), "Still Going Places," *The Australian*, 06/17: 28.

Chamberlain, F. (1943), "So Nobody Listens to Canadian Radio," *CBC Program Schedule*, 03/14: 17–18.

Commonwealth Bureau of Census and Statistics (1924), "Chapter XIII: Labour, Wages and Prices," *1301.0—Year Book Australia, No. 17*, Melbourne: Government Printer.

Culf, A. (1995), "Women's Radio 'Men-Friendly'," *The Guardian*, 05/05: 8.

Daly, E. (1996), "*Woman's Hour* Will Be 50 Tomorrow, and Really Doesn't Mind Who Knows It," *The Independent on Sunday*, 20/06: 7.

Dixon, C. (1992), "'Feminists' Hour' under Fire from Listeners: *Woman's Hour*," *The Sunday Times*, 2/06: ST.

E.C.W. (1947), "News Outdoes Jules Verne," *Sunday Mail*, 02/02: 6.

E.C.W. (1948), "Radiopinion," *Sunday Mail*, 04/11: 4.

E.C.W. (1949), "Male Announcers Move in on Kitchen Sessions," *Sunday Mail*, 12/11: 17.

E.C.W. (1951), "Radiopinion: Tide Turns on Serials," *Sunday Mail*, 07/22: 4.

Greenwood, I. (1939), "Women, World Events and Radio," *The Broadcaster*, 02/11–18: 30–31.

Greenwood, I. (1940), "Wavelengths: Woman's Work in the Wide World," *ABC Weekly*, 12/28: n.p.

Halsted (1938), "Roundabout: People and Events—International Letters," *West Australian*, 1/04: 5.

Halsted (1940), "Women's Realm: Roundabout—People and Events—Well-Known Broadcaster," *West Australian*, 10/02: 12.

Henry, G. (1991), "Radio 4: Sounds Fit for Nineties," *The Guardian*, 09/02: 23.

Housewife (1944), "Women's Opinions: Mine," *Sunday Times*, 04/09: 10.

Howard, J. (1964), "ABC's *Impact* Dreadful," *Canberra Times*, 08/24: 11.

Isbister, C. (1980), "A World Controlled by Women," *The Australian*, 7.

James, H. and MacIver, C. (1954), "For the Lonely Housewife: Eyes, Ears and Legs [Morning Stars of the CBC]," *CBC Times*, 11/21: 1–2, 7.

Johnston, I. (1940), "Points from Letters: ABC Women's Session," *West Australian*, 20/08: 11.

Karpf, A. (1996), "Radio Days: *Woman's Hour*," *The Guardian*, 09/16: 4.

Knight, H. (1938), "The Shades Discuss Sex Equality: Famous Women of the Past Are Critical of the Independent Modern Miss," *The Argus*, 20/03: 10.

Lambert, A. (1991), "Can BBC Radio Four's *Woman's Hour* Survive a Move to a New Morning Slot?" *The Independent*, 01/23: 15.

Listening-Insect (1924), "Radio for Mothers, Babes and Sucklings, III," *The Australian Woman's Mirror*, December 9: 22.

Listening Post (1939), "No Man's Land," *Australian Women's Weekly*, 11/25: 16.

Long, E. (1950), "A Welcome Guest in Every Home [Mattie Rotenberg]," *CBC Times*, 06/18: 1–2.

Long, E. (1960), "The International Standing Committee on Radio and Television of the International Council of Women," *European Broadcasting Review*, 63 (September): 19–21.

MacLean, J. (1997), "Whisky Marketing," *Herald Scotland*, 05/30: 23.

Marriott, J. (1969), "Contentment Is a Quarry," *Australian Women's Weekly*, 02/12: 17.

McEnaney, M. (1945), "Should Women Return to the Home," *National Home Monthly*, 46 (May): 56, 58.

McEnaney, M. (1950), "Press Conference," *CBC Times*, 11/10 III (47): 5.

Midgley, C. (1996), "*Woman's Hour* Marks 50 Years of Domestic Service," 20/08: 5.

Moir, J. (1992), "Public Lives: Female Trouble: BBC Radio 4," *The Guardian*, 2/09: GRDN.

Morris, L. (1952a), "Pops and Serials," *Advocate*, 02/28: 15.

Morris, L. (1952b), "Radio—Film: Woman Announcer Disappears," *Advocate*, 07/31: 15.

Musgrove, N. (1968), "A Happiness of Ten Children—and Always Room for One More Baby," *The Australian Women's Weekly*, 03/06: 2.

O'Hanlon, M., Mrs (1970a), "Politics and Education [Letter to the Editor]," *Canberra Times*, 09/25: 2.

O'Hanlon, M., Mrs (1970b), "Politics and Education [Letter to the Editor]," *Canberra Times*, 10/06: 2.

O'Hanlon, M. V. (1975), "ABC Programs Criticised [Letter to the Editor]," *Canberra Times*, 02/24: 2.

Pallis, M. and A. Doctor (1934), "The Woman's Side of Unemployment," *The Listener*, May 16, XI (2179): 811–812.

Quinn, J. (1951), "Radio Roundup: Change," *The Mail*, 11/17: 26.

Secretary (1940), "Letters to the Editor: No Question of Merit," *Daily News*, 10/16: 4.

Segal, M. (1952), "Five Million Ears to Please," *Brittania and Eve*, 10/01 (4): 14–15, 74.

Skeates, P. (1970), "Politics and Education [Letter to the Editor]," *Canberra Times*, 09/30: 2.

Stirling, J. (1953), "Radiopinion Tells Our Male Announcers … Give That Gooey Nonsense Away," *Sunday Mail*, 07/19: 20.

Trilling, D. (2007), "The Liquid Murmur of Posh Ladies," *New Statesman*, 09/10.

Victorian Year Book 1941–42 (1944), Melbourne: Office of the Government Statist.

Wellington, L. (1939), "Radionews," *Gloucester Journal*, 03/18: 7.

Wittstock, M. (1991), "Men Open Hearts to *Woman's Hour*: BBC Radio 4," *The Times*, 11/06: T.

Woodruff, J. (1951), "Station of the Month: W9DXX, Alice R. Bourke," *The VHF News*, 4 (9): 4–5.

Broadcasts

Bond, R. (1939–1940), *Woman's World*, 09/ 1939-06/1940, CBC RA.

Casselman, B., Patterson, P., Loring, R., et al. (1968), "Royal Commission on the Status of Women," *Trans-Canada Matinee*, 05/03, CBC RA 680503-8 on TBN940703-13(06) slot #6.

Christie, R. and MacDonald, D. (1976), "The First Forty," CBC RA 761104-12/00.

Glover, E. (1967), "Claire Wallace," *Luncheon Date*, 12/22, CBC RA 671222-07/00.

Hilliard, D. M. (1959a), "Fighting Fatigue," *Trans-Canada Matinee*, n.d., CBC RA 590000-2 on 971122-20(42).

Hilliard, D. M. (1959b), "Four Fears That Prey Upon Women," *Trans-Canada Matinee*, n.d., CBC RA 590000-4 on 971122-20(42).

Hilliard, D. M. (1959c), "Woman's Greatest Blessing," *Trans-Canada Matinee*, n.d., CBC RA 590000-3 on 971122-20(42).

Hilliard, M., Dr. (1959d), "Of Life and Love," *Trans-Canada Matinee*, n.d., CBC RA 590000-1 on 971122-20(42).

King, C. (1982), "Talkback with Catherine King," *6WF 50th Anniversary Program*, 07/01, ABC RA 82/10/1030.

May, F. (1970), "Talk by Professor Frederick May: Goodbye," *At Home This Morning with Elizabeth Bond*, 12/09, ABC RA 85/ 10/1278-2.

Morrison, J. (1961), "25th Anniversary Program: Jean Hinds," *Trans-Canada Matinee*, 11/02, CBC RA 644402-03/00, Box 990108-17(21).

Mugan, M. (1943), "Central Ontario's Women's Institute Broadcast & Canadian-Soviet Friendship," *At Monica Mugan's*, 01/01, CBC RA 430101-33/00 on 990424-21(06).

Patterson, P. and Reid, E. (1968a), "Reports from Royal Commission on the Status of Women," *Matinee*, 09/20, CBC RA 680920-02 at 940703-15(08) slot#8.

Patterson, P. and Reid, E. (1968b), "Royal Commission on the Status of Women," *Matinee*, 09/10, CBC RA 680910-10 on TBN 940703-15 (07) slot #4.
Queen Elizabeth (1939), "Message to the Women of the Empire," November 11, BBC BL SA 1CL0019530 HMV.
Wallace, C. (1943), "They Tell Me," *CBC National Network*, CBC RA 431214-01 on 990424-18(07) slot #3.

Oral histories

Belfrage, J. (2001), Interviewed by Shirley, G., 07/20, NFSA Ref. 535333.
Greenwood, I. (1976), Interviewed by de Berg, H. 03/07, NLA Ref. ORAL TRC 1/916. Available online: http://nla.gov.au/nla.obj-214733674/listen (accessed November 1, 2018).
Isbister, C. (1975), Interviewed by de Berg, H., 09/30, NLA Ref. ORAL TRC 1/861.
Jenkinson, C. (1987), Interviewed by Walker, J., 02/23, ABC RA Ref. 88/7/1096B.
West, J. (1991), Interviewed by Walker, J., 04/15, ABC RA Ref. 93/7/848D.

Theses

Gill, R. (1991), "Ideology and Popular Radio: A Discourse Analytic Examination of Disc Jockeys' Talk," PhD diss., Loughborough University of Technology.
Graham, S. (2014), "As Canadian as Possible: The Canadian Broadcasting Corporation, 1936–1939," PhD diss., University of Ottawa: Ottawa.
Korinek, V. J. (1996), "Roughing It in Suburbia: Reading Chatelaine Magazine, 1950–1969," PhD diss., University of Toronto: Toronto.
Kotai-Ewers, P. (2013), "The Fellowship of Australian Writers (WA) from 1938 to 1980 and Its Role in the Cultural Life of Perth," PhD diss., Murdoch University: Perth.
Leman, J. (1983), "Capitalism and the Mass Media: A Case Study of Women's Magazines and Radio Programmes, 1935–1955," M.Phil diss., University of Kent: Canterbury. Available online: https://librarysearch.kent.ac.uk/client/en_GB/kent/search/detailnonmodal/ent:$002f$002fSD_ILS$002f0$002fSD_ILS:368080/one.
MacLennan, A. F. (2001), "Circumstances beyond Our Control: Canadian Radio Program Schedule Evolution during the 1930s," PhD diss., Concordia: Montreal. Available online: http://www.collectionscanada.gc.ca/obj/s4/f2/dsk3/ftp04/NQ59220.pdf.
McCarthy, A. (1995), "Outer Spaces: Public Viewing in American Television History," PhD diss., Northwestern University: Evanston, Illinois, USA. Available online: http://simsrad.net.ocs.mq.edu.au/login?url=http://search.proquest.com.simsrad.net.ocs.mq.edu.au/docview/304225293?accountid=12219.

Murray, K. (2002), "Irene Greenwood: A Voice for Peace," PhD diss., Edith Cowan University: Joondalup. Available online: http://ro.ecu.edu.au/theses/722.

Razlogova, E. (2003), "The Voice of the Listener: Americans and the Radio Industry, 1920–1950," PhD diss., George Mason University: Fairfax, VA.

Rewinkel, K. E. (2013), "Representations of Housewife Identity in BBC Home Front Radio Broadcasts, 1939–1945," MA diss., Bowling Green State University: Bowling Green, OH.

Richardson, J. A. (1988), "The Limits of Authorship: The Radio Broadcasts of Irene Greenwood, 1936–1954," BA Hons diss., Murdoch University: Perth. Available online: http://wwwmcc.murdoch.edu.au/Readingroom/ozradio/Richo/RichCont.html.

Rossiter, P. (2002), "Problematising the Political: Feminist Interventions," PhD diss., University of Western Sydney: Werrington. Available online: http://handle.uws.edu.au:8081/1959.7/579.

Skoog, K. (2010), "The 'Responsible' Woman: The BBC and Women's Radio 1945–1955," PhD diss., University of Westminster: Westminster, UK.

Taylor, A. N. (1985), "'Window onto the World': A History of Women in CBC Radio Talks and Public Affairs, 1936–1966," Master of Arts diss., Carleton University: Ottawa.

Wang, J. H. (2006), "Convenient Fictions: The Construction of the Daytime Broadcast Audience, 1927–1960," PhD diss., University of Wisconsin–Madison: Madison. Available online: http://search.proquest.com.ezproxy.lib.uts.edu.au/pqdtglobal/docview/304978963/fulltextPDF/E52D8C9EB53149D2PQ/1?accountid=17095.

Archival documents

"Current Affairs Contributions to *Woman's Hour*," (1959), 04/29: In BBC WAC.

"Extract from Minutes of Conference of National Talks Advisory Committee Held at ABC Building, 171 William St, Sydney from Tuesday to Thursday, 17th–19th August, 1948," (1948), 08/17-19: In ABC General NAA.

"Facts about *Woman's Hour*," (1962), 05/: In BBC WAC.

"Minutes of *Woman's Hour* Meeting," (1953), 10/26: In BBC WAC.

"Minutes of *Woman's Hour* Meeting," (1959), 11/24: In BBC WAC.

"Points for Discussion with D.G. 15th March," (1946), 03/15: In BBC WAC.

"*Woman's Hour* in Search of 'the Modern Woman'," (1953), 12/: In BBC WAC.

"Women's and Household Talks," (1936–1938), n.d.: In BBC WAC.

Acting Talks Producer, Glasgow (1947), "Suggestions for *Woman's Hour*," 10/31: In BBC WAC.

Anonymous (1954), "[Letter from Male Listener on His 'Inversion']," n.d.: In BBC WAC.

Audience Research Department (1951), "*Woman's Hour*," 10/19: In BBC WAC.

Audience Research Department (1955), "An Enquiry about Afternoon Television Programmes for Women," 11/07: In BBC WAC.

Audience Research Department (1965), "Listener's Opinions of *Woman's Hour*," n.d.: In BBC WAC.

Barker, P. (1946), "*Woman's Hour* Experts," 10/02: In BBC WAC.

BBC Broadcasting Research (1982), "*Woman's Hour* (Opinions of the Programme Explored during Group Discussions)," 01/: In BBC WAC.

BBC News (1953), "Soviet Zone Fashions Portray Socialist Realism," 03/29: In BBC WAC.

BBC Radio 2 (1972), "The *Woman's Hour* Diet": In BBC WAC.

Benzie, I. D. (1947), "Suggestions for *Woman's Hour*," 08/14: In BBC WAC.

Benzie, I. D. (1947), "*Woman's Hour—*Housewives' Exchange," 09/19: In BBC WAC.

Benzie, I. D. (1947), "*Woman's Hour* Psychiatrist," 03/04: In BBC WAC.

Benzie, I. D. (1954), "Taking Trouble: Attached Anonymous Letters," 11/05: In BBC WAC.

Benzie, M. I. D. (1951), "Memo to Chief Assistant—*Woman's Hour*," 12/04: In BBC WAC.

British Broadcasting Corporation (1936), "BBC Announcement," 03/26: In BBC WAC.

Byth, E. F. (1948), "For the Women's Session, Feb 4th [What Should Be Its Format?]," 02/04: In ABC WS NAA WBS.

Canadian Overseas Telecommunication Corporation (1954), "Cable Transmission Card," 06/30: In KSAF CNA.

Chalmers, T. W. (1948), "*Woman's Hour*," 04/16: In BBC WAC.

Collins, N. (1946), "Letter to Director General about *Woman's Hour*," 10/30: In BBC WAC.

Collins, N. (1946), "Letter to DS about New *Woman's Hour* Program," 08/28: In BBC WAC.

Collins, N. (1946), "Letter to Radio Times about *Woman's Hour*," 10/28: In BBC WAC.

Collins, N. (1946), "*Woman's Hour* Inaugural Programme," 10/02: In BBC WAC.

Counsellor (1949), "[Talk on Legal Highlights of 1949]," 12/28: In ABC WS NAA WBS.

Cox, D. (1966), "Letter to Elizabeth Long," 04/10: In ELF CNA.

Derville, A. (1952), "Some Ideas and Thoughts about the Coming Session of *Woman's Hour*," 06/20: In BBC WAC.

Gibbs, E. (1950), "Gordon McConnel's Report on *Woman's Hour*," 05/08: In BBC WAC.

Gibbs, E. (1950), "*Woman's Hour* Report," 06/05: In BBC WAC.

Gordon, A. (1947), "Current Affairs Talks in *Woman's Hour*," 01/17: In BBC WAC.

Greenwood, I. (1936–1950), "Women in the International News; Australian Broadcasting Commission; Irene A. Greenwood [Scrapbook]": In IG MU.

Greenwood, I. (1937–1940), "Women in the International News, Station 6WN from August 8th 1937 to July 26th 1940": In IG MU.

Greenwood, I. (1938–1946), "Short-Wave Talks over Station VLQ 'the Voice of Australia' and Correspondence": In IG MU.

Greenwood, I. (1939–1940), "Women in the International News Station 6WN from August 4th 1939 to July 26th 1940": In IG MU.

Hill, M. (1948), "Suggested Talk on Refrigerators Etc," 08/19: In BBC WAC.

Hill, M. (1951), "*Woman's Hour* in the Evening or Weekends," 03/29: In BBC WAC.

Hunt, S. (1951), "*Women's Magazine* [Last Broadcast of Program with This Title]," 06/08: In ABC WS NAA WBS.

Kirke, B. W. (1943), "Memo to Federal Director of Talks and Federal Controller of Talks," 11/15: In ABC WS NAA WBS.

Knowles, W. (1971), "Letter to Radio Times—*Woman's Hour* 14th February," 12/20: In BBC WAC.

Knowles, W. (1971), "*Woman's Hour* from Israel: October 14, 1971," 11/19: In BBC WAC.

Knowles, W. (1972), "Possible Transfer of *Woman's Hour* to Radio 4," 08/04: In BBC WAC.

Knowles, W. (1972), "Program Plans in *Woman's Hour*," 01/14: In BBC WAC.

Knowles, W. (1973), "Radio Times Feature on *Woman's Hour*, Week 27," 03/05: In BBC WAC.

Knowles, W. (1974), "Weekend *Woman's Hour*," 12/12: In BBC WAC.

Knowles, W. (1979), "Competition," 02/06: In BBC WAC.

Knowles, W. (1979), "Joanna Scott-Moncrieff [Memorial Service]," 02/22: In BBC WAC.

Langley, M. (1953), "Audience Research Report: Week 44, Paragraph 6," 12/03: In BBC WAC.

Lee, M. (1968), "Audience Research," 12/20: In BBC WAC.

Lee, M. (1969), "Notes on *Woman's Hour* for Board Report," 03/16: In BBC WAC.

Lee, M. (1970), "Attitudes to Women in Radio Programmes," 10/14: In BBC WAC.

Lee, M. (1970), "Interests of Women Viewers and Listeners," 02/02: In BBC WAC.

Lee, M. (1970), "New Weekend's *Woman's Hour*," 09/10: In BBC WAC.

Lee, M. (1970), "Weekend *Woman's Hour*," 04/03: In BBC WAC.

Lewin, R. (1961), "Repeats on Home Service," 11/23: In BBC WAC.

Listener Research Department (1946), "Planning for Housewives: Best Hours and Days," 04/: In BBC WAC.

Listener Research Department (1947), "Record of Interview [Audience Research on Dr Jacques, *Woman's Hour* Psychiatrist]," 03/17: In BBC WAC.

Maloney, M. (1948), "[Budget—Typical Incomes]," 01/28: In BBC WAC.

McConnel, G. (1950), "*Woman's Hour*: Monitoring Report: General Impressions," 03/31: In BBC WAC.

McConnel, G. (1950), "*Woman's Hour*—Monitoring Report (Supplementary Notes) [Based on Programmes 21–28 March 1950]," 04/08: In BBC WAC.

McConnel, G. (1950), "*Woman's Hour*—Production and Presentation," 06/18: In BBC WAC.

McDonald, L. (1968), "Weekend *Woman's Hour*," 12/13: In BBC WAC.

McEnaney, M. (1955), "CWPC Overseas Trip 1954–1955," In WPCTP UoW.

McMillan, J. (1948), "*Woman's Hour*: Friday 16th March," 03/16: In BBC WAC.

Mitchell, C. (1947), "[Introduction of 60-Hour Week for Housewives]," 12/31: In ABC WS NAA WBS.

Mollinson, J., Mrs (1947), "Letter to *Woman's Hour*," 07/29: In BBC WAC.

Molony, M. (1947), "*Woman's Hour* Schedule," 08/28: In BBC WAC.

Molony, M. (1947), "*Woman's Hour*: Housewives' Exchange," 09/10: In BBC WAC.

Molony, M. (1948), "Budget Week—March 1st–March 9th Inclusive," 02/03: In BBC WAC.

Paterson, G. (1952), "Sophisticated *Woman's Hour*," 07/02: In BBC WAC.

Perowne, L. (1946), "Letter to Norman Collins about Direction of *Woman's Hour*," 11/11: In BBC WAC.

Powys-Lybbe, U. (1987), "The Touring Camera in Australia": In SLVIC PC.

Prince, V. M., Mrs (1956), "The Gate," 07/27: In BBC WAC.

Quigley, J. (1951), "Astrology and Graphology," 07/04: In BBC WAC.

Quigley, J. (1951), "Some Notes for Consideration in Connection with Proposed Reduction in Length of *Woman's Hour*," 07/23: In BBC WAC.

Quigley, J. (1951), "Suggested Repeat of *Woman's Hour*," 07/02: In BBC WAC.

Quigley, J. (1951), "*Woman's Hour*—Some Autumn Projects," 08/[n.d.]: In BBC WAC.

Quigley, J. (1953), "Audience Research," 12/31: In BBC WAC.

Quigley, J. (1953), "Report on Correspondence to *Woman's Hour* Editorial Office," n.d.: In BBC WAC.

Quigley, J. (1955), "Commercial TV Programmes for Women," 03/11: In BBC WAC.

Redcliffe, M. (1972), "Women in the BBC," 11/27: In BBC WAC.

Rhys-Evans, M. M. (1951), "Letter to *Woman's Hour* Editor," 11/[n.d.]: In BBC WAC.

Robertson, M. (1951), "Suggestions for OBs," 03/02: In BBC WAC.

Rotenberg, M. (1940–1964), "Radio Talks—Various," 11/[n.d.]: In MRF CNA.

Schofield, J. M. (1946), "Letter Suggesting a *Woman's Hour*," 03/03: In BBC WAC.

Scott-Moncrieff, J. (1951), "Audience Research Figures," 07/03: In BBC WAC.

Scott-Moncrieff, J. (1951), "Suggested Discussion on House Design," 03/13: In BBC WAC.

Scott-Moncrieff, J. (1952), "Digest," 11/27: In BBC WAC.

Scott-Moncrieff, J. (1952), "Making a Little Go a Long Way," 07/03: In BBC WAC.

Scott-Moncrieff, J. (1952), "Sophisticated *Woman's Hour*," 07/01: In BBC WAC.

Scott-Moncrieff, J. (1952), "Windows on the World," 06/06: In BBC WAC.

Scott-Moncrieff, J. (1953), "Public Affairs in *Woman's Hour*," 09/08: In BBC WAC.

Scott-Moncrieff, J. (1953), "Your Edition of *Woman's Hour*," 03/23: In BBC WAC.

Scott-Moncrieff, J. (1954), "Advice Please: Urgently," 12/16: In BBC WAC.

Scott-Moncrieff, J. (1954), "Contribution to *Woman's Hour*: Thursday 24th June," 06/11: In BBC WAC.

Scott-Moncrieff, J. (1954), "*Woman's Hour* Looks at the Modern Woman," 02/26: In BBC WAC.

Scott, M. (1951), "*Woman's Hour*—Listener Figures," 01/18: In BBC WAC.

Scott, M. (1953), "Teenager's Week—*Woman's Hour*, Week 16 (Checked with Schools Dept.)," 03/03: In BBC WAC.

Scott-Moncrieff, J. (1961), "Repeats on Home Service," 11/16: In BBC WAC.

Scott-Moncrieff, J. (1962), "*Woman's Hour*: Two Long-Term Policy Points," 01/02: In BBC WAC.

Somerville, M. (1948), "*Woman's Hour*: The Older Woman," 03/21: In BBC WAC.

Thompson, S. (1982), "*Woman's Hour*: Long Term Trends (1973–1982)—Summary," 06/[n.d.]: In BBC WAC.

Trenaman, J. (1948), "*Woman's Hour*," 05/05: In BBC WAC.

Various listeners (1947), "Letters Attached to Memo—Suggestions for *Woman's Hour*," 08/14: In BBC WAC.

Wallace, C. (1942), "*They Tell Me*: CBC National: Wartime Savings": In CWP UoW.

Wellington, L. (1954), "Television Programmes for Women," 03/31: In BBC WAC.

Whitby, A. (1972), "*Woman's Hour* Audience," 08/25: In BBC WAC.

Whitby, A. (1973), "New Radio 4 Pattern," 08/30: In BBC WAC.

Woman's Hour Editor (1956), "*Woman's Hour*—Horoscope," 10/02: In BBC WAC.

Wyatt, H. (1951), "Memo to Editor, *Woman's Hour*," 10/17: In BBC WAC.

Yorke, J. (1956), "Home for the Day," 10/18: In BBC WAC.

Other

Aitken, K. (1948), "Notable Women of 1948," Canadian Broadcasting Corporation. Available online: https://www.cbc.ca/player/play/1801487869 (accessed November 12, 2017).

Aitken, K. (1953), "Fruitcake Leftovers and International Politics, 1953," Canadian Broadcasting Corporation. Available online: http://www.cbc.ca/player/play/1648760107 (accessed January 12, 2017).

BBC (1976), "Olive Shapley [Interview]," 18/06, *Woman's Hour: Highlights from the Archive*, BBC Online. Available online: http://www.bbc.co.uk/programmes/p01ldcsc.

BBC (2010), "Olive Shapley: Centenary of Her Birth," 09/04, *Woman's Hour: Highlights from the Archive*, BBC Online. Available online: http://www.bbc.co.uk/programmes/b00rqqyj.

BBC Four (2015), "BBC: The Secret Files: Episode 2." Available online: http://www.bbc.co.uk/programmes/b077xcd6 (accessed November 1, 2016).

Carter, S. (1996), "Riding the Airwaves: Three Models of Women's Access to Broadcasting," December 9, *Association for Education in Journalism and Mass Communication Conference Papers*. Available online: https://list.msu.edu/cgi-bin/wa ?A2=ind9612B&L=AEJMC&P=R21141 (accessed February 1, 2017).

Cayley, D. (1986), "Turning Points in Public Broadcasting: The CBC at 50," Available online: http://www.davidcayley.com/podcasts/2016/11/26/turning-points-in-public-broadcasting (accessed November 5, 2017).

Clarke, P. (2012), "Rudduck, Loma Butterworth (1914–2005)," September 20, *The Australian Women's Register*, The National Foundation for Australian Women (NFAW) in conjunction with The University of Melbourne. Available online: http://www.womenaustralia.info/biogs/AWE4785b.htm (accessed November 1, 2017).

Consandine, M. (2006), "Varley, Gwendoline (1896–1975)," *Australian Dictionary of Biography*, Australian National University. Available online: http://www.adb.online.anu.edu.au/biogs/A160531b.htm (accessed November 7, 2018).

Donovan, P. (2004), "Benzie, Isa Donald," *Oxford Dictionary of National Biography*, Oxford University Press. Available online: http://www.oxforddnb.com/view/article/65410 (accessed November 26, 2015).

Fisher, C. H. (2017), "Greenwood, Irene Adelaide (1898–1992)," *Australian Dictionary of Biography*, National Centre of Biography. Available online: http://adb.anu.edu.au/biography/greenwood-irene-adelaide-25528 (accessed July 1, 2017).

Hastings, C. (2016), "*Woman's Hour*? Obviously It Must Be Presented by a Man … Or So Decreed Sexist BBC Chiefs When They Launched a New Show for 'Middle Class Housewives Who Don't Want Their Brains to Go Mouldy,'" 03/04, *Daily Mail*, Mail on Sunday. Available online: http://www.dailymail.co.uk/news/article-3520950/Woman-s-Hour-Obviously-presented-man-decreed-sexist-BBC-chiefs-launched-new-middle-class-housewives-don-t-want-brains-mouldy.html#ixzz4zmFckQ24 (accessed November 29, 2017).

Hicks, R. (2012), "Fairfax's *Daily Life* Launches Today," *Mumbrella*, Available online: https://mumbrella.com.au/fairfaxs-daily-life-launches-today-75185 (accessed November 1, 2017).

Hills, R. (2012), "On #Dailywife and Writing for the 'Women's Pages,'" *Musings of an Inappropriate Woman*. Available online: http://rachelhills.tumblr.com/post/17940722684/on-dailywife-and-writing-for-thewomens-pages (accessed February 1, 2017).

Hunter, F. (2012), "Matheson, Hilda," *Oxford Dictionary of National Biography*, Oxford University Press. Available online: https://doi.org/10.1093/ref:odnb/49198 (accessed November 8, 2018).

Nicholson, J. and Nattrass, S. (2003), "Pioneer Was Courageous Voice at ABC [Elizabeth Bond, Obituary]," n.p. *Sydney Morning Herald*. Available online: https://www.smh.com.au/articles/2003/01/10/1041990093670.html (accessed November 1, 2017).

Pease, S. (2006), "The *Woman's Hour* House," 06/02, *1950s British TV and Radio Snippets*. Available online: http://www.turnipnet.com/whirligig/tv/memories/ snippets/snippets39.htm (accessed November 1, 2016).

Pierce, D. and Hoyt, E. (2011), "Lantern: Search, Visualise & Explore the Media History Digital Library," *Media History Digital Library*, University of Wisconsin-Madison, Department of Communication Arts. Available online: http://lantern.mediahist.org/ about/index (accessed November 4, 2017).

Powys-Lybbe, U. (1948–1987), "The Touring Camera in Australia," State Library of Victoria. Available online: https://trove.nla.gov.au/picture/result?q=%22Powys-Lybbe%2C+Ursula%2C+1910-1997%2C+%28photographer.%29%22&l-format=Photograph (accessed November 1, 2017).

Rosen, R. (2010), "The 'Women's Pages' Go Online: Good or Bad News?," *Ms. Magazine Blog*. Available online: http://msmagazine.com/blog/2010/06/17/gender-apartheid-online (accessed November 1, 2017).

Tom K8CX. (2011), "Re: Vintage QSL Cards Found," *AMfone*. Available online: http:// amfone.net/Amforum/index.php?topic=26214.25 (accessed December 1, 2018).

Wedge, P. (2007), "Claire Wallace (1900–1968)," December, *History of Canadian Broadcasting*, Canadian Communications Foundation. Available online: http://www. broadcasting-history.ca/personalities/wallace-claire (accessed January 11, 2017).

Winnicott, D. W. (1939–1968), "Winnicott's Broadcasts," *The Collected Works of D. W. Winnicott: Volume 12, Appendices and Bibliographies*, Adès, R. (ed) Oxford Clinical Psychology Online. Available online: http://www.oxfordclinicalpsych.com/ view/10.1093/med:psych/9780190271442.001.0001/med-9780190271442-chapter-10 (accessed November 1, 2017).

Archives consulted

ABC NAA KFS	ABC Files, *Kitchen Front* Scripts, National Archives of Australia, Sydney
ABC WS NAA 2NU	ABC *Women's Sessions* Files, Tamworth *Women's Sessions*, National Archives of Australia, Sydney
ABC WS NAA General	ABC General correspondence including Administration, Policy, and Artists' Contract files, National Archives of Australia, Sydney
ABC WS NAA WBS	ABC *Women's Sessions* Files, Women's Broadcast Scripts, National Archives of Australia, Sydney,
BBC BL SA	BBC British Library Sound Archive, London
BBC WAC	BBC Written Archives Centre, Caversham Park
CBC RA	CBC Radio Archives, Toronto
CWP UoW	Claire Wallace Papers, University of Waterloo

ELF CAN	Elizabeth Long Fonds, Canadian National Archives, Ottawa
ELP UoW	Elizabeth Long Papers, University of Waterloo
HCF CNA	Helen Carscallen Fonds, Canadian National Archives, Ottawa
IG MU	Irene Greenwood Collection, Murdoch University, Perth
KSAF CNA	Kate Scott Aitken Fonds, Canadian National Archives, Ottawa
MMcEF CNA	Marjorie McEnaney Fonds, Canadian National Archives, Ottawa
MRF CAN	Mattie Rotenberg Fonds, Canadian National Archives, Ottawa
SLVIC PC	State Library of Victoria Pictures Collection, Melbourne
WPCTP UoW	Women's Press Club of Toronto Papers, University of Waterloo

Index

www.ingramcontent.com/pod-product-compliance
Lightning Source LLC
Chambersburg PA
CBHW050442280326
41932CB00013BA/2215

* 9 7 8 1 5 0 1 3 1 8 7 7 1 *